Acclaim for Song of Gaea: Paean to the Soul of Nature

SONG OF GAEA is much needed in the world of children's literature as we face the great crises of ecological destruction and climate change our human presence has caused Earth. Children need an holistic and, as the author says, 'loving call for humanity to live in balance with the Earth.' This book is a lovely integration of lyric poetry, mysticism and current science… it works!!!
~Elisabet Sahtouris
Author of *EarthDance: Living Systems in Evolution*

Lessons learned in our childhood contribute to forming the kinds of adults we become. Oberon Zell and Kirsten Johnsen have written both a wise and lovely tale that will delight children curious to know about Gaea the Earth, and all living beings that comprise her complex existence, and a powerful new mythology that supports ecological responsibility and the acknowledgement of the interconnectedness of all. **SONG OF GAEA** is a lesson in ethics as well as a compelling picture of the wonder and mystery of the natural world.
~Carole M. Cusack
Chair, Studies in Religion, Arts, Social Sciences
The University of Sydney, Australia
Co-Editor, *International Journal for the Study of New Religions*

SONG OF GAEA brings the simplicity of a child's eye view together with the wisdom of old souls from ages long gone into perfect harmony with a melodic rhythm that captivates even as it enchants and inspires. This mesmerizing and insightful account of our creation and place in the multiverse is not only suitable for children from 2-10, but all peoples of the world. You owe it to yourself to wander into this wondrous web of words and immerse yourself in their beautiful meaning.
~Lynn Santer
Director, Saris Trust Film Production, Australia

Children have an innate awareness of the personalities in nature. **SONG OF GAEA** helps to strengthen that connection in a generation where children are rapidly becoming socially isolated and disconnected from their environment. Buy this book if you want to help your child enjoy getting away from the computer screen and foster in them the desire to get back out into nature. As a publisher of children's books, I can heartily recommend this gem.
~Shé D'Montford
Founder, Shambhallah Awareness Centre
Principle, The Happy Medium Publishing Company

Oberon Zell is one of the truly creative spirits emerging from the American religious experience. Deeply committed to human relationships and to the wellbeing of the world within which we all live, he has long championed the venerable belief that our planet is no lifeless lump, but is itself a living organism to which we owe all and from which we gain all. This composition of poetry and art by Oberon, his student Kirsten and his friends Sage and Pratima, is a deeply devoted tribute of praise and thanks and should be welcomed by all as a genuine contribution to our spiritual understanding.

~Michael Ruse
Lucyle T. Werkmeister Professor of Philosophy
Director of the Program in the History and Philosophy of Science,
Florida State University

Poetry and art open doors of understanding to the sacred, and with them **SONG OF GAEA** guides young children to celebrate the beauty and mystery of our beloved Earth. Our hope for humanity's future rests in the hands of our children, and that hope is well placed if they absorb the love and wisdom of works like this.

~Amber K
Executive Director of Ardantane Pagan Learning Center
Author of *True Magick, RitualCraft, How to Become a Witch*

The greatest stories are not presentations of fact, but nor are they fiction—they are expressions of belief and memory, imagination, experience and wonder, rich with emotion and consideration, and the magic of communication. **SONG OF GAEA** is a great story written in the gentle rhythm of verse, weaving together science and sanctity, reason and vision, to inspire our children to be wide-eyed, wakeful and thoughtful.

~Emma Restall Orr
Author of *The Wakeful World: Animism, Mind and Self in Nature*

This lovely book, **SONG OF GAEA**, seeks to retrieve the beauty of our Earthly home from the clouds of carelessness that surround it. Kirsten Johnsen and Oberon Zell are teachers to our children, who know that poetry and song are the vital connecting links, which allow us to become fully human. This is a poignant but powerful work because it touches the soul and the emotional being. The child who feels connected to the Earth will become Her lover and protector. **SONG OF GAEA** is an introduction for that child and a gift to all of us.

~Roger Nelson
Director, Global Consciousness Project

Books by Oberon Zell

1. *Occult Crime & Ritual Abuse: Who's Who & What's What* (Church of All Worlds; 4 editions, 1989-1992)
2. *Grimoire for the Apprentice Wizard,* with the Grey Council (New Page, 2004)
3. *Companion for the Apprentice Wizard,* with the Faculty of the Grey School of Wizardry (New Page, 2006)
4. *Creating Circles & Ceremonies: Rituals for All Seasons & Reasons,* with Morning Glory Zell (New Page, 2006)
5. *A Wizard's Bestiary,* with Ash DeKirk (New Page, 2007)
6. *Green Egg Omelette: An Anthology of Art and Articles from the Legendary Pagan Journal* (New Page, 2008)
7. *Prophecy & the End of the World (as we know it): Apocalypse or Solartopia?* with Harvey Wasserman (Solartopia, 2012)
8. *Barsoom: A New Map of the Mars of Edgar Rice Burroughs' "John Carter of Mars" Novels* (TheaGenesis e-book, 2012)
9. *The Wizard and the Witch: Seven Decades of Counterculture, Magick, and Paganism: An Oral History of Oberon Zell and Morning Glory,* by John C. Sulak with Oberon & Morning Glory Zell (Llewellyn, 2014)
10. *Death Rights & Rites: A Practical Guide to a Meaningful Death,* with Judith Fenley (Llewellyn, 2020)
11. *That Undiscover'd Country: A Traveler's Guide to the Afterlife,* with Phaedra Bonewits (Black Moon Pubs, 2021)
12. *Song of Gaea,* with Kiri Johnson (a children's book) Art by Oberon, Sage Lampros, Pratima Sarkar (TheaGenesis, 2021)
13. *Goodbye Jesus, I've Gone Home to Mother* (Left Hand Press, 2021)
14. *The Wizard and the Witch: Special two-volume expanded edition,* by John C. Sulak with Oberon & Morning Glory Zell (Left Hand Press, 2021)
15. *Barsoom: Mapping the Mythic Mars* (Ingram, 2022)
16. *A Wizard's Bestiary* (2nd Edition), with Ash DeKirk (Left Hand Press, 2022)
17. *GaeaGenesis: Conception and Birth of the Living Earth* (Left Hand Press, 2022)
18. *Hystory's Mysteries: Turning Points that Changed Our World,* with Nicholas Kingsley (Left Hand Press, 2024)
19. *Handbook For Our Future Parents: Raising the Magickal Child,* with Haleigh Isbill (Left Hand Press, 2024)

Handbook For Our Future Parents
Design and layout by Oberon Zell

Black Moon Manifesto
It is the Will and mission of Bate Cabal/Black Moon to effectively manifest unique and insightful occult Works for the esoteric community in a manner that is unfettered by commercial considerations.

ISBN: 979-8-9865228-7-6

Published by Left Hand Press
Cincinnati, Ohio USA

Left Hand Press is a subsidiary of Black Moon Publishing, LLC

BlackMoonPublishing.com
blackmoonpublishing@gmail.com

United States • United Kingdom • Europe • Australia •
India • Japan • Brazil

Handbook For Our Future Parents:
Raising the Magickal Child

Oberon Zell
With Haleigh Isbill

Left Hand Press
Cincinnati, Ohio

Acknowledgements

This book is dedicated to the Children. The Children of yesterday, today, and tomorrow. Children to whom I have been a parent, a god(dess)father, and an honorary uncle. Children of my flesh, and Children of my Spirit. Children I may never even meet in person, but whose lives have been (and will be) touched by my words and works.

In particular, my now-deceased son, Bryan—child of Martha and the only issue of my loins. My stepdaughter, Rainbow Galadriel, daughter of Morning Glory, and her daughter—our granddaughter—Alessandra. My stepson, Zachariah, son of Diane. Jenny Wren, daughter of Wolf. Our Goddess-daughters, Tam and Fayth. And Diana, daughter of my new wife, Rhiannon, and now my awesome stepdaughter.

And all the kids of Greenfield Ranch, when Morning Glory and I lived there from 1977 to 1985, raising Unicorns. We were the honorary Aunt and Uncle of the whole wild kid pack, then and afterwards. And to all the kids that they came to bear in their turn over the years.

I would also like to acknowledge Haleigh Isbill, my Las Vegas friend, editor, and co-conspirator on this book and others. She has handled soliciting and editing submissions for the most important aspect of this book—the personal stories from fellow travelers on this journey through incarnations.

And thanks to all who have contributed stories, anecdotes, and chapters to this Handbook—especially Cat Gina Cole, William Hegeman, Judith Barnett, Alayne Griffin, Kathleen Mugnolo, Christine Glass, Ed Hrafnskald Conway, and Marylyn Motherbear Scott.

And here's to the wonderful folks at Black Moon/Left Hand Press—Maegdlyn, Louie and Joe—who have believed in me enough to publish this and others of my books, since 2021. And more to come!

To my very dear friend, personal manager, technomage and business partner, Mama Maureen. She has been my good right hand for the past 15 years, competently handling every aspect of my myriad enterprises. I couldn't have done any of this without her. Thank you!

And finally, to my lovely Bride, Rhiannon. She took me in and decided to keep me. I cannot imagine a more perfect lifemate for the years ahead. May we live happily ever after to the end of our days!

Foreword by Cate Dalton

RANK AND I MET OBERON ZELL AT CRAFTWISE 1995. Since then, he has been a friend, a peer, and like a grandfather figure to our kids. We feel blessed to know Oberon, and truly honoured to have been asked to write this Foreword.

First, I'm not a mom; I was a stepmom. It was not easy, but I found it by turns to be fun, challenging and in a lot of ways more fulfilling than I ever expected. I had a chance over the years to watch my beloved husband Frank raise his kids; sometimes, I even helped.

Our kids were always included in rituals, in running our own event (CraftWise), in marching band, in travel (an education in itself and an important aspect of expanding their horizons.) We did whatever we could on our limited budget to expose them to experiences they could learn from, to people from various walks of life, to different Pagan paths. We have watched many kids in the community grow up, at events we attended, events we hosted, and in regular kid activities.

Frank is a self-taught solitary Pagan. He discovered his Path in early adulthood. He read, he studied, he researched, he created his own practice. Once we met and began melding our practice to become a fluid working priest and priestess, it was a natural step to include the kids.

As solitaries, we decided to try working in a coven. While the kids got a kick out of it, we chose to leave—it didn't serve us and tho the kids had fun, as a learning experience it didn't serve them either.

Covens are not for everyone. So we learned a lesson—and by extension, so did the kids. Trial and error is a fact of life. It may be a good experience, or a bad experience, or it could be just meh. But it is always a chance to learn.

Our kids were instrumental in whatever success we had with our Pagan event, CraftWise. One manned the registration desk (at age 15), one was in charge of the Speaker Hospitality Suite (at age 12), the last (age 9) was training to take charge of the Merchant Hall. They were, in a word, AMAZING. Truly, we could never have done it without them. Never let any adult sell kids short. Give them a minute and they will astound you!

I was an only child, raised by an Irish Pagan mom, who literally hid the Irish Family Tradition I was raised in inside the Catholic church.

Mom was active—a Girl Scout leader, the woman who ran the White Elephant table at church fairs, who was so active in the PTA she actually got our old grammar school shut down and a new school built because the old one was full of asbestos!

Mom knew all the neighbors AND the neighborhood kids. And she kept a watchful eye on us all. And it was Mom who impressed upon me the importance of our Pagan beliefs, the importance of Nature—our place in it and our connection to it, and that Community is everything. And she provided experiences for me to explore them all.

Of course, it wasn't 'til I was an adult that I fully realized the importance of the role Mom played in shaping my life—how she guided my feet from a young age. She introduced me to Gods and Goddesses thru her wonderful stories, taught me about working with the Fair Folk, and kept me interested in everything. It was a gift every parent can give their children.

Pagan kids are a bit different. They are bright, inquisitive, open to the energies around them, and eager to learn. They are AWARE in ways other kids their age are not. They see ghosts, trust their instincts, can be prescient, are talented and creative and often think outside the dodecahedron. They can come up with the BEST rituals all on their own! They may be more work for their "parental units," but they are DEFINITELY worth it!!!

In this book are the experiences of Pagan parents—their ideas, events observed, lessons learned, life milestones, dealing with the non-Pagan world, teaching Tolerance and Respect for the beliefs of others—adventures in guiding these young folks into their lives in the "Big World."

Frank and I are sure you will find valuable insights from other Pagan parents in this book. We hope your parenting is filled with Joy, Hope, Fun, a few Challenges, fewer Tears, but most of all—LOVE. Enjoy the Journey!!

Blessed Be,

Cate and Frank Dalton
2/20/2024

Ħandbook for Our Future Parents
Raising the Ɱagickal Child
Contents

The Stars in His Eyes

by Aurora May

Do you see the stars in his eyes,
The way time both lengthens and flies?
Learn through the maturity of his gaze,
He will show you old magic ways.
His knowingness, beyond his tender years,
Somehow allays my deepest fears,
Of my understanding of what this could be,
The mystery of his great energy,
That courses through his veins wild,
What will become of this gentle child?

Meet him with openness, curiosity, the heart of a dove,
And he will flourish with great love.
Make sure to not tell him lies,
For truth itself will always rise,
As he needs to feel the warmth of trust,
His parent must be true and just,
To help him find his path,
Through tears and aches and joyous laugh.

Together we work as a team,
To understand past lives,
a different dream.
Take my hands,
and son, we'll fly,
Through time and space
and lives gone by.
We'll learn again,
and this time, we'll soar,
With eternity's grace,
a journey now, and more.
Over and over,
the cycle repeats,
Mother and son,
gentle heartbeats.

~Art by Aurora May

Introduction

by Oberon Zell

And the circles they go round and round
And the painted ponies go up and down
We're captives on the carousel of Time
We can't go back, we can only look
Behind from where we came
And go round and round and round
In the Circle Game!

~Joannie Mitchell: "The Circle Game"

FTER THE DEATH FROM CANCER ON MAY 13, 2014, of Morning Glory—my beloved Wife and Lifemate for 40 years—I worked for a few years with our dear friend and Death Doula, Judith Karen Fenley, to compose a handbook for the loving care and graceful passing of someone going through the process of dying. All about home funerals and green burials—as we had done with Morning Glory. Our *Death Rights & Rites* was finally published by Llewellyn in 2020.

My subsequent book, *That Undiscover'd Country: A Traveler's Guide to the Afterlife* (Black Moon, 2021) was a companion and sequel, dealing with the journey of the soul between lives—from death to birth.

The present work picks up from there—not about afterlife, but afterbirth. Consider these three books a trilogy: for dying, dead, reborn.

For many years I've wanted to write a little handbook as a guide for parents who find themselves with a "black sheep" or "ugly duckling" child who just doesn't seem to fit in. "Old Souls" reincarnating with uncanny abilities, insights and attitudes, memories of former lives, nightmares of previous deaths… Us. Me.

I wrote the *Grimoire for the Apprentice Wizard* (New Page, 2004) with the Grey Council specifically with the intention that it would be gifted to us on the 11th birthday of our next incarnation. And much later, with MG's and my apprentice Kiri, *Song of Gaea* as a bedtime story to be read to me (us) as a child next time around.

I suspect that many of you—like me—were "Changeling" children, born into families that had no idea what to make of weird kids like us. Cuckoos hatching in a nest of robins. We identified more with *The Addams Family* than with *Leave it to Beaver* or *Father Knows Best*. Some of our families handled the challenge well, with love and patience. But far too many blew it badly, often including serious abuse.

When I see all the happy kids at our Pagan gatherings, I am always struck with a poignant sense that in my next incarnation, this is the community I want to be born into and grow up into, with these parents!

For all the millions of us modern Pagans alive today—with more coming out every day—eventually it will come our time to leave this life; perhaps to return to begin a new one down the road. As the fastest-growing religion in the Western world, we Pagans will comprise entire generations to come. What advice and counsel do we want to offer our future parents to guide them in raising us?

This book is a "message in a bottle" tossed into the River of Time for future generations. If it feels like it was written to you, it was…

The vast marvel is to be alive… The supreme triumph is to be most vividly, most perfectly alive. Whatever the unborn and the dead may know, they cannot know the beauty, the marvel of being alive in the flesh. The dead may look after the afterwards. But the magnificent here and now of life in the flesh is ours, and ours alone, and ours only for a time. We ought to dance with rapture that we should be alive and in the flesh, and part of the living, incarnate cosmos. I am part of the sun as my eye is part of me. That I am part of the Earth my feet know perfectly, and my blood is part of the sea. My soul knows that I am part of the human race, my soul is an organic part of the great human soul… There is nothing of me that is alone and absolute except my mind, and we shall find that the mind has no existence by itself, it is only the glitter of the sun on the surface of the waters.

~D.H. Lawrence (9/11/1885-3/2/1930) as he lay dying at the Villa Robermond in Vence, France, from complications of tuberculosis.

Art by Craig R. Miller, from the Wheel of the Year Songbook, *by Gwydion Pendderwen*

Part I:
Born Again

And in the Spring, yeah, I'll be back
Like the grass in yonder field.
I'll be reborn into this wo-o-orld
When the Lady's will is revealed!

~Gwydion Pendderwen, "I'll be Reborn!"
On his album, *The Faerie Shaman,* 1982.

THE MAJOR WORLD RELIGIONS THAT HOLD A belief in reincarnation are Hinduism, Jainism, Buddhism and Sikhism, all of which arose in India. Rebirth is also the core theme of the ancient Mysteries of the Mediterranean world: Sumerian, Isian, Eleusinian, Orphic, Attic, Bacchic…the Descent (and rebirth) of Inanna, Kore, Osiris, Orpheus, Adonis, Attis—the Green Man and Maid.

Theosophy, modern Witchcraft (Wicca) and most NeoPagan reconstructionists also embrace the concept of reincarnation as an Afterlife option, if not necessarily for everyone.

In all of these systems, it is a basic assumption that we may or may not come around again in the same sex/gender, race, culture, religion, country, or even planet as we knew in our previous life. Indeed, Eastern religions teach that experiencing different forms in each lifetime is how we learn, evolve, and eventually attain enlightenment.

"What's past is prologue" (~William Shakespeare, *The Tempest)*

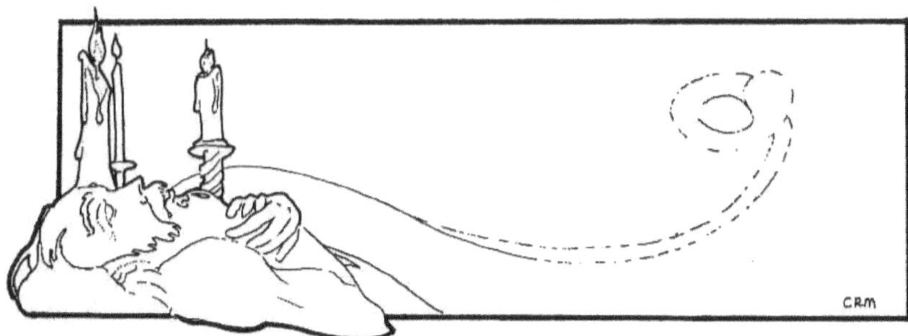

Art by Craig R. Miller, from the Wheel of the Year Songbook, *by Gwydion Pendderwen*

1. Reincarnation

By Oberon Zell

EWTON'S FIRST LAW OF THERMODYNAMICS, also known as the Law of Conservation of Energy, stipulates that *"Energy can neither be created nor destroyed; energy can only be transferred or changed from one form to another."*[1]

If we can conceptualize "soul" or spirit as a kind of living vortex or energy field that animates our corporeal bodies, we might apply this same principle to our individual consciousness, and conclude that it too "can neither be created nor destroyed, but can only be transferred or changed from one form to another."

There do, however, seem to be many options for the soul's post-corporeal journey and destination, and these differ widely among various cultures and religions. Noting that many are not mutually exclusive, here are some of the possibilities:

1. The departed soul may journey on to a particular culture-specific Afterlife realm. This may be a paradisal place of reward (Heaven, Elysium, Sekhet-Aaru, Valhalla, the Summerlands, the Isles of the Blessed) or punishment (Hell, Tartarus, Jahannam, Dante's Inferno), depending on various criteria (works, faith, Grace, karma). Afterlife realms may be vague and nebulous, but many are described and mapped in considerable detail.

2. The departed soul may lose all memory of its former life (drinking from the waters of *Lethe*—forgetfulness); or it may retain full memories of its previous life and identity (drinking from the well of *Mnemosyne*—memory).

3. The soul may pass through a gauntlet of Afterlife trials and judgements to prove itself worthy and deserving of its ultimate destination (Egyptian Hall of Judgement, the Bardos, Xibalba, the Christian Final Judgement…).

4. The soul may pass permanently into the realm of The Dreaming, which it has visited nightly throughout its life. Or conversely, we may find ("merrily, merrily, merrily") that *this* "life is but a dream," from which death is but an awakening into a truer reality.

---

[1] Boundless. "The Three Laws of Thermodynamics." *Boundless Chemistry*. Boundless, 02 June 2016. https://www.boundless.com/chemistry/textbooks/boundless-chemistry-textbook/thermodynamics-17/the-laws-of-thermodynamics-123/the-three-laws-of-thermodynamics-496-3601/ accessed 4/21/17.

5. *Apotheosis:* the soul may ascend to the realm of the Gods, to attain divinity and join the divine pantheon of ancestral spirits (Greek Heroes, Saints, Prophets, Angels, Loa).

6. The soul may just hang around in the *aether,* as a discarnate spirit or ghost, just on "the other side," but unable to interact with the realm of the living. It may be trapped between the worlds, awaiting release of some sort to continue its journey. In this state, the spirit may make contact and be consulted via mediums and *necromancy* (Spiritualism).

7. *Reincarnation:* the soul recycled to be reborn into another body—usually human, but not necessarily. Successive incarnations may be at higher or lower status according to how the person had conducted their previous lives, or they may be more random. Reincarnation may be immediate (*transmigration*) or occur after a period of time.

8. Or, as Dr. Michael Newton,[2] Sylvia Browne,[3] and others claim, the soul may return to an elaborate and complex astral realm of further learning, reuniting with other souls who have been associated though many lifetimes, and moving up the ranks of a celestial hierarchy towards Divinity. From such a realm, the soul may choose eventual reincarnation, or remain there as a guide and mentor to other souls.

9. Released from the confines of a physical body, the soul/spirit may return, like water spilled from a broken vessel, to the vast oceanic Well of Souls (the Collective Unconscious; the Quantum Field), from whence it may in time be poured again into a new vessel.

10. According to the Quantum *Simulation Hypothesis,* all the realms, worlds, and afterlives we experience (including this one) are actually *simulations*—like 2nd Life, video games, and "The Matrix."[4] Gods and souls are extensions of the quantum field (which is pure consciousness), entering into these various "sim" realms via *avatars*. It is all a game, and what we call "birth" and "death" are just entries and exits as we *res* from one sim into another. There may be infinite levels of such sims; worlds within worlds within worlds—like *Matryoshka* Russian nesting dolls.

11. Or the soul may just dissipate, lose all consciousness, and fade into oblivion, like the light of a lamp when the current is turned off (Atheism). Quantum physicists and virtually all religions consider this the least likely scenario, but it may be true for some. Who knows?

---

[2] Newton, Michael, *Journey of Souls: Case Studies of Life Between Lives*. Llewellyn Publications, Woodbury, MN, 1994.

[3] Browne, Sylvia, *Life on the Other Side: A Psychic's Tour of the Afterlife.* Berkeley, 2001.

[4] Merali, Zeeya, "Do We Live in the Matrix?" *Discover*, Dec. 2013, pp. 24–25.

> According to people under deep hypnosis (based on the 200 sessions I've filmed and the thousands that Dr. Helen Wambach and Michael Newton examined) people claim that prior to coming here our "consciousness" is "back home." (Their term). They claim that we work out the details of our next lifetime with loved ones and guides, and while we are here, only about a third of our consciousness is here with us, and roughly two thirds is always "back home." Once we're done with our journey here, they claim that we return "home" and reconnect with the rest of our conscious energy (that can access and remember previous lifetimes).[5]

In all fairness, one can only conclude that all these options must be available, and whatever any individual may experience after death is a product of the expectations of that person's faith, beliefs, and convictions. What you expect is what you get.[6]

Ŋear Death Experiences

Sometimes people who—by all indications—have died, are revived. Many revivers report a common series of experiences that have become known as "near-death experiences," or NDEs. Such experiences have been identified in religious literature since ancient times; 95% of world cultures are documented as making some mention of NDEs.

Many researchers (as well as revivers) cite the NDE as evidence that human consciousness can become separated from the body and brain under certain conditions, and glimpse the spiritual realm to which souls travel after death. Interpretation of these events tends to correspond with the cultural, philosophical, or religious beliefs of the person experiencing it.

Where do these near-death experiences come from? What causes them? New studies may offer some answers. Not all NDEs happen during actual life-threatening events—only about half of them happen during times of duress or even during something as relaxed as meditation, times when the body is not at risk of actual harm. But do people who actually die have the same experiences?

Based on recent data (as of this writing in May of 2023),[7] it appears that about half of those who die from cardiac arrest experience a surge in

---

[5] Martini, Richard, www.quora.com/Where-is-your-soul-before-you-are-born?

[6] Zell, Oberon, *That Undiscover'd Country: A Traveler's Guide to the Afterlife.* Black Moon Publishing, Cincinnati, OH, 2020.

[7] Pappas, Stephanie, "Surges of activity in the dying human brain could hint at fleeting conscious experiences." LiveScience.com, 5/1/2023. www.livescience.com/health/neuroscience/surges-of-activity-in-the-dying-human-brain-could-hint-at-fleeting-conscious-experiences

gamma waves in their brain for about 30 seconds before brain death. Now the question is—if the heart has stopped and the brain is surging with activity for 30 seconds, in what appears to be our brain's dream center, is the dying person having a true NDE or is the brain activity part of the natural body shut down process after the heart has stopped working? Is it possible that in those 30 seconds the spirit/consciousness of the dying person is being released from its confinement in a mortal shell into the next phase of the soul's journey?

Once they are irrevocably dead, the newly deceased must journey across the lands of the dead to settle their accounts. Devin Hunter allows up to ninety days for this process, which he calls "reorientation."[8]

Reincarnation

Also called *transmigration* or *metempsychosis, reincarnation* refers to the rebirth of some aspect of an individual that persists after bodily death—whether it be consciousness, mind, the soul, or some other entity—in one or more successive physical existences. Depending upon the tradition, these may be human, animal, or even spiritual. For instance, The Venda of southern Africa believe that, when a person dies, the soul stays near the grave for a brief time and then seeks a new resting place or another body—human, mammalian, or reptilian.[9]

The major world religions that hold a belief in reincarnation are Hinduism, Jainism, Buddhism and Sikhism, all of which arose in India. Rebirth is also the core theme of the ancient Mysteries of the Mediterranean world: Sumerian, Isian, Eleusinian, Orphic, Attic, Bacchic…the annual descent and rebirth of Inanna, Kore, Osiris, Orpheus, Adonis, Attis, even Christ—the Green Man or Maid. Gnosticism, Theosophy, religious Witchcraft (Wicca) and most NeoPagan reconstructionist traditions also embrace the concept of reincarnation as an Afterlife option, if not necessarily for everyone.

The Greek Orphic Mysteries held that a preexistent soul survives bodily death and is later reincarnated in a human or other mammalian body, eventually receiving release from the cycle of birth and death, and regaining its former pure state. Plato (c. 428-348 BCE) believed in an immortal soul that takes frequent successive incarnations.

The major religions that believe in reincarnation all hold in common a doctrine of *karma* ("act"): that one's actions (cause) in this present life will have effect in the next one. In Hinduism, the process of birth and

---

[8] Hunter, Devin, *The Witch's Book of Spirits.* Llewellyn Publications, , 2017.
[9] McKenna, Amy, "Religious belief: Reincarnation," *Encyclopedia Britannica.*
   https://www.britannica.com/topic/reincarnation

rebirth is perpetual until one achieves *moksha* ("release"), which is attained upon realization that the eternal core of the individual (*atman*) and the Absolute reality (*brahman*) are One. Only thus can one escape from the recurring cyclic process of death and rebirth *(samsara)*.

In all of these systems, it is a basic presumption that we may or may not come around again in the same sex/gender, race, culture, religion, country, or even planet as we knew in our previous life. Indeed, Eastern religions teach that experiencing different forms in each lifetime is how we learn and evolve, until we attain enlightenment and release from the cycle. Therefore, no incarnation can be "wrong," as there will be important lessons to be learned from the experiences of each lifetime. And there will always be another, as long as one remains on the Wheel.

Reincarnation Studies at the University of Virginia[10]

Ian Stevenson, MD (1918-2007) was a Canadian-born American psychiatrist, the founder and director of the Division of Perceptual Studies at the University of Virginia School of Medicine, where he was a professor for fifty years. Jim Tucker, MD has taken over for Dr. Stevenson at the University of Virginia.

For 40 years, starting in 1961, Dr. Stevenson investigated thousands of children who spontaneously remembered past lives that could be factually validated. He chose to only study children as he reasoned that children were unlikely to fabricate past life memories. Most of Steven-son's cases come from Asia, India, or other areas where the doctrine of reincarnation is generally accepted. Where reincarnation is not an accepted belief system parents tend to dismiss and inhibit their children's expressions of past-life memories.

Stevenson compiled more than 2,500 childhood past-life memory cases. In 1,567 of these, the person of the previous life was able to be identified through research. In another 150 cases, the past life personality was "tentatively" identified.

Stevenson found the median interval between the past life death and rebirth to be four and a half years. In cases of suicide, however, the average interval between death and rebirth is only three months.

A particularly important observation is that individuals may change religion, nationality, ethnic affiliation, race, and gender from one lifetime to another. In 1,200 validated past memory cases, 90% of the time

---

[10] Semkiw, Walter, "Gender Change in Reincarnation Cases and Homosexuality," *Reincarnation Research,* www.reincarnationresearch.com/tag/past-life-gender-change/

children reincarnated in the same gender as in their previous life. This implies that souls may have an innate masculine or feminine character.

But some of us may switch gender periodically, to learn what it is like to be a different gender, as in the myth of Tiresias of Apollonia, who was turned into a woman for seven years, then back to a man. When Zeus and Hera got into an argument as to whether men or women experienced greater pleasure in sex, they asked Tiresias, who had been both. Tiresias replied, "a man enjoyed one tenth the pleasure and a woman nine tenths."

It seems that some individuals who have gender identity issues may represent gender change cases, in which the person still relates to the gender of a prior incarnation. If a soul is accustomed to incarnating in one gender and then has a lifetime as the opposite gender, that soul may still identify with the previous, more usual gender. This may lead to gender dysphoria and transgender issues.

Common Patterns of Reincarnation

The childhood cases of reincarnation studied by Dr. Ian Stevenson have many common features:

1. **As soon as the child can communicate, they start to describe a previous lifetime**. Often, the child declares that their name is different from the name given by their biological parents. The child insists that the current family is not their true family, but that their real family lives in a different village or town. The child remembers the names of various family members and geographic locations from the past lifetime. The average age at which the child starts speaking about a past lifetime is 3 years and the average age when children stop talking about a past lifetime is 7½ years.

2. **The child remembers details of their death in the prior lifetime**. In approximately 66% of cases, a violent or premature death occurred in the previous lifetime. Dr. Stevenson found that individuals who died of traumatic wounds, such as bullet or knife wounds, often are born with birthmarks that mirror the wounds incurred in the past lifetime. In the contemporary lifetime, the child may have a phobia related to the cause of death in the past life. Of the children who remember a violent past life death, 35% have a phobia related to the cause of death.

3. **Based on information provided by the child, their family from the prior incarnation is eventually identified**. When the child meets this family for the first time, the child is able to identify family members by name or relationship. The child often knows family

secrets that only members of the prior family would know. As a result, the family from the past lifetime often accepts the child as the reincarnation of their deceased relative.

4. **Personality traits, personal preferences, and habits often persist from one incarnation to another**.

5. **Gender usually stays the same**. In 90% of cases, the child returns assuming the same sex as in the past lifetime. But in 10% of cases, gender is reversed from one lifetime to another.

6. **Physical appearance can be similar from one lifetime to another**.

7. **Relationships are renewed through reincarnation.**

8. **Children may remember the interval in-between lifetimes.** In 20 percent of Stevenson's cases, children report memories of what happened in the spirit world in-between lifetimes.[11]

Ħeligious Comparison Ħegarding Afterlife
By Edward Hrafnskald Conway

First, my background: My godfather was the Hindu scholar Raja Rao. I was born and raised Advaita Vedanta Hindu, for 16 years. Then I followed a seva *(service) and* shakti *(feminine divine ecstasy) focused guru for another 3 years. This was followed by 3 years of Wicca and the past 16 years as an Asatruar Heathen. I am speaking from 19 years on experience of devout practice as a Hindu, and 19 years of similarly devout practice as a Pagan.*

The fundamental basis of Hinduism and other dharmic religions is different from, and I would argue, the opposite of, the fundamental basis of Paganism.

First, what you probably are already familiar with: Christianity and Islam teach that the life you are living should be spent praising God, serving God, doing good deeds in God's name, and suffering for God. The reward is an afterlife spent in paradise/heaven. You serve, submit, suffer for, praise, and keep faith with God, and in return you get a great afterlife.

For Christianity and Islam, the transaction is: Service Now, Reward Later.

For Hinduism and other dharmic religions, the teaching is that life, and this world, is filled with suffering, illusion, attachment, and endless

---

[11] Semkiw, Walter, "Advances in Reincarnation Research: A Tribute to Ian Stevenson." *Reincarnation Research.* https://www.reincarnationresearch.com/childrens-past-life-memories-and-the-research-of-ian-stevenson-md/ Accessed 4/21/2023.

pain. The way out is to cease to do things that cause suffering, to cease to care and attach to outcomes, and/or to find a guru who can enlighten you. The world and this life is seen as inherently painful. To live is to suffer. To seek enlightenment is to seek an end to that suffering.

For dharmic religions including Hinduism, the transaction is: Follow our rules, and you will cease to exist by achieving enlightenment, liberating yourself from the pain, suffering, and attachment of this world/life.

For Paganism, the teaching is that this world and this life is inherently good. This life is made up of people, places, seasons of tremendous beauty, and above all, a chance to change the world for the better. Pagans worship the Gods and Goddesses not because we will be rewarded later, but because the act of worship makes our lives richer and more meaningful right now.

For Paganism, the transaction is: embrace the Gods, Goddesses, ancestors and spirits of the world, and they will make your current life rich and joyous.

Christianity and Islam see this world as a thing to endure for the glories and rewards to be found in the next life. This life has meaning only in the rewards it can gain you for good behavior and for maintaining faith.

Dharmic religions including Hinduism see this would as inherently evil: filled with karma, attachments, and illusions. For dharmic religions, the world is something to escape.

Pagan religions embrace this world and this life, and focus most of their time and energy on this world and this life.

Paganism and Hinduism teach diametrically opposed lessons: Hinduism that one should abandon the world and seek an exit, Paganism that one should embrace the world and seek to integrate oneself into it.

Tell a Hindu they will be reborn again a hundred times, and they will see it as a horrible fate because the world, and being born into it, is full of pain for a Hindu. Tell a Pagan they will be reborn again a hundred times, and they will embrace it and see it as a blessing, because being born, being alive, and celebrating that gift of life is what Paganism is about.

The Well of Souls [12]

From OZ's journal; May 25, 1986—

Death is a passage, not a destination. We are born from the womb of the Mother of Life, and to Her we eventually return, to be clothed with new

---

[12] Zell, Oberon, *op cit.*

flesh and born again, and again, and again. We are like drops of water spewed from a fountain, to sparkle and dance for a time in the sunlight, only to fall eventually back into the pool, from which we are continually being drawn up and sprayed forth again. There are no endings, only endless beginnings, as we cycle round and round through night and day, winter and summer, death, and life.

All living creatures are like cups of diverse sizes and shapes, with which the waters of life are scooped from the Well of Souls. And all the cups are emptied back into the pool when they are periodically broken. New cups are continually fashioned of living clay and dipped in their turn into the same Well to be filled. But it is rare that a new cup will scoop up the exact same batch of molecules as in a former cup. Usually, there will be a considerable mix. And so, it is that a human may have bits of "past life" memories of several other people, as well as assorted animals—or that a human-sized cup may contain a number of entire birds and other small animals, but at most, only a fraction of a single whale.

And in the proper balance of Nature, each new generation replaces the previous, so that the number of each kind of cup remains constant. Now what do you suppose happens when one species proliferates greatly at the expense of others? When there are no more cups of Moa, Steller's Sea Cow, Carolina Parakeet, Passenger Pigeon, Thylacine, Sperm Whale, Condor, Mammoth, Giant Lemur, Great Auk, Cave Bear, Megatherium, Dodo, Roc, or countless others, but the cups labelled "Human" are being produced by the geometrically increasing billions? In that case, I believe, the human soul-stuff would become increasingly diluted with other decimated species, and all the vanished animals would return in human form.

In their 1962 book, *Warriors of the Rainbow*,[13] William Willoya and Vinson Brown claimed that many years ago, the Indigenous Hopi had prophesied that the spirits of all the dead Indigenous tribes would return in a single generation in the bodies of the white conquerors. This generation, they said, would be recognizable by their native affinity for the ways of those native peoples. They would wear beads and leather and feathers, let their hair grow long and hold it back with braids and headbands. They would assume the Indigenous ways and return to the reverence of Nature and the Great Mother. They would learn the native chants, and purify themselves in sweats, fasts, and vision quests. And they would come to be known by a name like *Hopi,* which means "the Peaceful Ones," for they would also be the Children of Peace.[14]

---

[13] Willoya, William & Brown, Vinson, *Warriors of the Rainbow.* Naturegraph Pubs, 1962.
[14] Morton, Chris & Thomas, Ceri Louise, *The Mystery of the Crystal Skulls: A Real-Life Detective Story of the Ancient World.* Vermont, Bear & Company, 1998.

Around 1970, the Hopi elders declared that this prophecy had come to pass, and they summoned shamans from all the tribes to come to the Four Corners of the ancestral Hopi Land, to learn the full extent of the prophecies and to go forth and instruct those who would be receptive. This was done.

I believe that the generation now coming of age will be a generation of noble heroes in an age of future legends, for it will be their task to undertake that Heroic Quest, through all manner of perils, to the Fortress of Ultimate Darkness, to restore the Light, save the world, and usher in the Golden Age of Aquarius. For this is one of those great Ages of Magic—when the fate of all living beings turns on a tiny pivot, and all things are possible. More than at any such time in all history, the choices have escalated to the ultimate: Apocalypse or Apotheosis; planetary annihilation or planetary illumination. And with such a wide range of possibilities comes the return of true Magick in the form of coincidence control through manipulation of probabilities.

There are now more people alive at one time than have ever lived before in the entire span of human history! It has been a great show, and I, for one, think we should take it on the road. I find it no coincidence that the very technology which presently threatens all life on this planet could be used to build starships to carry our children's children throughout the galaxy, to "plant the seeds from star to star." We create our world by the myths we live and believe in, and for the first time in our history, we are creating myths not just of a golden age long past, but of one yet to come. What shall it be; Mad Max or Star Trek? Consciously or unconsciously, we are all choosing sides...

Here's an Indian Bedtime Story. The current Hell Cycles began when the White Minds crossed the Great Waters and anchored on the Land of the Red-Hearted Ones. There they met, broke and defeated the Red Hearts. Blood was spilled and heads, they rolled. Thirteen hundred moons later, the Souls of the dead Red Hearted warriors reincarnated as the newborn of the White Minds. These new Red-Hearted Souls were recognized by the Red Hearted Ones of that time by the way thy dressed and wore their hair to look like the Red-Hearted. The first wave brought the "hippies" who marked the beginning of the end for the White-Minded. One-hundred and thirty moons later, the "mohawk punk fashions" signaled a new wave of Red warriors and two-hundred and sixty moons afterwards... crystal channeling, pop shamanism and Mayan nostalgia. This is how the Red Hearts initiated the Great Collapse and finally defeated the White Minds. The Reds were defeated because of their weak hearts and the Whites, their weak minds. For

> *now we know what happens when a people's strength grows too strong…yang turns to yin, hurly burly hits Broadway and everybody is hereafter proclaimed a Pope. Is Nothing Really Sacred? Of course it is, my cherry blossom…of course, it was…*
>
> ~Antero Alli *The Akashic Record Player*, 2015[15]

References

1. Alli, Antero, *The Akashic Record Player: A Non-Stop Geomantic Conspiracy.* The Original Falcon Press, 2015.
2. Browne, Sylvia, *Life on the Other Side: A Psychic's Tour of the Afterlife.* Berkeley, 2001.
3. Hegeman, William, *Magic, Mind, Emotion and Body, The Praxis: Magic No Woo, The How and Why Book.* People Embracing Change Tribe, 2021.
4. Keirle-Smith, Gordon, *Another Egg, Another Life: A Book designed to Stimulate Children's Past Life Memories.* CreateSpace Independent Publishing Platform, 2017.
5. Martini, Richard, https://www.quora.com/Where-is-your-soul-before-you-are-born?
6. Morton, Chris & Thomas, Ceri Louise, *The Mystery of the Crystal Skulls: A Real-Life Detective Story of the Ancient World.* Vermont, Bear & Co., 1998.
7. Newton, Michael, *Journey of Souls: Case Studies of Life Between Lives.* Llewellyn Publications, Woodbury, MN, 1994.
8. Semkiw, Walter, *Born Again: Reincarnation Cases Involving International Celebrities, India's Political Legends, and Film Stars.* Pluto Project, 2007.
9. Stevenson, Ian, *Twenty Cases Suggestve of Reincarnation.* University of Virginia Press, 1966. Revised and Enlarged edition, 1980.
10. ________, *Children Who Remember Previous Lives: A Question of Reincarnation.* University of Virginia Press, 1987
11. ________, *Reincarnation and Biology: A Contribution to the Etiology of Birthmarks and Birth Defects.* Praeger Publishers, 1997.
12. Steiger, Brad, *You Will Live Again: Dramatic Case Histories of Reincarnation.* Blue Dolphin Press, Grass Valley, CA, 1996.
13. Tucker, Jim. B., *Return to Life: Extraordinary Cases of Children Who Remember Past Lives.* St. Martin's Griffin, 2008.
14. ________, *Life Before Life: Children's Memories of Previous Lives.* St. Martin's Press, 2013.
15. Willoya, William & Brown, Vinson, *Warriors of the Rainbow.* Naturegraph Publishers, 1962.
16. Zell, Oberon, *That Undiscover'd Country: A Traveler's Guide to the Afterlife.* Black Moon Publishing, Cincinnati, OH, 2020.

---

[15] Alli, Antero, *The Akashic Record Player: A Non-Stop Geomantic Conspiracy.* The Original Falcon Press, 2015.

2. Which Life Are You In?
A Philosophy of
Progressive Reincarnation[16]

by Gavin Frost, Church of Wicca

I died as a mineral and became a plant;
I died as a plant and rose to animal;
I died as animal and I was a man.
Why should I fear? When was I less by dying?
Yet once more I shall I die as man,
To soar with spirits blest.
But even from this I must pass on:
All except God doth perish.

~Jalalu'd-Din Rumi, 1241 CE

HUS IN THE THIRTEENTH CENTURY DID THE leader of the Mevlevi Dervishes set down in the *Mathnawi* one of the finest explanations of basic reincarnation theory, which in dramatic terms separates Christian belief from Pagan. For at the second Council of Constantinople in 553 CE it became Christian dogma that reincarnation was heresy, Jesus' atoning sacrifice having broken the cycle for all true believers. Ever afterward, belief in reincarnation has been superfluous and unnecessary to Christians, even though such a belief is clearly indicated in the writings of many famous Christians; for instance, St Francis of Asisi.

For modern Christians also, the dogma is being replaced with new belief in reincarnation based on the Hindu ethic of the lawgiver, Manu. However, to many philosophers this transmigration, or degenerate form of reincarnation, has many flaws. If you are "bad," says transmigration, you will be punished by coming back as some loathly beast; so you must *ipso facto* be "good." Further, transmigration implies that you must endure any present misfortune passively because at some time in the past you were evil, and your present misfortune is the natural evening-up of the score. In that Great Ledger in the Sky, the Akashic Record, your name is on a page of debits and credits which must in some unspecified way be balanced if you are to get off the Wheel.

---

[16] Reprinted from *Green Egg,* Vol. VIII, No. 76; 2/2/1976.

These theories of transmigration and of resurrection do not seem to fit in with what has been learned from regression techniques 1, 2, 3 nor with concepts of an afterlife as described by Ruth Montgomery's communications with Bishop James Pike, nor yet with the famous Myers experiments.

Reincarnation in Early Societies and Thought

It would be comfortable if we could flatly say that prehistoric peoples believed in reincarnation. But it is fairly clear from boat burials and from barrow graves that Indo-European peoples shared with Egyptians a belief in an afterworld where existence was similar to that known here, where dead spirits required a wide range of goods and many servants. These funerary rites and grave goods also tended to indicate a belief in the final resurrection of the actual physical body and hence the need to preserve the Earth-plane shell. The brief change to cremation in the Urn Field Cultures can tentatively be interpreted as indicating a dramatic change of philosophy and may, as in the eastern cases which retained cremation, indicate a belief in reincarnation. We can say that the propitiation of spirits—both animal and human—indicates a high-level understanding of the spirit-and-shell concept; though little belief in reincarnation or transmigration is detectable.

This concept of spirit and shell can be seen in the very ancient writings of the *Rig Veda,* where we read,

The Spirit is likened to the Charioteer;
The Body to the Chariot;
And the reins are Wisdom.

We must also look to eastern writings for the first thoughts on reincarnation, for the *Bhagavad Gita* says,

As the soul passes in the body
Through childhood, youth, and age,
Even so is its taking on of another body.

Soon after this we get the Pythagorean and Platonic doctrines of progressive reincarnation which swept the Old World. Thus early Christians, especially the followers of Origen, were heavily oriented toward reincarnation, though of what type it is difficult to define.

There is some evidence for a belief in reincarnation in various extant books from Ireland and Wales. The prevalence of "I have beens" in the Triads seems to us a clear indication of such beliefs.

I have been in many shapes
Before I attained a congenial form.
I have been a narrow blade of a sword,
I have been a drop in the river,
I have been a shining star.

Despite Robert Graves' out-of-hand rejection of a literal interpretation of this type of poem, still we in Celtic Wicca tend to believe that the old Bards were quite capable of including both obvious and hidden meanings in their writings. The only other source is own (Celtic) oral and written tradition; from these sources the following philosophy is drawn.

A Philosophy of Progressive Reincarnation

Let us consider the idea that a spirit comes from some unspecified Source and inhabits an Earth-plane (or planet-plane) shell so that it may learn and grow. Referring to Figure 1, we see a situation which might have occurred some five billion years ago, just after the very first spark of life carne to our planet. A spirit came from a pool of what we like to call Divine

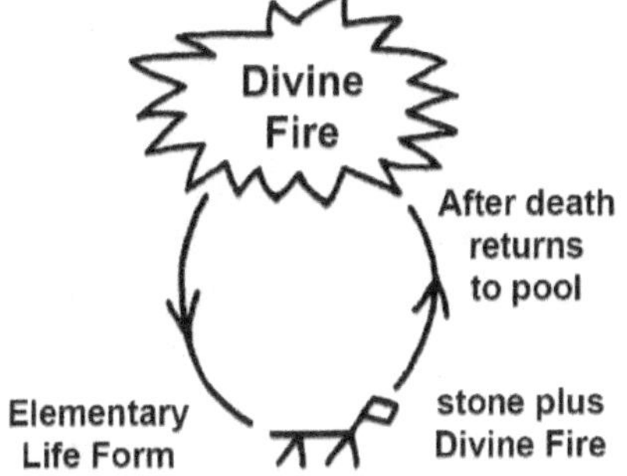

Fig. 1. And thus came Divine Fire.

Fire, inhabited the first elementary creature, and gave it life. By inhabiting this living body, the spirit grew; then in returning to the pool of Divine Fire, it caused the pool to expand as well. Thus as the Cosmos and the living beings therein grew and expanded, so the controlling Divine Fire also expanded, keeping pace with the needs of the Cosmos. This pool of energy has been called the '5th dimension' or 'eternity' by a British mathematical team headed by Professor Bennett, who finally formulated a Unified Field Theory—something which Einstein worked toward during his entire life. As the Cosmos expands, it loses energy, since theoretical physics requires that the energy level be constant. Only by formulating the Energy-Pool theory were the mathematicians able to explain a structured Cosmos.

As the Cosmos expanded and life became mere complex, the Divine Fire correspondingly expanded to keep everything in balance, as might be depicted in Figure 2. We see here an illustration of the idea attributed to Hermes Trismegistus: "As above, so below." For as we get levels

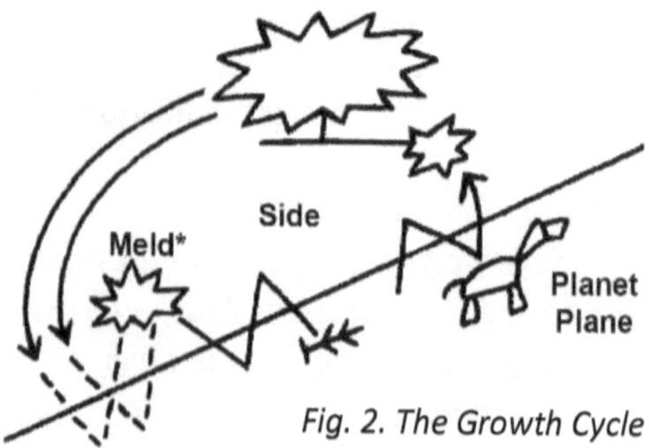

Fig. 2. The Growth Cycle

of development on the planet plane, so levels of spirit development occur on the other side of the Invisible Barrier, a place which is often called 'heaven' but which we simply call *Side*.

Returning to Figure 2, we see here the minute spirit growing through several levels of progressive reincarnation so that the mere spark now becomes a large energy mass which will ultimately re-meld with that pool of Divine Fire from whence it originally came. This figure also introduces the concept of several small spirits melding to run around a larger (that is, more complex) body; e.g., maybe three virus-spirits are required to run a lichen body.

The *raison d'etre* for our existence, then, is a growth system: As the Cosmos grows, so do our spirits. And the total amount of energy stored in the pool also grows. When we examine this schema in more detail for any given entity, we get a situation like that depicted in Figure 3. This has often been called the "boarding-school hypothesis." The spirit inhabiting the lowest level of any given animal species, perhaps homo sapiens, has come from a less-complex being. Thus we can detect in some levels of mankind animalistic, anti-social behavioral patterns.

The being on the Earth-plane learns, grows, and dies. That spirit then progresses through a short time at home in Side to another more complex assignment in a suitable body. This assignment can be likened to a further learning experience at boarding school. The progress shown here is upward, as the spirit grows and learns to handle assignments of ever-increasing complexity.

The time the spirit spends at Home—in Side—serves to assimilate and synthesize new knowledge and (in conjunction with guide spirits) to select the spirit's next school and assignment.

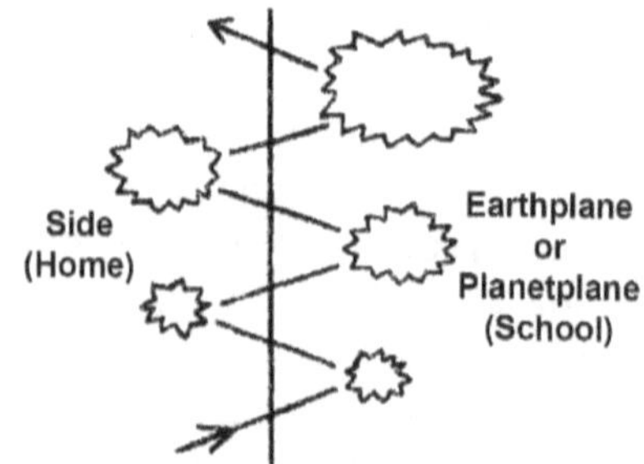

Fig. 3. The Boarding-School Metaphor.

The spirit is thus its own Akashic Record. It has within itself all the knowledge gained in previous lifetimes in the Boarding School of Life. Its mistakes, blunders, false starts, wild-goose chases, abortive efforts, are to be considered as an essential part of the learning experience, rather than as "evil" or "sin."

It is worthwhile here to consider the third-grader who—purely by accident—smashes a dish. We don't consider him to be inherently evil; rather, he lacks experience. So if indeed socially acceptable behavior is one of the goals of this learning process, how irrational it is to believe that anti-social behavior deserves demotion clear back to kindergarten—or to an eternity in the burning sulfurous pit of the principal's office. Such a sentence would serve only to increase the spirit's wish to rebel against the system.

It is important to recognize that many thinkers do not place human beings at the top of the ladder of progression. For if social behavior or intelligence is to be the criterion of spiritual development, dolphins are far more advanced than mankind. Many philosophers have attempted to decide what criteria should be used to define development at the human level. Apart from a definition of nine levels on the Earthplane (and congruently—as above, so below—nine levels in Side), our tradition is silent on these criteria.

Let us for a moment speculate on one set of criteria: selflessness versus competitive behavior. Consider an assortment of your acquaintances. Can you separate them into, say, four or five groups which are progressively less competitive? Start with those who love violence, roughhousing, and blood sports; and end with those selfless individuals who refuse to compete. Which group would you place highest on your personal ladder of progression? The selfless ones? If a life of total selflessness is a means to avoid reincarnating again as a human, though, might it not actually be selfish to live a selfless life?

The progressive-reincarnation theory outlined above, with its concept of continuing and orderly growth, gives us all a reason for living; additionally it fits with the British Unified Field Theory. It seems essentially rational and it negates the karmic threat system. It is also important to note that this reincarnation system replaces the concepts of "sin" and "evil" with an acknowledgement that less-compassionate and more hurtful behavior is the sign of incomplete spiritual development (the actions of a third-grader rather than those of an adult).

Logically, if you really have a drive to do a given thing, such as learning to tap-dance or going round the world on a raft, you should do the thing, thus filling the gap in your experience. Otherwise you will be obliged to return yet again into another identity to complete that assignment. We explain infant deaths and incurable, crippling disease as fulfilling the individual's need to complete his particular. assignment.

Such death and disability can also be regarded as a learning process, a semester in school, both for the individual and for his family and friends- -not as a retribution for previous negative acts.

Conclusion

Any religion requiring a threat system to keep the faithful in line is probably not worth the powder to blow it with. The transmigration system devised by the Hindu Manu has probably caused more suffering in the world than any other philosophical concept; and it is important for those now embracing the idea of reincarnation to understand that transmigration was not the original philosophical ideal.

"Why should I fear? When was I less by dying?" asks the Mathnawi. We should look upon death as a gateway to further and greater opportunities; not as a threat, not necessarily to be staved off at immense expense until the last possible second.

The reincarnation system described in this chapter, using the metaphor of the boarding school, is simple and straightforward. It does not deny anyone his or her individual rights. Remember that in a modern Unified Field Theory the energy which may be "spirit" must increase as the universe expands so that cosmic energy is kept constant. But the system is also reversible: When the Cosmos starts to contract, spirit energy will necessarily have to diminish.

So the reincarnation cycle will then flow backward, approaching zero at the ultimate single-nucleus cosmic state.

As a final thought: Beware the Catch-22 of reincarnation. That is, if you expect to be reincarnated at the human level again after this present experience, you probably will be. For thoughts are real.

3. The Passing

By Cat Gina Cole

EINCARNATION, WHAT A FASCINATING AND MYS-
terious subject, and I think many of us have heard stories
that have left us wondering if reincarnation is real or not.
Having been raised in a closed magical family tradition, I
had heard about reincarnation like it was a fact from a very
young age. I did not question that until I was much older and wanted to
know more for myself. I read books and listened to many stories, none of
which gave me the concrete proof I thought I was seeking; so the mystery
remained.

The Grandma I grew up with was Beulah White, a "family friend"
who took my mother in when both moms parents passed by the time, she
was sixteen. I only knew them from photographs shown me as a child. As
for Beulah, she was just Grandma because she was the only grandma-type
person in my life.

Once in my early twenties, while staying with Beulah, I had a past
life experience in my dreams. The dream was set in a time long ago where
some village was being invaded and I was suddenly one of those villagers
and I was killed. Startled I woke panting, in a sweat and all tangled in my
blankets, fighting to get free of them.

That morning, "Beulah/Grandma" took one look at me and said
"Rough night?" Still shaken I sat down and told her about the dream. I
learned so much more about past lives and reincarnation from her that
day. I learned what Unverified Personal Gnosis was, an event one experiences that cannot be verified by others but is real and true for the person
experiencing it. That past lives and reincarnation are considered a UPG,
but many people over the span of all recorded time have experienced them
that many in society have come to accept it as real and true. I also learned
that many will not accept a UPG as real and true until they have had such
an experience. Hence the mystery of reincarnation remains.

In my time with "Grandma", she talked about "The Passing." She described the passing as an event that occurred when an elder was dying and
they "Passed on" all their knowledge to the next in line, that it was all part
of reincarnation. This too was discussed as a fact of life, but it was an
unknown mystery to me as I grew up.

Now in my late thirties, I was living four hundred miles from Beu-
lah/Grandma, when the passing occurred. It was a day like any other, I
had gone to work, made dinner and so on, but as I slept Grandma called

to me. I was transported to her bedroom where it was very clear she lay dying. She reached for my hand from her bed and as I took her hand she said, "I must show you."

I took her hand, and we were transported to a foreign land sometime in the past. We stood holding hands as we watched many people fleeing their homes. They were bundled up, carrying what they could with their children following, babies bound to their chests with scarves. I saw children crying over parents who died on the trail and were carried away by another adult as they screamed for their mothers. I cried too.

"This is where our people come from," Beulah said, shaking me from the intensity of what I was seeing. "This is Poland, after the great war. But the fighting never stopped, and we were never safe. This is what we call the Trail of Souls." I felt heartbreaking sadness from her as she said, "You see that screaming child taken from her dead mother? That was me."

Before I could respond she said "come" and turned away.

I began to see images flash in my mind like clips of an old movie. A young girl playing with flowers, then she was in school. It took me a moment to realize I was seeing Beulah/Grandma's life flash before us. The clips of her life stopped for a moment, and we were now standing in a barren land, dust blowing around a clapboard house. Now inside I saw Beualah/Grandma as a thirty-year-old woman pregnant for just a moment, then with a baby in her arms.

In the room were also the couple I had known as my "biological grandparents," the Roberts, also about thirty years old. The Roberts took Beulah/Grandma and the child in and raised the child as their own, it was 1932, the year my mother was born. As I considered this, I realized the vision was telling me that Beulah *was* actually my biological grandmother, and the child I was seeing was my mom.

Then more movie clips of Grandma's life
began again and when they stopped,
we were in a cave.

Art from The Mighty Thor, *Marvel Comics, No. 301, Nov. 1980 - p. 5*

As my eyes adjusted, I could see before us a long line of people to our right and to our left as far as the eye could see in either direction, walking past us. As each one walked in front of me, I got a glimpse of their life; what they were, how they lived, what they knew, I could see and feel it all entering into me. They were all some kind of oracle, visionary magician, mage, wise woman, monk, and on. Then grandma said, "They are all you, this is your line. Their knowledge, their lives are your knowledge and your lives; and now you have mine too."

With that we were transported back to her bedroom where I was holding her hand. I was crying as grandma said, "Let go now girl and carry on, stop fussing" she patted my hand and let out her last breath.

Four hundred miles away I woke sobbing and crying out for my grandmother. An hour later the phone rang, it was my mom, she told me Grandma had passed.

"I know" I said.

"How?" she asked.

"It was the Passing, Mom, she gave me the Passing."

"So, you know then, everything?"

"Yeah Mom, Everything."

My dreams for the next month or two were loaded with past life dreams—mine, Grandma's and those of the many who we had been before. In each of them more magic and family traditional knowledge came and so the passing goes.

Is this the magnitude and depth of reincarnation? Will science ever prove reincarnation? Will I be able to do the same for those that come behind me? I guess those questions will be a great Mystery yet to be revealed.

4. The Village[17]

By Oberon Zell

I am Death, I touch all, I will come as I must,
Bringing comfort and rest, for your souls are my trust.
And reunion, my gift beyond death is the prize,
For your heart, for your soul, for your eyes.

I will pulse in your blood, I will ring from your core,
When the Lady, my Love, gives you flesh once more!
You will meet and remember the loves of your lives;
For your heart and your soul are my eyes.

~Kathy Mar & Gwen Zak, "In Your Eyes"

U

PSET BY HIS SATIRICAL BROADSIDES AGAINST the Christian establishment, a woman once asked Samuel Clemens (Mark Twain) whether he believed in Holy Baptism. "Be*lieve* in it?" thundered the irascible journalist; "Why, Madam, I've seen it *done!*"

This is the way the members of my expanded Family – the Ravenhearts – feel about reincarnation. It is not a matter of belief for us; it is a matter of personal experience. It is a matter of re-cognition (literally, "knowing again").

As Pagans, we consider the myths and legends that have been passed down to us through the generations to contain the essential stories and lessons conveyed from our ancestral selves to our present incarnations. And we Ravenhearts have a story we share amongst ourselves; a Family Myth, if you will. We call it The Village...

Thousands of years ago (or Once Upon a Time, if you prefer), somewhere in central Europe, we all lived together in our little Village. We had lived there from the earliest time, from when the great walls of Ice retreated from the valley. Other villages, of course, also came into being across the Earth, all with similar stories and destinies...

We farmed the fields, hunted in the forests, picked herbs and berries on the hillsides, planted apple trees, and erected standing stones to mark the risings and settings of the Sun, Moon and stars. We learned to grind and polish stone; to fire pottery; to forge bronze—and later, meteoric iron.

---

[17] Oberon Zell-Ravenheart, "The Myths of Oberon" –*Green Egg* Vol. 32, No. 132, Jan. 2000.

Our houses had ancient walls of stone and ever-renewed roofs of thatch. We honored the Earth our Mother, and celebrated the turnings of Her seasons through Summer's life, Winter's death, and Spring's rebirth. And when we died in our time, our bodies would be buried in the apple orchard, with sapling trees planted on our graves. And we would be remembered, and invited to return as children conceived by those who had loved us.

And generation after generation, in this way we kept returning to The Village, and the ones we loved. For we were reborn among the souls we had grown to know and love, familiar beacons calling us Home to become brothers, sisters, sons, or daughters to those we had just left. And we grew strong in our love for each other, our bonds of Family, Clan, and Tribe, as well as the wisdom accumulated through countless returning lives.

Sometimes wanderers would find their way to The Village, to become part of it ever after. And sometimes some of us traveled far afield, and returned with mates from distant lands, whose lives and destinies became interwoven with The Village forevermore. These stories are also recalled and told among us.

Over the centuries, our Village suffered hard times as well as good. Periodically, raiders would cross the river to pillage and plunder, stealing what they could make off with, whether it be food, tools, goods—or women. But always we defended our homes, drove off the invaders, recouped our losses, and rebuilt our lives. And when women who had been carried off in those raids eventually came to the ends of their lives, they often returned to The Village in their next incarnations, sometimes calling to join us the souls of children they had borne far away.

And then one terrible day, the Romans came. These were not simple raiders, intent only on plunder. These were disciplined armies of conquest in the name of Empire. When we would not capitulate, they burned The Village to the ground. Most of us were killed defending our homes and families. The few survivors were taken prisoner, back to Rome, far from our destroyed home—which was lost to us forever.

For now, when we died, there was no Village to return to. No one to receive our spirits back into the welcoming wombs and arms of those who had known us and loved us. We were homeless souls, cast adrift; orphans of the storm.

And so we became scattered across the world. We took incarnation wherever we could find it, in other lands both near and far. We all have our stories of these past two thousand years, always seeking each other, through life after life, driven by love and longing. Sometimes two of us would meet, would love, would live a life together for a time. And then, death would separate us once again.

In these many lives we have lived—and in many lands—since The Village, we have each met and loved other lost souls and forged new bonds. Some of us have returned in each new life to the essential roles we had held in the Village: potter, smith, warrior, farmer, healer, hunter, herder, builder, priest/ess, storyteller, poet, wizard, witch... And some of us have lived successive lives very different one from the next.

Never quite fitting in with the societies in which we kept finding ourselves, for we carried a secret alienation deep in our souls, many of us were particularly targeted by the Witch Hunters and Inquisitors, and we were brutally tortured and murdered in life after life during the Burning Times. Only to keep returning, relentlessly—courageously—again and again.

For always we have sought each other; sought to recover the Village. Because, in our deepest heart of hearts, we remember the Home.

And now, in this time, two millennia later, some of us have found each other again. We have remembered who we truly are, and what we have always meant to each other. And we have forged a new Family—a core seed of The Village that once was, and shall be again. It is an open Family, seeking reconnection with those others of The Village who may show up. All that our Family members have done in working to create (and re-create) new (and old) religious and social movements and structures (Church of All Worlds, Neo-Paganism, *Green Egg,* polyamory, Mythic Images, Grey School of Wizardry...) has been towards setting up a beacon to draw Home again those of our kindred so long lost from each other.

How often have we heard the words of a newly-discovered Pagan, spoken through tears at their first Festival: "I feel like I've finally come Home! I feel like I've finally found my People!" How many of us have spoken those words? How many of us have said to another that most beautiful of all phrases, "Welcome Home, brother (or sister); welcome Home!"

And now we have a great work to do together—beyond merely finding each other and recreating The Village. We must make certain that our Home is never destroyed again, and that, once reunited, we who love each other will never be torn asunder again.

For the whole world is our Village. If our world is destroyed, there will be no Home to return to; no more wombs to receive back our sundered souls. Our task in the coming Millennium is to ensure that there will always be a Village to welcome us Home.

Through the Ages many races have arisen and have gone
Yet disbursed among the nations of the world we linger on
Now the time has come to take the sacred Cauldron of Rebirth,
And fulfill our ancient pledges to the Earth!
~Gwydion Pendderwen (5/21/1946-11/6/1982) "We Won't Wait Any Longer"

5. The Meaning of Life[18]

By Oberon Zell

CHERISH DIVERSITY! FIND FASCINATION IN THE strange and unusual. Live passionately. Explore everything, especially things forbidden, with boundless curiosity. Read voraciously. Grow a garden. Establish and maintain altars in your home. Celebrate the ever-turning Wheel of the Year. Go camping and hiking in the wilderness. Work on yourself. Love and be loved unconditionally, without reservation. Be kind. Help others. Do as you would be done by. Have fun. In short, become what you potentially are.

Don't just "think outside the box;" think "Box? There's a box?"

According to some leading thinkers in quantum physics, this "real life," as we so naively call it, is but a living virtual world simulation, like "Second Life," or "World of Warcraft" —only infinitely more sophisticated than anything we are presently able to create, with many layers of sentience. More like *The Matrix, Total Recall, Jumanji,* or *Ready Player One.* Or the simulation holodecks on *Star Trek* and *The Orville.*

Humanity (i.e. *Homo sapiens*) is maybe 300,000 years old; agriculture 14,000; writing 5,000; the "Common Era" 2,024. It's been 424 years since Giordano Bruno was burned at the stake for insisting that the Earth revolves around the sun; and the United State of America is only 248 years old—close enough in recent memory to inspire a hit musical play: *Hamilton.* And the Internet was invented only 44 years ago.

Given the accelerating rate of advances in our own lifetimes, now moving into quantum computing, try to imagine our virtual gaming worlds in another 44 years… 248 years… 424… 2,024 years… 5,000… mere drops in the ocean of Eternity. Remember, Dragons ruled the Earth for *170 million years!* And over the last *13 billion years,* how many civilizations may have arisen throughout the galaxy to our present technological level…and beyond? Maybe way, way beyond…to what? Can we even imagine? We're just getting started, on this one tiny speck of dust in an infinite cosmos!

We perceive ourselves as individual entities—just as a cup of water appears to be separate and distinct from all other cups of water. But it's only the vessels that are separate—not the water they contain. There is no death of the Spirit. Only a release when the vessel it contains can no

---

[18] Zell, Oberon, from *GaeaGenesis: Conception and Birth of the Living Earth.* Left Hand Press, 2022.

longer hold it. What we think of as God or the Gods is just the next layer of Spirit of which we are extrusions.

The only difference between us and the Gods (as well as the Beloved Dead) is that They are non-corporeal (i.e. not currently animating avatars). But They are real personas just as much as the rest of us. Moreover, when we "die," our own consciousness returns ("ascends") to the next level up… And beyond the next level, there are presumably an unknowable number of further levels, like *Matryoshka* Russian nesting dolls…

Like a Fairy Circle of mushrooms springing from a common invisible mycelial network beneath the surface of "reality," we are extensions/ projections of Universal Consciousness (Spirit; Divinity; the Quantum Field) into this realm of "materiality." We/I inhabit/incarnate/animate these marvelous avatars for a brief "lifetime" of lessons, adventures, emotions, love, family, relationships and entanglements, agony and ecstasy, trials and tribulations; then we res out and take a little break before we/*I* decide to play another game with new avatars.

It's all a game, and the goal—as in any game—is to win, to complete each level, and then advance/ascend to the next level. Indeed, the ultimate goal is for *everyone* to advance/ascend to the next level—"Enlightenment;" "Awakening." And then perhaps to create another even more advanced game… For that's what Gods do.

Psalm 82:6: I said, *"You are gods, and all of you are sons of the Most High."*

John 10:34: Jesus answered them, *"Is it not written in your Law: 'I said you are gods'?"*

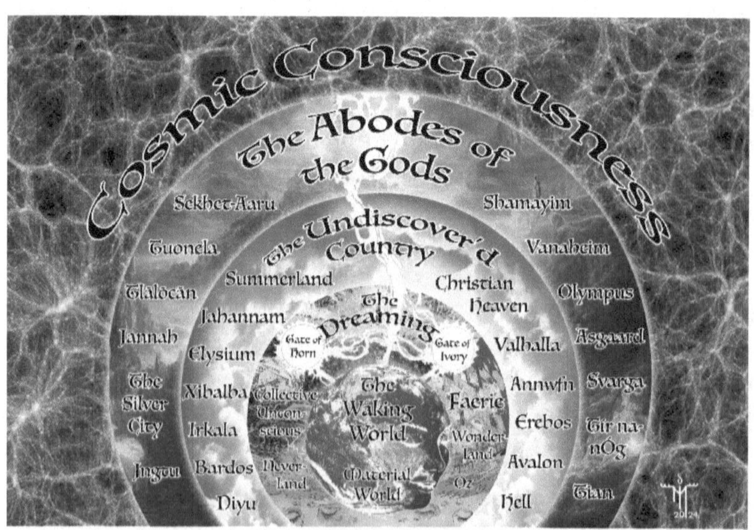

"Concentric Realms of Spirit," by Oberon Zell (2024)

Part II:
Starting Off Right
(Birth to Toddler: age 0-3)

Welcome to the World![19]

Welcome, Child.
You are a part of this Earth.
You are cradled in blue oceans;
you are bathed in golden light;
you are wrapped in green grasses;
you are made shining by the stars.

Welcome, Child.
The redwood is your friend,
and the Joshua Tree;
the fern is your companion,
and the wild berry garland.
There will be rain for you, hushing;
and thunder for you, roaring;
and lightning for you, dancing;
and all this perfect world for you, turning.

Welcome, Child.
Amen.

~Erica Lynn Frank

---

[19] from the *LovingKindness Survival Kit,* at http://www.forlovingkindness.org/lksurviv-alkit.html

6. Magickal Birthing

By Alayne Griffin of The Farm in Tennessee
(Farm Midwifery Center https://thefarmmidwives.org/)

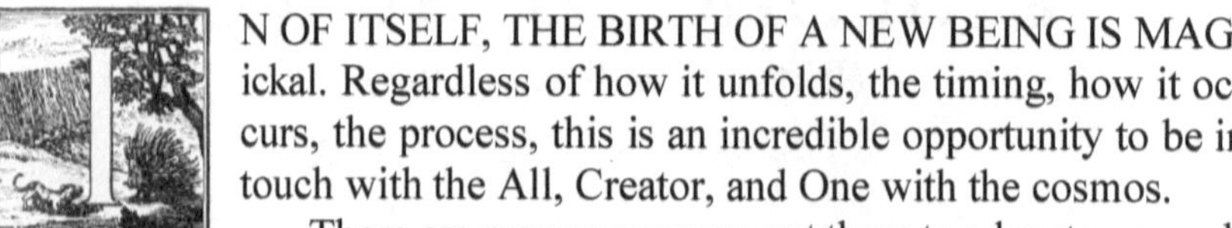

I N OF ITSELF, THE BIRTH OF A NEW BEING IS MAGickal. Regardless of how it unfolds, the timing, how it occurs, the process, this is an incredible opportunity to be in touch with the All, Creator, and One with the cosmos.

There are many resources out there to educate yourself on how to have a healthy birth, and I encourage you to investigate all that is available to you. My thoughts and experiences here are meant to give you inspiration and by no means should be used in lieu of sound advice from a professional. What I share here is from my personal birth experience, community living, and what I gleaned from my interviews with midwives. Use what resonates and discard the rest. May these musings be a jumping start for your own journey with a magickal birth.

Birth is a sacred sacrament here on The Farm community in Summertown, Tennessee. It is held in utmost honor as one of the most illuminating rites of passage that one can go through. If it is the birth of the first child, or the fifth, each time it is magickal. To bring forth new life is holy.

But how does one have a magical birth? As with all magical events, you start with yourself. To Know thyself is one of the pillars of a spiritual and magickal life. Who are you? What is your purpose? Go deeper. What is your intent? What are your fears and concerns regarding birth? How do you handle stress and unexpected pivots? Who are your allies (animal, Deity, Goddesses, Gods, Angels, Ancestors, Fae, Plant spirits, elementals, land spirits, etc.)? From whom do you draw strength and guidance? What brings you peace and comforts you? Items for your altar could be crystals, plants, chants, songs, incense, music, treasured keepsakes, specific clothing and textiles, pictures, tapestries, statues, icons, oracle, and tarot cards…The possibilities are endless and dictated by you. What practices ground you? Meditation, particular songs, chants, candle gazing? The more adept you are at drawing on your well of strength and endurance, focus and adaptability, the more you can rest in the knowledge that you have prepared yourself well for this most auspicious rite of passage. Practice your craft, begin to create time and space for self-care and inner peace to ready yourself for this transformation.

At the birth, who is on your team? Partner, Midwife, doctor, doula, friend, family? Who do you count upon to advocate for you, to support you? Interview the midwives, doulas, and the doctors. Do you feel that your goals, wishes, concerns and plan are being heard and honored by those on your team? Do you trust them with your life? They are working for you and your baby. Establishing a healthy and supportive relationship with your birth team is paramount in ensuring everyone is clear and ready for this sacred event. Create a birthing plan that is flexible. Talk through possibilities and incorporate steps that do "the next best thing,' recognizing that it may not go as planned. For example, you want a water birth, but the portable tub has a hole in the liner. So, the next best thing is labor in the bathtub and then move to the bed for the birth. You want a home birth, but you or the baby may be at high-risk as discovered by you and your medical professionals, so choosing a reliable birthing center that has immediate access to a lifesaving medical team is the next best thing.

What environment makes you feel safe and supported? Home? Hospital? Birthing center? Sweat lodge? Woods? Meadow? Nearby creek? Ocean? Generally, the safest place to have your baby is where you are most comfortable. Birth is a natural process. Your body was made for this! Once you and your Providers are clear on your health and abilities, as well as the baby's health, what makes sense to you and your team? Does your choice account for flexibility if necessary? Sometimes babies or moms need extra care. Considering what you decide with your team, check that your choice of environment also meets your needs of safety and support. You may want to consider infusing a small magickal tool like a stone, a rattle, or a charm ~ with the sense of this magickal space you intended to create for your birth process. Imbue this tool deeply with the vision of your ideal environment as you ripen and ready. That way, if, during your birthing process, you or your Provider suggests a plan change, you could have this magickal talisman to help ground and center you in time of need.

The Pregnancy

How do you prepare yourself? Nourish your body and your spirit with good wholesome food, meditation, spring water, herbal teas, vitamins, and gentle exercise. You know your body best. Advocate for yourself and re-

Art by Derek Dominic D'souza from Song of Two Worlds *by physicist Alan Lightman.*

search supportive resources as well as your primary care team who will assist you with the practices to help nourish you and the baby.

I strongly encourage reading *Birthing From Within, An Extra-ordinary Guide to Childbirth Preparation* by Pam England and Ron Horowitz. This book gives several tools to utilize during pregnancy, birth, and beyond. The techniques offered help the mother work through her fears, concerns, hopes, and dreams are of supreme importance in fostering a magickal birth. Journaling, painting, walking meditations, are just a few explored in this dynamic book recommended by home birth professionals.[20]

One of my favorite ways to honor the pregnant woman is a Blessing way. Here on The Farm, it is an intimate setting where we share birth stories, prayers, songs, and nourishing food. We each bring a bead and offer it to the mother with a blessing for her upcoming birth. As we regale our stories, laughter, and songs, one of the ladies will string the beads into a beautiful necklace for the mom. We also inscribe a candle with images and words to encourage a smooth birth. This candle is then briefly lit as we light individual candles that are taken home to be relit when the birth begins. This connection and prayer create a web of strength for the mother to draw upon.

Relaxing footbaths, massaging the mom to be, adorning her belly with henna, flower crowns, and doing a belly cast are just a few of the things I have seen in various Blessing ways. The feeling of camaraderie and sharing the different birth journeys is a beautiful way to celebrate the pregnant woman.

NOTES from OZ: It is recommended that pregnant mothers eat plenty of seafood, as certain brain-enhancing nutrients (*Docosahexanoic acid* or DHA) are richly found in ocean fish. Indeed, it has been proposed that eating ocean seafood is a prime factor in the high intelligence of all sea mammals—including our own aquatic ancestors![21]

The developing embryo is only inches away from the mother's environment, and thus acutely sensitive to the outside world. So be sure to surround yourself with appropriate lights and sounds, such as sweet music. Avoid loud and cacophonous noises, such as machines, motorcycles, barking dogs, fireworks, gunshots, or amped metal music.

And surely it doesn't need to be said that pregnant mothers should avoid all toxic substances; no alcohol, tobacco, marijuana, or other drugs and chemicals that could afflict a developing baby!

The Environment

It is imperative to create a space where the mother feels comfortable and safe. The birth may not progress much if the environment is tense or stressful and there is a lack of privacy. An ecstatic birth can happen when there is freedom for the mother to do what she needs to do, be it walking,

---

[20] England, Pam & Horowitz, Ron, *Birthing From Within.* Partera Press, 1998.
[21] Morgan, Elaine, *The Aquatic Ape Hypothesis,* Souvenir Press, 1997.

dancing, screaming, praying, shouting, crying, and all the messiness that comes with bringing a new being into the world.

Dim lighting, calming music, an area free from distractions such as the TV, sports, loud activities or conversations, machines, etc.

At-home births have made a resurgence thanks to the tireless efforts by the Farm midwives. If you can, I strongly advocate for this option if you and your provider agree you are a good candidate for a home birth. At home, you are in familiar surroundings, you can create a nest of safety and comfort for yourself—in your own time, your own way. Nourishing food and drinks are nearby. Your altar is set. Your team is solid, ready to either be there or on standby. Now you are ready to allow the unfolding and let the rhythms take over as this new being begins to come forth.

One of the magical processes that occurs during birth is the altered states that take over. Some liken this to a rosy golden glow that permeates the room. It is an auric change that many sense and feel as they witness the emergence of the new child.

The hormones oxytocin, endorphins, and adrenaline are the key players to induce physiological birth. I will simplify the roles of each of these hormones and encourage you to read about their roles and effects elsewhere as well.

Oxytocin is the love hormone which was likely present in the creation of the baby. This hormone encourages bonding and falling in love, deepening the connection between people, to their spirituality, awareness, and the ability to speak on a telepathic level. This helps the uterus contract during labor.

What I found out from Corina Fitch, Midwife, is that oxytocin does so much more. This hormone assists us to be instinctual, able to multitask, and propels us out of the neocortex thinking region of the brain which tends to lead by over-thinking, over-analyzing, and dropping one into an anxiety ridden realm because the birth is not following the textbook. When anxiety rears its ugly head, refer to your tools that you cultivated during the pregnancy, such as breathwork, mantras, music, somatic stretches, loud toning, prayers, etc.

Endorphins are painkillers that assist in rising above the pain of labor. Allowing the mother to transcend into an altered state of focus upon her body and yet at the same time feeling a connection to All That Is. It is a realm that can be fuzzy, ethereal, and omnipotent.

Adrenaline chimes in to bring you back into awareness and facilitate channeling the energy to push the baby. As many have experienced this fight or flight hormone, it heightens our instinct to protect and be vigilant.

Now I must insert here, that it is common in hospitals to induce labor and pushing with epidurals and other such drugs. If possible, give the mother time, give the baby time. Using a hands-off approach and allowing it to unfold naturally encourages and fosters a smooth birth. A magickal birth can still occur in the hospital if medical procedures are used, because in the end, a new being has entered your world. It is a divine gift no matter the journey it took to get here. Sometimes medical intervention is necessary, and we are blessed to live in a time where we have access to many life-saving techniques and trained professionals. If a c-section is necessary and welcomed, this intervention is a win for mother and child. You have brought new life into this world! Yes, our bodies were made for this, but in certain circumstances, we need specific assistance to achieve the goal of health and safety of mother and child.

Birth centers utilize low lighting in the rooms and create a welcoming atmosphere for the birthing family. Having quick access to medical care if the mother is at risk cannot be understated. Again, it comes back to where the birthing woman feels safe and supported.

A birthing tub is ideal to aid the mother as she enters the final stages of labor. The water suspends her as the surges course through, increasing the endorphins and decreasing the risk of tearing. Floating in the warm tub can transport the mother into the primordial birth waters of Gaia, being in the womb as she IS the womb. Transcending the pain as her body shifts and opens up.

The Birth

The crowning of the child is the epitome of magic. The child's spirit has been brought forth from the astral plane and incarnated into a body. All the months of waiting, growing, connecting has resulted in a new being. Yes, it is painful. The mother's body is morphing to bear a child. It is not easy, but it is a rewarding journey.

The Farm Midwifery logo.
© The Farm Midwifery Center.

Once the baby is born, that first hour is the Golden Hour. A momentous event has occurred. Be still. Pause and bask in the glow, become fully present and allow the first bonding between mother and child to occur without intervention.

The largest surge of oxytocin courses through the new mother's body that facilitates falling deeply in love with the baby. Lay the child upon the mother's chest. Allow them to synchronize their heartbeats as the babe also learns to breathe on their own. Most will instinctively crawl towards the breast for their first feeding.

The brain waves of a baby are six times slower than ours. Flow into this rhythm. Pause and breathe into this space, be present with the baby.

After this first hour with this new being, the midwives and birth attendants will want to check the APGAR, weight, length, etc.

Cutting the cord is a sacred moment when the child is no longer physiologically connected to its mother. Most midwives allow it to stop pulsing on its own, then the partner, sibling, or another trusted individual cuts the cord, and the midwife will tie the knot to create the baby's belly button. The Placenta can be buried in a special place to nourish the soil. We planted a pink flowering crabapple tree chosen by my daughter many years later. Placenta encapsulation is a service offered by some doulas and midwives. This nutritious supplement will aid in replenishing the mother after birth.

Pamel Hunt, CPM, related one birthing story that happened on The Caravan[1]. This was the second birth the group experienced as they were traveling. Folks had heard how magickal the previous birth was, and many wanted to witness this next one firsthand. The bus was so crowded with people that the midwives could not even make it towards the bed where the mother labored. The energy and the vibe was "jangly and stuffy." Ina May Gaskin asked that all males who were not the husband leave the bus. This shifted the atmosphere, enabling the birth to progress.

Afterwards, the midwives adopted that "...The birth is a natural life process as well as a holy event. That it belonged explicitly and only to the birthing mother and her family. The midwives and her helper could come into this sacred space, but it was not for everybody to attend. It was the families' own special sacrament to be honored and protected. We as midwives vowed to protect this event for all families in the future."

Birth is not a spectator event. It is private, the mother deserves to be held as the most holy divine being who is doing sacred work and be undisturbed (unless an emergency develops, then apply common sense throughout the process and refer to the experienced trained professionals).

After Birth

Postpartum care is key for the new family. The mom has undergone a life changing event and needs time to bond with the baby and recuperate. Your team can continue the nurturing care with prepared meals, a meal train, delivered groceries, Uber meals. Finding dependable folks to assist with chores is a boon. Have a reliable person organize this as well as scheduling the meals. There are calendars and such online to help navigate and keep people informed with reminders.[22]

---

[22] MotherFly https://www.motherfly.mom/

If you have other children, involve trusted caregivers to engage with them with visits to a park, arcade, zoo, library, and play dates so that they too feel seen, heard, and to have one on one attention.

Ideally, I recommend having these planned for at least a month or several months after birth. Recovery takes a long while. Life has irrevocably changed, there is no return to the previous routine. There is a new path taken and patterns are changing. Give yourself time to adapt. Speak honestly with your children that changes are coming and that all are welcoming a new sibling into the family. Life grows, and the family has as well. Reassure them that they are important and loved. Their new sibling will need a lot of care and attention because they need protection, and it is an honor to be chosen by this baby to join as family.

One of the fascinating ceremonies offered by Corina Fitch is "Closing of the Bones." She was introduced to this in Uganda. This weaves the woman back into herself. Like the Blessing way, this is a spiritually intimate healing. Corina incorporates many modalities to create a wholistic ceremony. She begins with a steam bath, then applies a clay mask all over the mother's body and has her sit in the warm room meditating on what she wishes to leave behind. Then they wash the clay away with a cleansing salt scrub. Leading the cleansed mom into the next room to lay upon a soft pallet where several long swathes of cloth are laid out. One is for the head, the next at the shoulders, then the breasts, followed by the belly and pelvis, knees and finally the feet. These cloths are snugly wrapped around each area. Acknowledging all the expansion the body underwent that brought forth new life impacted every aspect of your being. Enveloping the mother in the warm, soft, and secure embrace as each cloth is tied lends this ceremony not unlike a chrysalis. Ruminate on what you most desire to call back into your life. How are you realigning? Call your essence back into your body, gather what was scattered, reincorporate, and breathe into this pause. Invite what you want and desire for your mothering journey, your health, your family, and your spiritual growth. This can be done at any time after the birth, 6 weeks to even years later.

Also, I must add here that do not beat yourself up for not getting everything perfect. Give yourself some grace, for we are all learning. How can we evolve into more dynamic beings if there are not challenges, and opportunities to grow?

It is my sincere wish that what I have shared will inspire you to explore how you and your family can experience a magickal birth. With your support team of cherished friends, family, and dedicated birth workers, may you have a most dynamic and mystical birth.

7. Baby Blessing Ceremony[23]

By Morning Glory Zell

RITE OF BABY BLESSING, CALLED *SAINING*, should be conducted within the first lunation after birth. It may be a very simple ceremony, so as not to put a strain on the baby. The assembled guests should include God- and Goddess-parents. The ceremony should take place within a traditionally cast and consecrated Circle. Small altars should be set up at each of the quarters, holding burning sage and bird's wing fan (E), a lit red candle (S), a chalice or shell of water (W) and a small dish or half geode of salt (N). The quarters should be called by individuals stationed at those points. Parents are stationed in the East, and God- and Goddess-parents in the West. After invoking the God and Goddess (who should be particularly parental deities, such as Isis & Horus, etc.), there are traditionally four phases of a Seining:

1. Presentation & naming of the Baby
2. Presentation of God- & Goddess-parents
3. Anointing
4. Offering of Blessings

Presentation & Naming

The parents, standing in the East and holding the baby, turn it to face the Circle, saying, *"We are greatly blessed this day. A new life has entered our Circle. Let us give joyous welcome to (baby's name)."*

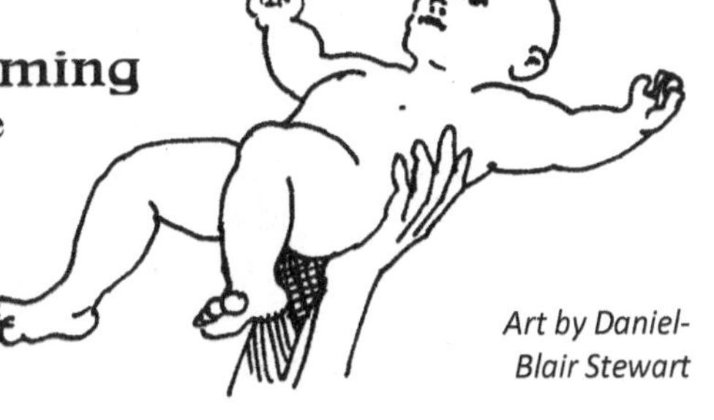

Art by Daniel-Blair Stewart

Everyone responds with something along the lines of *"Welcome, (baby's name), into our Circle of Life!"*

Presentation of God- & Goddess-parents

The parents ask, *"Who would come forward now to be God- and Goddess-parents to (baby's name)?"*

From their places in the West, the God- and Goddess-parents step

---

[23] Zell, Oberon & Morning Glory, *Creating Circles & Ceremonies: Rituals for All Seasons & Reasons,* with Morning Glory Zell. New Page, 2006.

forward into the center of the Circle, saying "We do."

The parents pass the baby over to them, saying, *"May your love and support nourish (baby's name) through good times and bad as (s)he grows in strength, wisdom and beauty. May you always be there for him/her in times of need. Do you accept this charge?"*

God- and Goddess-parents reply, *"We do."*

Anointing

God- and Goddess-parents carry the baby around the Circle. At each quarter they stop, and the blessing of that element is conveyed, by the person who originally called that quarter, thusly:

East— smoke from the burning sage is wafted around the baby using the bird's wing fan: *"By the Air which is Her breath, may you live long and prosper!"*

South— the baby is passed over the candle flame: *"By the Fire which is Her radiant spirit, may you live long and prosper!"*

West— water is sprinkled over the baby: *"By the Water which is Her blood, may you live long and prosper!"*

North— salt is sprinkled over the baby: *"By the Earth which is Her body, may you live long and prosper!"*

When they return to the East, the God- and Goddess-parents give the baby back to the parents, and return to their place in the West.

Offering of Blessings

This is just like the baby blessing in the beginning of Disney's *Sleeping Beauty*. The parents begin the offering of blessings by saying something like, *"(Baby's name), I offer you the gift (or blessing) of (music, dance, fine speech, good health, love of reading, insight, compassion, creativity, many friends, beauty, love, intelligence, coordination, etc.). May this gift serve you well."*

Then they pass the baby to the person on their left, who says, *"Baby's name), I offer you the gift (or blessing) of (whatever),"* and then passes the baby on around the Circle, with each person taking the baby and offering their own special blessing.

When the baby has been passed around the full Circle, and is returned to the parents, they say, *"Thank you all, friends and family. We are all blessed this day."*

The God and Goddess are thanked, the Quarters dismissed, and the Circle is opened. The rite is ended.

8. Laying the Foundations

By Kathleen Mugnolo
Professional Childbirth Consultant
Family Advocate and postpartum care provider

 **ANGUAGE DISCLAIMER* I ACKNOWLEDGE AND** respect every person's chosen identity. I never want to assume that I know someone better than they know themselves. That being said, I use the term *Mother* to refer to the being who gave birth. To me Mother refers to the body, or planet, gifted with the power to pull consciousness from the ether, pull it through her body, and bring said consciousness into physical form. The word "Mother" to me is elemental, like air or water. I suppose "mother" could not be gendered, but I do use "her" pronouns when speaking to this female energy and power because I have made a career of working with women. By using "mother" and "her" I am choosing to streamline my language and speak from my direct experience. I use Father to refer to the being who brings the spark of life and/or assures safety for the family unit. When working directly with a family, I honor any language they choose for themselves.

So often I've heard, when it comes to being a new parent, "if only there were a map/handbook for this." My learning informs me that there is, most definitely, a map, and that is our physiologic design. That which makes us well, the practices that put us in alignment with planet and source, are the articulated path forward. This is the voice that, through colonization, we have been trained to ignore. This is the voice that informs us through how our bodies, this Gaian endowment, responds to stimuli and input. Among these answers we find more than "eat clean food" and "drink live water," and "a right to safe shelter." We are physiologically designed to need each other, and in order for food, water and shelter to be truly nourishing, robust community support is essential. All children are magical children. Each one carries with them into the world and unadulterated knowing of liberated expression. It is our sacred duty to tend these soul seeds as extensions of divine creation.

For a new mother to be held in robust community support means that she is being fed warm, nourishing food. Food made for the Mother by community while she heals and bonds with her baby is medicine. Food made and prepared by the Mother in the immediate postpartum time is not medicine. Rather, it is a source of exhaustion and evidence of survival, not thriving. A Mother can be fortified in the six weeks postpartum by being provided warmth and body work. The practice of receiving is a muscle many mothers in our culture need to develop. Learning to receive helps her heal more efficiently, and builds her into the ever-changing person it takes to parent a magical child. For the Mother to be held in robust community support she must rest. She must trust and feel safe with the people that surround her. It is the Father and her community that will be loving on this baby when Mama needs sleep, or when she wants to poop alone. Rest is a revolutionary act. It is imperative that, as parents, we develop a healthy relationship with rest. Rest is a key component in raising whole ass beings. Rest restores our intuition. Our small developing piece of fleshy creation requires us to listen to our intuition. Seven hours sleep of heals the body and nine hours restores the intuition. Rest is crucial. Cultures all around the world support the postpartum mother through a traditional rest period. Staying close to the bed for 6-8 weeks is physiologically appropriate for healing and bonding.

Paganism can be defined by cosmologies formed around direct human experience/relationship with the Earth and rhythm of the cosmos. Pagans were village people, with the village consisting of more than the humans co-habitating in one space. Magic was synonymous with medicine. Much magical understanding was lost when the church and colonial powers forced us away from the dirt that held our placentas and severed our connection to the heartbeat of creation. Arbitrary schedules were imposed, and isolation led to parents (especially mothers) doing the work of an entire village. Overwhelm, exhaustion, and punitive systems created a culture of survival instead of thriving. In our depleted state we began to accept the voice of colonization when it said, "I am your ancestor now," leaving behind the rites and ceremony of our lineages. It is time to sing these bones and reclaim ritual that witnesses the Mother, Father, and Child so they become their fullest expressions. Central to raising magical children is divesting from harmful systems, and investing in the fortification of new parents.

Mother is the terrain of the newborn, just as the Earth is to all living creatures, and it is from this secure attachment that the child learns to develop into their own distinct creation on the planet. In order to support this creation, we must create a nourishing environment for new parents to thrive. Quantum mechanics provides us a definition of entanglement which refers to two particles being connected in such a way that they are dependent on each other's state. We can observe this theory in that Mother and baby swap DNA during the womb time. Mama creates the baby from her body, and also receives fetal cells into her blood stream, thus changing her for life. She carries her child within her, always. Honoring the magical infant means aligning with the frequency of the Great Mother so they may unfurl, in very much the same way, as the leaf on the tree. Becoming the expression that Creator intended just for us, is to participate in and support thriving life. The dyad of Mother/Child reflects the health of the ecosystem where they are held. Proper care for new parents in the immediate postpartum time (birth to toddlerhood) is the medicine for raising magical people.

Nursing

Proper support of the mother so she can develop a healthy breastfeeding relationship with her newborn has global healing implications, both physiologically and spiritually. Breastfeeding is built into the road map of the Mother/Child dyad, evident by the wellness promoted by the relationship. Breast milk is how the baby's immune system develops. Antibodies from the mother empower the baby to fight illness for the first several months of life. Saliva from the newborn speaks to the mother's body. Mother's milk changes according to the information she receives from the baby's mouth. This is magic. This is by no means an attempt to shame anyone who did not, for whatever reason, breastfeed. And breastfeeding is a birthright of Mother and Child that colonized culture has attempted to downplay or dismiss in importance.

For the first three months after birth, the milk supply is hormone driven. This gives the dyad time to learn. For this learning to be efficient, the mother having a regulated nervous system is ideal because this is where the infant first learns to regulate their nervous system. For a regulated nervous system to be present, the dyad must be held securely in loving community. What is good for the baby, is good for the Mother, is good for the Father, is good for the community.

The inherent chemistry provided by Mother's milk and the breastfeeding relationship informs the trajectory of the infant's development. Cannabinoids exist in breast milk. A perfect example of physiology being an instruction manual is the endocannabinoid system. We have receptors for cannabinoids as embryos. This system is designed by the creator to bring us back into homeostasis. Our first message from our Mother, as a blastocyst, is a cannabinoid signal that informs us where to implant in the uterus. Again, after birth, we find cannabinoids in breast milk that are important for human development as they teach the new child how to eat, boosts immune function, and play a neuro-protective role. These specific cannabinoids cannot be made available to the infant outside of the Mother/baby dyad.

Bonding

Breastfeeding is a time when both Mother and baby produce oxytocin, the feel good bonding chemical. In infancy, the more we experience this chemical, in relationship with our Mother, the more receptors that we form for oxytocin. It's a feedback loop. The experiencing of oxytocin, and forming of receptors, which happens most efficiently in relationship with primary care providers, lays the foundation for the babe's secure attachment in the world and how they will relate to other beings throughout life. This chemistry of connection informs how the child will become a good community member. One day on the spiral, it will be their turn to nurture the new family, so the newest life in their village develops a somatic understanding of what it means to belong.

It is the fully formed relationship, actuated by deep listening, between baby and mother, that ensures the well-being of the child in the first formative years. When the Mother is fed, rested, and held by her community, she will be able to be present with her baby and know what they need. Rested and nurtured parents have the bandwidth and energy to wear their babies and participate in healthy attachment practices. Strollers and swings are handy tools for tired parents but are not compensation or a replacement for body contact, a requisite for healthy neurodevelopment. You cannot over-cuddle or spoil your baby with affection.

In the first years of life it is ordained by physiology that the infant learns from the parents' bodies during sleep. Safely co-sleeping with your baby is a facet to ensuring rest, and for appropriate development of the mother/baby dyad. Babies are not meant to be alone all night. Their sweet hearts learn to regulate to the rhythm of their parents. Their breathing is instructed by the lungs of the care providers. It is programmed into their DNA to be close to the Mother to be safe. Infants are physiologically designed to wake up throughout the night and need contact and food. Accepting that sleep will be different for a while, and that your baby is not malfunctioning, is important to your sanity. From birth we need at least twelve people tending to the needs of the new family to meet our physiologic design.

Ceremony

Another key to a regulated nervous system is ceremony. As feral children of the diaspora, it is our calling to reclaim ritual and ceremony within the context of community. Ceremony is influential to our development as individuals and as a collective. Cultures all around the world have ritual that witnesses and nourish the new mother, and all are informed by physiology. Ceremony brings us into a space where we are open to connection with the divine, where we can ask for help and open to possibility. Ceremony can be simple. With the arrival of the child Earthside, the community can gather, light a candle, and say a blessing that knits the family to the Earth.

Giving thanks to Earth
For the molecules that form our bodies
And for the freedom
of being able to discover Self
from the security of Her body
May this child be nourished
And the parents gifted the strength of mountains.

As I pull Air in and out of my lungs
I feel nourished and cleansed
Grateful for the kinship with
Brothers and sister that fly
And seeds that spread.
May this child be free.
And gift the parents with clear sight.

Water, who makes us supple
Our blood runs and tears flow
Our connection to all life
and pre planet ancestry.
May this child find joy
And the parents be protectors of water.

Our Sun, who gives us the day and our bread
Fire, that pumps my heart and inspires me
Who has witnessed us through the ages
And held our stories, thank you.
May this child relish in creativity
And may the parents remember.

As above, so below.
As within, so without.

Element circles by OZ

Ceremonial care of the placenta informs our belonging. Anchors us. Reminds us that we are dirt. Seri, a people of Northern Mexico greet each other by saying *"Miixoni quih zo hanta no tiij?"* In English this means, "Where is your placenta buried?" Nepalese people consider the placenta the baby's friend, and in Malaysia the placenta is thought of as an older sibling. We see placenta wisdom in cultures all over the world. Physiologically, the placenta is genetically identical to the baby, and is a creation of the combined effort of mother and baby with the purpose of fostering relationship and nourishment. Being mindful of the honoring and placement of the placenta impacts the babe's rootedness to the planet.

Big ceremony is important, but the little daily rituals add up. Bathing can be a sensual ritual for parent and baby to enjoy. Newborns don't need to be washed (I mean, if you think they stink, please wash them), but most do love being in the water. Getting in the tub with mom or dad is a return to the womb. A rose, chamomile infusion to add to the bath water will help regulate all the nervous systems. As the child gets older, small daily rituals with dirt and water (the Old Gods), or diapering, or visiting an old tree friend are anchors of joy and connection. The sheer wonder that young people experience when experiencing the elements surpasses any toy or gadget.

When new parents question their skill and sanity, or if their baby is OK, what I hear is a plea for nervous system regulation. Herbs, in conjunction with robust community support, are a beautiful way to create a simple ceremonial container. With herbs, we enter a covenant with the earth. Soaks can promote healing for the Mother's body and calm a restless babe. Infusions can support milk supply, elevate mood, bring people together, and soothe a gassy tummy. Plants cleanse us and heal us and put us in connection to the wisdom of the Great Mother.

Ceremony that holds the mother while her body heals and she relearns herself is in alignment with physiology and thriving life. Ceremony that celebrates the Father, that witnesses him in his maturity, and shows him who are his people, support his nervous system and promote thriving life.

Circumcision is an example of an unnecessary, harmful and arbitrary ritual that many parents unconsciously perform. There is absolutely no medical evidence that supports this as a means of health. Please do not cut your babies. This is a painful and traumatizing surgery that imprints our male-bodied people with violence and teaches them to not trust the world upon arrival to the planet. Many people's first experience of losing their agency is having a very sensitive part of their penis cut from their body while they are strapped helpless to a board. When the soul's body is aged enough to make a fully informed decision, they can choose to be circumcised, on their own terms, with anesthesia. Take the time to sink in and allow yourself to feel how this irrational practice has shaped our civilization. This is violence, and only serves to perpetuate violence in our world. Would creation have created foreskin only for it to be removed?

Being held in ceremony, witnessed and supported by the village, and having many care providers will gift to the infant the experience that the world is good and safe. All babies cry, but the more secure their ecosystem, the less their need to cry. Babies cry out of need and discomfort, or when they are scared. Sometimes the need is obvious, such as a messy diaper or they're hungry or they need connection. Sometimes crying seems inexplicable.

There are experts that speak to the need for the child to work out their birth experience as a facet of healing and just need to be held in love while they work some stuff out. "Excessive" crying is called colic. Colic is a blanket term for a fussy baby, possibly with a confounding set of symptoms. Often colic can be traced to gastrointestinal issues and is resolved by addressing food sensitivities in Mama and baby. A parent being rested and nourished properly allows them the grace to read respond, in real time, to what the needs of the infant are in the moment.

Supporting the development of magical children means recognizing the arbitrary structures we have adopted and making a deliberate move to living with the innate rhythms provided by the Earth and cosmos. Parenting is more a call, requiring deep listening, from the Creator to inform us, rather than a list of things to check off. Diapers, for example, are a personal decision. Do you have five children and want to reduce your impact on the environment? Does elimination communication fit your lifestyle?

These are personal choices that deserve exploring to fit your family's ethics and need for sanity. Same with toys. In my opinion, trees are the best mobiles, but your relationship will inform you what stimulation will get their wheels turning. Developing souls in fresh bodies really just want to experience what you are experiencing. They don't want a toy phone, they want YOUR phone. Infants are very much sensual beings, and are discovering the whole world through all the senses. Everything can be entertainment, everything is new. And the best part about parenting at this age is that you get to re-experience the world through this framework.

This relationship to Mother first, and then caregivers, is Gravity. Even into adulthood, if you can find some gratitude nestled in gravity, then you can know you belong here. This is the ultimate embrace. One can palpably feel the pull between Mother and her child, very much like gravity. As above, so below. As within, so without.

9. Recognizing the Magickal Child

By Oberon Zell

 MAGICKAL CHILD PERCEIVES SENTIENCE IN ALL Nature; talks to animals, birds, bugs, plants, flowers, trees, stones, water, fire… Sees Faeries. Has invisible playmates. Dreams of Gods, Goddesses, Dragons, Spirits…

My son Bryan was born in 1963. I'm pretty sure he was the first non-indigenous child of our time to be raised Pagan in a Pagan family, as none of the other Witches and Pagans of those days included their kids in their Pagan/Wiccan doings. Bryan had a natural sense of magick which I encouraged, as I identified it with my own as a child 20 years earlier. He spontaneously established an altar, and would put things on it that he found. He would find special stones, and by their shape, color, markings or whatever he would identify them as having special functions.

We were living in St Louis and I remember one April, when he was maybe 9, it hadn't snowed all winter. He told his schoolmates that he was gonna make it snow the next day. He came home and set up his altar with a "snow stone" that had white snowflake speckles all over it.

That night there was a blizzard, and the next day the schools were closed due to snow. We all played in the snow, had snowball fights, and built a big snow-mom in the front yard. The following day when he went back to school he got quite a bit of respect from the other kids!

We got him a couple of Guinea pigs for pets, and he would turn them loose in the unfenced back yard all day. At the end of the day he would go out and whistle, and they would come running back to their cage to be brought inside.

At Camp Tribe one summer he became the designated Shaman. One day, hiking in the woods with a counselor and some of the other kids, they came upon a branch that grew out of the ground, formed an arch, then went back into the ground. He noted that this was something special, so the counselor asked what they should do. Bryan said, *"We should build an altar. Look around for some stones."*

Just a few feet away they discovered a pile of bricks from a fallen chimney—all that remained of a totally overgrown burned-down house. So they built a fine altar, and they all camped out that night around it. In the middle of the night they noticed that some roots and wood around the altar were glowing. It was luminous foxfire fungus, but no one knew of that. To them all, it was pure magick. And so it was.

So on Mother's Day, 2023, I invited Pagan parents to answer this question: *"How can you recognize a magickal child? What are the signs to look for?"*

Here are some of their responses:

Archonstone

The child will have conversations with themself.

Most people (60%) do not have internal dialogues. 40% do and just about every magical person I know does.

Questions, There will be more questions, deep questions. Find good people to mentor them in those areas that they have deep focus in.

Hippie Matt Crowson

Wonder, curiosity, muchness, an ability to analyze a situation, and make out-of-box decisions. Magickal folk also tend to be very good at making connections in their thinking.

Victoria Brosnan

All children start out magical. It's how they are related with that allows them to hold that understanding or forget. All children are born Pagan.

Raven Ebonywing

From what I noticed with my oldest (9 year old) he is super empathic and always knows when someone is having a hard time emotionally. He puts himself last and makes sure that person is okay, talks them through and tells them they are okay. He's also attuned to nature, treats even rocks and ants with respect. Asks the Earth before he takes a stick home and knew crystals have meaning without me telling him so first.

He's also learning how to put healing energy and love into food. He knew on his own he could put love into food so people could feel loved from the inside.

It's little things that they pick up on which let you know they are a magical child.

Morgain Faye McGaughey

Extraordinary psychic. Willing to work hard for schooling. Historian of lore. Passion mainly.

Catt Foy

When daughter was about 2, I was on the phone with my mother-in-law when her husband suddenly had a heart attack. Millie said, *"I have to call an ambulance,"* and I said *"OK,"* and hung up. Mary Ellen brought me a pillow and said, *"Pop-pop's sick, Pop-pop needs a pillow."* There was nothing in the conversation that alerted her to her grandfather's condition and they were 1,000 miles away. That's when I knew she had my psychic ability.

My nine-year-old grandson has been through a lot in the last year, moving cross-country with his mother to come stay with us, only to have his Mom come down with cancer—lots of change and fear and worry and missing his brothers and sisters in Illinois. So when he came to me one night, frightened white, and told me about a box of candy that seemed to fly and flip itself over in midair. He was afraid it might be a bad spirit. I was able to reassure him that it was likely his own unresolved emotions. I've had poltergeist activity around me since my pre-teen years, usually when I am under a great deal of stress. He thanked b/c I was the only grown-up who ever could explain stuff like that to him. I got the feeling he'd had other experiences that were dismissed as his imagination. But I am now the best grandmother ever!

Becky Dale

For me it was when my then 2-year-old said something that my BFF called me. This one-time event happened the weekend my BFF was passing away. My child hasn't said it before or since that one weekend.

Cybeled Sernik

All children are majickal.. my daughter included.. she sees spirits and talks to them.. my husband and I have always encouraged her .. we tell her not to let anyone or anything put your light out.. she is majickal and is learning everyday.. we have told her never stop learning , the day you stop it's over... learn something new every day for the rest of your life... our daughter is gifted and she will be a healer when grown.

Lisa Mila Wilson

When I was little I would call the winds.

Judith Prueitt-Prentice

All children are magical as we all are. My grandmother called me the weird kid. Lots of compassion and clear communication and a healthy dose of consequences will allow the higher aspects to be nurtured.

Far too often mystics have traumatic early lives and hyper vigilance, and other survival skills like anticipation of events and outcomes get labeled as gifted, psychic, etc.

Many of us become healers, but we are healing external wounds. We must teach our children they are magical, loved for who they are in order for them to take their place in the cosmos.

Maria Shelley Leggett

My husband is a beekeeper. When he first started gathering hives he was having trouble filling one of the traps. No matter what he did he couldn't catch a hive in that box.

Our then 4-yr old granddaughter said *"Mimi, did PopPop ASK for the bees to come? You know the fairies rule animals; we just need to ask. You taught me that."*

I looked at her and smiled. I said *"I did, didn't I? I don't think PopPop believes in the fairies like you and I do."* I leaned down and said to her *"Will you do me a favor? When you go home tonight and go to bed, right before you go to sleep will you visualize the Queen Bee and ask her if she'd be willing to live in PopPop's box?"* She nodded her head.

Three days later she came over and ran up to me. *"Mimi, I need to talk to you and tell you sumfin."* We walked away from where her Mom was standing (my daughter doesn't believe either) and she told me she saw the Queen Bee two days before and asked if she'd come to PopPop's house to live. She said the queen agreed.

I told my granddaughter I had to show her something. She took my hand and we walked down the property to the now very busy hive box thriving with loads of bees that was empty 3 days prior.

My granddaughter looked at me and said *"I knew it. I knew the Queen wouldn't lie to me."*

That evening we left out mandarin oranges as a gift for the fairies

Daniel Michael

If they have regular conversations with an invisible friend or friends.

Cee Cee Bloom

I see the unending love for nature and connection of deep empathy. Our son takes his time studying and collecting stones and feathers and holds value in every single one. He talks to birds. He listens to the wind and the ripple of Thunder and tells us *"Mom!! Thor is not happy tonight!"* I would say if a child is gifted with magic...he or she is in tune and holds his or her surroundings and finds pure joy and connection with it.

Celene Wolf

The 1st thing I noticed with my daughter was she would go out into the flower bed and talk to the flowers and whatever insects were around. My son would do what I could only describe as out of body.

A.C. Fisher-Aldag

Them telling me, while still in the womb, *"I love this music"* and *"that food is really good"* and *"I dislike that smell.*

Mia Sirovetz

I think them knowing and discussing past lives at a young age and being drawn to sources in nature that feel magickal are two good indicators. But I agree, most children seem to have an innate ability and belief that is normally ignored or suppressed due to the parents' disbelief or distress at the idea.

Amy Nyteroze Slate

Every human is born with a connection to nature which makes them magical. It is up to us as parents and community members to nurture that connection and teach them to honor that part of themselves.

David Zunker

* knows their way respectfully around a Sabbat ceremony
* puts on different personalities and makes up names in play—obviously past life remembrances

Anji Wies

My youngest daughter has always been an old soul. Wise beyond her years, but also an incredible empath and kindness is paramount. That to me is a sign of intellect beyond what we usually see every day and specialness that the world could use more of.

Cody Kemmet

A born dreamer, quite possibly an Indigo.

I spent a lot of time with my family and they taught me many lessons.

I had positive creative support. This helped develop my interest in geometry. My favored symbol was the star or pentagram.

I was amazed it could be drawn without lifting my pen and could be drawn from each side.

Artistry has a way of teaching lessons on the universe as math can be a universal language.

I adored coloring bright imaginary worlds with paint and making board games out of cardboard.

The nights I had blanket forts and read stories all night with my string of pumpkin night lights and flash light to keep the boogie man away.

A child who is born to do great things is not always the child who makes few mistakes, but is the child who find his/her inner strength and rises above adversity.

With these skills I felt different than my classmates but what gave me strength is that I always chose the soft spoken words of love that were true to my heart.

A few of my early epiphany's were the presence of 7. Red, orange, yellow, green, blue, indigo, violet. Musical notes A-G. Days of the week. Classical astrology.

The older I became the more I would see these correspondences. This became clairvoyance.

I played card games like go fish and slap Jack. Eventually solitaire, eventually tarot.

If you take anything from what I wrote, notice a child starts small with little interests that can grow with ambition. What the fuel? You may ask, it's fun.

I found happiness from a young age through innovation and creation.

This might just be a guide to grow a wondering, intuitive, child that is timeless.

Reading material for the young? Folk/ fairytales from across time immortal. We like a good bedtime story, tell us before we become independent. We will thank you for years to come.

Tom ONeil

Their imagination and fascination with all of Mother Earth's gifts in Nature. Finding unique things in forests like Fae rings or holes in the base of a tree and wonder what lives in there. Feel sad when a tree is damaged. Curious about otherworldly places and things.

Mandi Galloway

Every child is magical, just as every adult is magical. It isn't so much about recognizing it as it is nurturing it and helping them to see it in themselves.

Some of the most pivotal work I did with my littles were doing meditations with them, helping them to build their creativity and imagination, and doing circles with them. This builds the groundwork for later, when they become a magical teen and being self aware and mindful is a blessing. This then rolls into being a well equipped magical adult.

Karen Godfrey Betts

Our middle daughter would trance out at drum circle. At age five she confided in me that she spoke to elders no one else could see.

Cassandra Hamlin

Their desire to stand against the grain…follow instinct, and be kind.

Michael J. Love

If you wish to find magical children, you need to look for magical adults, or as we Elves would say: children who have matured. Nearly all children are magical. It is as they pass into the world and are faced with myriad dark spells cast to encourage them to conform and fit it that they retain or, more often unfortunately, lose their magic. Most often, if you find magical adults, you will find children who are likely to retain much of their magic as they grow and develop. Still, evolution is not exclusively material in nature but spiritual or energetic and those who retain their magic, even when they had rather normal parents, do so because they have been upon the path of magic for ages and therefore many incarnations. And it is these beings, upon reaching maturity, that are most likely to provide an atmosphere wherein magical children can thrive as they mature.

Rhonda Peters

They have a special and intimate communication with animals and think innocently that everyone communicates and loves animals the same way.

Miracle Emery

It was pretty easy with my daughter from a very young age, aside from being very sensitive to others' emotions and needs, she saw and spoke to spirits, and said that one particular tree in a park in town had a fairy living in it; she would always run up, hug the tree and greet it like an old friend.

Michael Eric Bérubé

None of us becomes magickal. Most of us START with that magic and wonder and become mundane and single-minded as the magic and wonder are stripped from us by preconceived peer pressure notions of who we are SUPPOSED to be in order to fit in to our society.

I think our job as parents is primarily not to stunt or stifle that innate magic and wonder in our children, but rather to encourage and foster it that they hold on to that into their adulthood and aren't forced to have to find it again after it's lost or forgotten.

B'Joy Yumi

Dreams are often remembered and told to who to whoever is willing to listen. If no one is willing to listen then the artwork, poetry, story, song and many other methods of manifesting creativity comes out of the energy of that manifestation!

Forces of nature can't be stopped.

Rori Barnard

My entire life I knew I was different. I wasn't like the other kids. When I was little I could see Faeries. Later in life I discovered that's because I am one (Dragon specifically). A Faerie, I have discovered, is someone from the realm we call Faerie. It is like Earth but it can only be accessed by those from there (or you know, psychedelics).

I loved shows about mythical, magickal beings such as Wizards, Mages, unicorns, dragons, etc. I LOVE RPGs for this exact reason. What can I say? I'm a Talecrafter. Creativity is something I fully embody. I drew all kinds of things, concepts none of my family could comprehend. I could always feel when the full moon rose, when a storm was approaching, every time a seasonal shift happened, and when a tree or animal was sick. I have always been able to affect ambiance. I've always excited every-thing around me like I kick-started every molecule I came in contact with. What a chemist does with chemicals or a carpenter does with wood, I do with words, sounds, & colors. I've never felt I was the same at any given time. Even to this day I constantly shift & change. Why? Because I am a Metamorphomagus.

River Routen

I have had to fight to keep my magical nature. I'm a young wizard now at 56 winters. I grew up with fellow magical kids and watch them grow today. I had two of my own. It ain't easy being magical. You have to find a harmony of nurturance, acceptance, and the discipline to be here

Katara Thompson

The first book I read when I found out I was pregnant with my son in 1969 was *The Magical Child.* It set my theme for life with my children. They were all magical in a way, but some had that special connection. I saw when I took my four-year-old granddaughter to the ocean for the first time and she stood at the shore with her feet in the water and her eyes wide and arms reaching to the ocean and she called out, "Thank you, thank you, thank you," over and over. When my son would touch people and their pain would go away. When she spun beside the dancers for half an hour without stopping at Dance of Universal Peace. There are so many magical moments with those especially touched by magic.

Kelly Willow MacNeil

They say random thoughts early on like:
"Remember when you were little and I was big?"
These words spilled from my son's mouth around 4 years old .

Rita Knight

I have 3 lovely girls whom of which I think are going to be excep-tionally good should they continue to choose an interest in magickal pur-suits. The eldest (14) whom we see on the weekends comes over and is absorbed in the books we have on magickal practice. We often have a Q & A which when I answer her questions she seems to be in deep conversation and often is quite engaging and gives different perspectives that I wouldn't have thought possible.

My Eldest (9) often couldn't grasp magickal pursuits and had no interest after the age of 5. She began going through my things and found a Fae decor to which we had different conversations about the Fae. Now, this sparked her interest greatly and she is now more keen on celebrating Beltaine. Her interest in Fae has grown since and asks me if she can be a Fae witch. This fueled her fire even more for knowledge of the Fae and another mythical beast.

My youngest (4) I see such a natural gift develop in her it's stunning. She has many toys and items to play with along with a TV tablet etc. Yet she will show more interest in plants and tries to eat them. I often find myself running after her to make sure she doesn't eat anything toxic. She enjoys mixing things she finds outside and in the grand cauldron. She can also be seen constantly putting our driveway in her pockets which contain plenty of quartz.

I feel like any child can be a magickal child if you find the right angle that piques their interest.

Tibor Gajdács

At an early age she could made a cocoon to protect herself.

Bryan Stafford

My daughter spoke to spirits when she was young. This went beyond imaginary friends as the details and descriptions she gave were reminiscent of past loved ones and ancestors, etc. Now an adult, she is still guided by her intuition.

Dyan Brown

When I was raising my son he had no interest in magick, only baseball, hockey, football, and every sport. But one of his friends would borrow my books, found an old cauldron, started coming to our circles, spending nights going on wild hunts out in the woods, and had a natural urge to connect with the magickal energy around him. Some kids just feel the pull and have natural curiosity and aptitude for magick!

Amy Mertes Fernandez

I agree with all children being magickal. It's just important to recognize that not all children manifest it the same way. I have 4 incredibly individual children, with different personalities and different drives. Each of them are magickal in their own way. And not all of them necessarily want to maximize their potential in that area.

My job as a parent is to allow them the opportunity to grow and explore in a safe environment.

Caitlin Haralson

In my experience sleepwalking can be a good tell, especially if they are doing things in their sleep...for example my daughter pulls her runes in her sleep. So maybe not in all cases but I'm also a sleepwalker so it seems too much of a coincidence.

Mia Sirovetz

I think them knowing and discussing past lives at a young age and being drawn to sources in nature that feel magickal are two good indicators. But I agree, most children seem to have an innate ability and belief that is normally ignored or suppressed due to the parents' disbelief or distress at the idea.

Mandi Pandi

All children are magical ♥my son I notice he is particularly connected to nature and feels very deeply for all living creatures. We identify everything as a big helper and talk about how it helps the planet, except mosquitos cuz what do they even do?

Christopher Bridges

Some may say that all children are magical, but certain children do have a special affinity for magic. These children have a propensity to turn things on their head and, depending on the family, may be labeled as trouble-makers. Their imaginations fire on all cylinders and they tend to test the limits of authority.

Everyone is an individual. You cannot identify a magical child based on their interest in the trappings of ritual, feast days, or ceremony. The hallmark of a magical child is the fluidity of their thinking. As other children move on into more concrete modes of thinking, magical children remain connected to the evocative forms of their own imaginations. They shape the world as much as it shapes them, and it's difficult to get them to settle for a world that doesn't accommodate their special vision.

A magical child may be extra sensitive to particular elements of the natural world in a way that goes beyond a simple appreciation for "nature." There will be certain aspects of nature that speak to them. They may also become fascinated with ancestors and things that make other people uncomfortable, like death. You very well may find them lingering around the hearth fire after other children have gone off to play and they may take a special interest in meditation or divination. Magical children are frequently singled out as favorites by quirky elders, and will have a lot of support, even if they don't see it themselves.

If you are a magical person, you may have potent dreams about the magical child in your life. Whether or not they take an interest in magic, you will find that they intuitively understand the uncanny.

It's important to recognize that the lives of magical people can be difficult. Magical children may come across as disruptive or with special needs and may be especially vulnerable to abuse and exploitation. However, if they are loved, their differences accepted and their precocious interests fostered, they can become great assets to their communities, restoring the frayed social fabric in a way that only their special touch can. Chances are, if there is a magical child in your life, you'll know.

Leslie Caradina

They seem unusually astute. They seem particularly drawn toward touching magical jewelry I'm wearing. They have complex imaginary friends. They can tell if something is bothering you.

Edward Buck Shomo

When you're hiking in a hilly, wooded area of central Indiana (the bones of a mountain range from 300 million years ago), and as you walk with your 4-year-old up a dry creek bed between two ridges, he says, "The elephants used to like to come back here looking for food."

Amanda Allen

For mine it was having the child look at me and say *"Really soon I want to go to x or get y."* Then hours later having dad call and say *"How do you think child will feel about going to x or getting y when I get home?"*

Rachel Wheeler

When I was pregnant with my daughter, I just knew there was something different about her. She was my first (and only) and I'm sure many parents feel that way, but this was a distinct sixth sense that there was something exceptional about this child. When she was born, she held up her head and tracked her father's voice at minutes old. She was extremely alert and interested in everything. She was very sensitive to other people's emotions, not liking people crying around her, for example, and to noises and energies. There were certain places she'd just refuse to go in, for example, and would cry until we left, usually because there was something off about the energy there that she picked up. She was also very sensitive to textures and tastes and had (and still does) a photographic memory.

With all this, she also struggled with conversational speech and walked later than some with no physical cause. At age 5, she was diagnosed with Autism and ADHD. I've read that many children with this diagnosis are actually dialed in to a higher plane than most people all the time, hence their seeming need to be on their own, their sensitivity to noise, remarkable memories, decreased need for speech. They often don't understand the rules for socialization as they are as they think outside the box and these norms don't occur to them.

She also had spiritual experiences very young. As a toddler, she would point to the ceiling and say she saw someone named "Michael" and would giggle and play with whoever it was. She also said she saw a lady in the kitchen when no one was there, and told me she saw eagles etc. when none were to be seen. These things all faded as she grew older, as it does with many children, but a heightened awareness remained. She has an affinity with animals, especially horses, and shows no fear of them.

All the women in my family line have had some kind of psychic ability. My mother and grandma taught me to pay attention to dreams from the time I was young, we all had precognitive dreams and my mom and grandma had visions. We all had strong spiritual impressions of different buildings and spaces. My daughter seems to be the most psychic of the lot.

I would say to look for extreme sensitivity, different ways of socialization, a need for solitude, strong emotions, great awareness. I think also many times magickal children are often also autistic, have ADHD, or other neuro differences as their brain is wired differently.

Michele Bailey

The one that gets me is the total stranger child that walks right up and wants you to hold it or wants in your lap. Happened to me at a work function, toddler of a coworker waddled over to me got into my lap and put her head on my shoulder, proceeded to eat my chips and sleep. Took mom over an hour to notice.

Tchipakkan Fair Richards-Taylor

In my experience, we all have the potential, and I have simply explained things like energy healing, dream-work, magickal intent, how lying, messes up your magick, how to tell if a spirit is messing with you (dangerous) or benevolent, how to deal with ghosts, etc. as the topic comes up. That's how you teach kids anything from cooking to taking care of animals. (Also herbalism, weather working, using a pendulum, the same stuff adults want to know.)

One of the big things is teaching them how to avoid getting into trouble with folks who have strange ideas about everything from entities (from Santa Claus to fairies) so that they don't draw unwanted criticism either from adults they encounter or other kids. Many kids have already learned to ask questions obliquely so that they won't get in trouble by the time they hit school age. You have to reassure them that there's nothing wrong with what they are experiencing, and it's normal (for them, even if not for everyone). I usually liken it to artistic talent, some people have natural abilities others don't; most kids understand that. So if they see ghosts, or auras, etc. don't let other adults 'scare it out of them'. But you have to be really careful around other people's kids- unless the parent has brought them to you. "You know about this stuff, right?" In which case you sometimes have to reassure the parents, as well as the kids.

Maybe the biggest thing is to not insist that something they are telling you as real is from their imagination. That can really confuse them about what's imagination and what they perceive.

Sorry, I could go on about raising kids with magick forever, having raised my own that way.

Eva Marie Shaw

My son told me when he was a toddler that before he was born he was in the sky and was tasked with choosing his family....

Avianne Ivy Zen

My granddaughter who is 4 would talk to her little brother while he was still in her mommy's belly. She would tell us things that happened before she was even born. For instance, in great detail how one of my dogs passed away, what he looked like, how it happened, and where we were. When asked who told her, these things, she said her baby brother. She said she talked to him a lot.

When her dad (my son) was her age, he often spoke of past lives.

Glo Blades

I felt everyone was born with their own way of magical thinking and was utterly confused attending Catholic School.

My parents did not raise a magical child but I never gave up my affinity for all that is magic!

I remember my confirmation. My mouth would recite the script, (I renounce Satan, blah, blah, blah) and in my mind I was screaming *"but I don't even believe in Satan!!"*

Many years later, I happened to go to my first ritual, Samhain. I was in complete shock! It was dizzying when I heard the HPS speak of the thoughts, feelings, secrets, philosophy, and perception of existence that I held to be true for me. What I never told another person. I didn't know others thought like I have my whole life!

I was 3 the first time I asked to be dressed as a witch for Halloween (every year for 30+ years)!

I know I was born magical. As a child, I thought so was everyone else!

I never understood why Christianity, Judaism, or Islam forces its people into the Abrahamic schools of thought. Then they make it the congregants' responsibility to proselytize!

I would often question people about it.

To raise a magical child, you must simply foster their natural curiosities. Listen to their thoughts just like you would an adult. Respect their experiences, thoughts, feelings and their analytical processes. And not try to force them. away from their natural inclinations. Arm them with knowledge of other religions to better handle themselves in the world at large and understand people rather than arming them with fear.

In coming out of the broom closet to my brothers, I was asked if I was converting.

I never converted to Paganism because I was never Christian.

My mother was present to attest to my truth, because she and I had an ongoing conversation gathering all the evidence of those moments when my Magick shone brightly throughout my life.

Henry Karl Scherr

When my younger son Evan was a little boy, he used to talk with the dead when we visited cemeteries. One time he saw a photo on the wall that included his grandmother and her deceased sister as teenagers with their dog. He blurted out "That's me with my sister and our dog Rosie!" He often talked about his experiences "Back before I was little."

Jaime Cowley Jeffer

My daughter was born magical. She has a Faery's heart, and all through her life animals have found their way to her. One morning when she was little I opened the door to find her curled up with a strange black dog. They love her. And she has embraced the Goddess all on her own.

10. Indigo, Crystal and Star Children

By Oberon Zell

**NDIGO CHILDREN** ARE CHILDREN WHO ARE believed to possess special, unusual, and sometimes supernatural traits or abilities. The idea is based on concepts developed in the 1970s by Nancy Ann Tappe. In 1982, Tappe introduced the concept of "life colors," defined as *"the single color of the aura that remains constant in most people from the cradle to the grave."*[24] Her ideas were further developed by Barbara Bowers, Pamala Oslie, Lee Carroll and Jan Tober.

The concept of "Indigo Children" gained popularity with the publication of a series of books in the late 1990s and several films in the following decade, concerning "Indigo Children" and their nature and abilities. Claims range from Indigo Children being more empathic and creative than their peers, to the belief that they are the next stage in human evolution, whose purpose is to usher in a new and improved phase of our species.

Indigo Children are usually described as being born in 1978 or later, but Tappe claimed to have been noticing "indigo" children beginning in the late 1960s. And I have to say, the characteristics of "Indigo Children" do seem to me descriptive of my own generation, born in the early 1940s and coming of age in the "New Age" of the psychedelic sixties—the previous 60-year Cultural Renaissance Cycle.

Indigos are often described as "old souls." They may be immature in body, yet seem older than their years. They like animals and Nature. They may seem to have low self-esteem while simultaneously acting grandiose. The rebellious spirit of the Indigo seems to say: *I know I'm here for a purpose. I know that the way we treat each other and our Earth is supposed to change. I'm tired of waiting. Let's get on with it!*[25]

---

[24] Tappe, Nancy Ann, *Understanding Your Life Thru Color: Metaphysical Concepts in Color and Aura.* Starling Publishers. 1986

[25] Lipson, Judith E. "Indigo, Crystal, Rainbow and Star Children." *Metro You Magazine,* May 29, 2012. https://www.spiralwisdom.com/indigo-crystal-rainbow-and-star-children/

Common Indigo, Crystal, Rainbow & Star Child Traits

- "Old soul" qualities, with wisdom far greater than their age;
- Are often perceived by friends and family as being strange;
- Are often socially awkward;
- Are often introverted and feel isolated, unless around people on the same "level;"
- May feel "superior" or that they may have been "royalty" in a previous life;
- Have a strong feeling of entitlement;
- Are empathic, curious, and strong-willed;
- Have high intelligence quotient;
- Are highly creative—often drawn to writing, art, music, etc.;
- Often have psychic & intuitive abilities;
- Show a strong innate subconscious spirituality;
- Possess a clear sense of self-definition and purpose;
- Feel a strong calling, or "mission," to make the world a better place;
- Have a deep, innate knowledge of better ways to do things—are often "paradigm busters;"
- Are non-responsive and resistant to controlling people and authority figures;
- Love nature, plants, and animals.[26]

According to Tober and Carroll, Indigo Children may function poorly in conventional schools due to their being smarter or more spiritually mature than their teachers, and their consequent rejection of rigid authority and guilt-, fear- or manipulation-based discipline. They come across as wise, intuitive, caring, and curious and they often have a "spark" —which seems to challenge the existing educational and societal constructs.

Pagan author Lorna Tedder notes that every Pagan mother she knew believed their child was an Indigo Child. S. Zohreh Kermani states that *"Despite their problems with authority, uncontrollable tempers, and overbearing egos, Indigo Children are many Pagan parents' ideal offspring: sensitive, psychic and strong-willed,"* but also notes the concept

---

[26] Are You an Indigo, Star, Rainbow, or Crystal Child / Adult? How to Maximize the Potential of an "Advanced Soul."

https://eocinstitute.org/meditation/meditation-indigo-children/?mind_power&gad

is less about the child's psychic abilities than the parent's own hopes and desire for *"distinction from the less-evolved masses."*[27]

Many children who have been diagnosed with attention deficit hyperactivity disorder (ADHD) may be considered Indigos. The characteristics that define one describe the other: out–of–the–box, right-brained, and otherwise unconventional learners and global thinkers.[28]

Sarah W. Whedon suggests that the social construction of Indigo Children is a response to an "apparent crisis of American childhood" in the form of increased youth violence and diagnoses of ADHD. Whedon believes parents label their children as "Indigo" to provide an alternative explanation for their children's inappropriate behavior stemming from ADHD.[29]

Crystal Children, a concept related to Indigo children, has been linked by autism researcher Mitzi Waltz to the Autism spectrum. She says that proponents recategorize autistic symptoms as telepathic powers, and attempt to reconceptualize *"the autistic traits associated with them as part of a positive identity."*[30]

According to Doreen Virtue,[31] Crystal Children reflect the new generation that began incarnating in the late 1990s—the spiritual children and grandchildren of the Indigo Children. Like Indigos, these children are highly psychic and sensitive—but without the rebellious edge and vigor. Crystal Children are said to have crystal or clear auras. They are considered the next stage in human evolution, and are harmony-builders meant to continue the work started by Indigos.

As babies, Crystal Children may take longer than normal to begin talking. They are highly telepathic, and their tuned-in mothers communicate with them nonverbally. Because they're so sensitive, the Crystal Children babies may fuss and cry a lot in crowded places. They're also very fond of Nature.

"Crystal Children are beautiful inside and out, like magnificent little high-priests and priestesses. One look in their eyes, and you'll recognize Divine love and wisdom. Their auras are bright, radiant, and

---

[27] Kermani, S. Zohreh, *Pagan Family Values: Childhood and the Religious Imagination in Contemporary American Paganism.* NYU Press. pp. 66–67. (2013)

[28] Lipson, *Op cit.*

[29] Whedon, Sarah W. *"The Wisdom of Indigo Children: An Emphatic Restatement of the Value of American Children".* Nova Religio. 12 (3): 60–76. (February 2009).

[30] Waltz, M. "From Changelings to Crystal Children: An Examination of 'New Age' Ideas About Autism." *Journal of Religion, Disability & Health.* 13 (2): 114–128. (2009)

[31] Virtue, Doreen, *The Crystal Children: A Guide to the Newest Generation of Psychic and Sensitive Children.* Hay House, 2003.

opalescent—they seem to glow from the inside! They talk about past lives, distant galaxies, and profound insights concerning peace and love."[32]

Rainbow Children and **Star Children** are similar to Crystals, but they don't have the karmic "baggage" of unresolved issues carried forward from other lifetimes. Star Children are said to be partly or fully extraterrestrial in origin and possess extrasensory and psychic abilities, deep spiritual connectivity, extraordinary creativity, and high levels of intelligence and empathy. They may have difficulty learning in traditional school environments, experience discipline problems, and/or be diagnosed with ADD or ADHD. They are entirely self-identified.[33]

Star Children tend to be geniuses in the sciences. They're supposed to play a key role in transforming the world.

> "I call them the 'children of now' because I'm really trying not to specifically label them too much," said Meg Blackburn Losey, the author of *Children of Now.* "There are several different labels. Indigos, most of them are in their 20s now, some in their early 30s. Since then, we've had other kids with more refined gifts coming in, telepathic, intuitive, little healers. My estimate is 20 to 25 percent of the total population of children is some form of what we're talking about."[34]

Indigos, Crystals, Rainbows, Star Children. Regardless of the name, we are all interconnected as members of the Family of Earth, even the Universe. As parents of these remarkable children, help them to:

- Understand and accept their sensitivities, empathy and intuition;
- Develop self-confidence and be empowered;
- Establish personal and energetic boundaries;
- Minimize their sensitivities, fears and the effects of anxiety;
- Remember that they are spiritual beings having a human experience.

Hold the Indigo, Crystal, Rainbow and Star Children in your life in light and love. May we all recognize our purpose and live our lives to their fullest potential.

---

[32] Crystal Children website: www.crystal-children.com

[33] Holman, Desirée, *Sophont*, 2015. https://www.sfmoma.org/read/desiree-holmans-indigo-children/

[34] Lucas, Beth, "Are indigo, crystal and star people among us?" Jun 13, 2008 Updated Oct 7, 2011 https://www.eastvalleytribune.com/get_out/are-indigo-crystal-and-star-people-among-us/article

---

Ṫraits Ḟor a Ḟully Ậwakened ẞ Ậctivated Ïndigo, Ꞓrystal, Ṟainbow ẞ Ṡtar Child

- A bulletproof sense of inner peace.
- True happiness, no matter the circumstances in your life.
- Feeling "at one" with everyone & everything.
- Unconditional love for all living beings.
- Finding your true self and your true path.
- A worry/stress/anxiety free natural existence.
- A very fulfilled, meaningful life.
- Deep healing of mind, body, and spirit.
- A permanent higher shift in consciousness & understanding.
- Fulfilling your life mission or calling.
- Having the ability & capacity to fundamentally "change the world."[35]

All these Indigos, Crystals, Rainbows and Star Children were born in the late 20th century. Here in the 21st, as I write this, we are now the aging grownups who look forward to reincarnating as your children. By the time you bear and raise us, these paradigms will likely have little relevance, as new names and descriptions will no doubt have come to be applied to us "Old Souls" next time around! But I expect we'll still exhibit the same traits. I wonder what you'll call us in your time?

Ṟeferences.

1. Carroll, Lee; Tober, Jan. *The Indigo Children: The New Kids Have Arrived.* Hay House, 1999.
2. Kermani, S. Zohreh, *Pagan Family Values: Childhood and the Religious Imagination in Contemporary American Paganism.* NYU Press, 2013.
3. Lipson, J.E. "Indigo, Crystal, Rainbow & Star Children." *Metro You Magazine,* 5/29/2012. www.spiralwisdom.com/indigo-crystal-rainbow-and-star-children/
4. Losey, Meg Blackburn, *Children of Now.* Weiser, 2006.
5. Lucas, Beth, "Are indigo, crystal and star people among us?" 6/13/2008; 10/7/2011 www.eastvalleytribune.com/get_out/are-indigo-crystal-and-star-people-among-us/article
6. Tappe, Nancy Ann, *Understanding Your Life Thru Color: Metaphysical Concepts in Color and Aura.* Starling Publishers. 1986.
7. Waltz, M. "From Changelings to Crystal Children: An Examination of 'New Age' Ideas About Autism." *Journal of Religion, Disability & Health.* **13** (2): 114–128. (2009).
8. Whedon, Sarah W. "The Wisdom of Indigo Children: An Emphatic Restatement of the Value of American Children." *Nova Religio.* **12** (3): 60–76. (February 2009).

---

[35] Are You an Indigo, Star, Rainbow, or Crystal Child / Adult? *Op cit.*

11. Changelings

By Oberon Zell

N EUROPEAN FOLKLORE, "CHANGELINGS" ARE creatures left in place of human babies or children taken by Faeries. The changeling may be an elderly or a sickly fairy. The rational for this exchange was that a changeling would be cared for by the family while the human child would become a servant to the Fae. Of course, changelings would never grow up to be someone who could help the family or take care of themselves. Instead they would use up family resources. Because changelings were seen as a burden to families, this legend may have come about as an excuse for getting rid of unwanted children.[36]

Many people today claim descent from "Faerie" ancestors, and the *Faerie Tradition* is well-respected in the Pagan/magickal community. Many Medieval Witches claimed that their lore and teachings came from the Fae, and Witches and Faeries are often conflated in myth. A common profession of both was midwifery. Deformed or unusual babies were often considered to be *changelings*—a Faerie child substituted for the human infant. The ramifications could be quite terrible and traumatic, as mistreatment would be inflicted upon developmentally disabled children whose parents believed that their own babies had been kidnapped by the Good Neighbors.

In our current enlightened times we label such children as "developmentally disabled." When I was studying for my teaching certificate in the late-1960s, they were called "special" or "exceptional." Unkind terms included "retarded." Later labels were more clinical, such as "autistic," "Aspergers" or "ADHD." Now the accepted term is *neurodivergent.* Neurodivergence includes conditions like autism, ADHD, dyslexia, and others. It underscores that there is no single "normal" way the brain functions. The opposite of neurodivergent is *neurotypical.*

New Agers call them "Indigos," "Crystals," "Rainbows" or "Star Children." In science fiction and comics they are called "Mutants." But this category

---

[36] Kathleen Listman, M.Ed. from The University of Texas at Arlington. www.quora.com/In-fairy-lore-what-are-changelings/answer/K-N-Listman-1?

also includes geniuses and savants. Avatars. *Homo novus;* the next stage in human evolution.

But for many of us who have been so labelled, our personal experience is that of our souls (if not our bodies) being from "Elsewhere"—"The Island of Misfit Toys." Maybe Faerie, maybe aliens. "Ugly ducklings." As children, we felt we must have been adopted, or fosterlings, like Harry Potter, and so many foundlings in so many tales. Definitely not of the same stock as our "parents." And many of our parents seemed to have felt the same way—"This is *not* my child!" Child abuse against misfit kids has always been rife—and not just in the Middle Ages.

"Changelings" is a term many of us feel is particularly descriptive and apropos, and many of us relate and identify with it. I certainly do! As a child, I used to go out in the backyard at night and shine a flashlight into the sky, hoping to signal the flying saucers to come get me and take me home—wherever that might be! Clearly, it wasn't here.

However, Fiagái Faeborne says that "generally across the board autistic/ADHD/neurodivergent people really do *not* appreciate *Indigo Child, Star Seed,* or *Changeling* as titles being ascribed to us in any way. All of those terms carry a lot of baggage for the ND community, unfortunately. Many parents will just say their child is a Star Seed or an Indigo Child, and then not actually get them support for their needs, or have them diagnosed. It can be really hard for ND folks to be put on that pedestal, but never supported in real life skills and support. Many parents use those terms to simply be in denial about their child being neurodivergent, and so it puts a sour taste in the mouth of most ND people."

There is a genetic disorder called *Williams Syndrome,* first described in 1961, which affects about one in 20,000 births. Those who have it "are loving, caring, and sensitive to the feelings of others. Despite having low IQs, many are good storytellers and have a talent for music, notably perfect pitch.

"Most striking of all is their appearance. A relatively large number are short. They have childlike faces, with small, upturned noses, oval ears, and broad mouths with full lips and a small chin. They look and behave like the traditional depiction of Elves."[37]

---

[37] Highfield, Roger, *The Science of Harry Potter: How Magic Really Works,* Penguin Books; Reprint edition 2003. pp. 192-193

12. Nightmares[38]

by Oberon Zell

 "NIGHT-MARE" MEANS LITERALLY A MONSTROUS black spirit-horse which carries us away on a terrifying and uncontrollable ride through dark and scary places. Nightmares are like a stuck replay, with added dramatization and special effects, of experiences too frightful to think of in our waking state. In very young children, such nightmares may often be remembrances of a tragic death in their previous life. Especially if they died by violence, these "night terrors" can be so frightening that they cause insomnia and the child will suffer from sleep deprivation. Sleepwalking can be expected. Talking and crying too, when they are not fully awake. For that type of nightmare, a really good antidote is to have the child draw pictures and talk about them. Let them keep a light on in their bedroom so they can fully awaken. That way they can go back to sleep. And sing them to sleep with a familiar lullaby.

> Nightmares not so much last death, but night hags from sleep paralysis. Liminal sleeping where sleep paralysis the mind makes up monsters. Sleepwalking can be expected. Talking and crying, but they are not fully awake. Leave a light on so the child can fully awaken. That way they can go back to sleep. (~Archonstone)

Throughout my own early childhood, I was haunted by nightmares in which I kept reliving my last death. I had died of a heart attack, and I experienced this as if I was falling backwards down a bottomless well, with the world I knew shrinking into a smaller and smaller circle until it was gone from my sight, and I kept falling endlessly through total darkness…until I awoke as a baby in my new life.

Another source of nightmares can be traumatic experiences in this current life. Children (and even adults) who have been exposed to violence or abuse; who have lived through tragic accidents or fires—especially if others have died; who have had severe and life-threatening illnesses; or experienced other traumas; will have nightmare in which they will continue to relive these horrors—often symbolically.

Particularly frightening nightmares are sometimes caused by a disconnection between the brain and the body as one is falling asleep or just

---

[38] *Grimoire for the Apprentice Wizard,* pp. 41-42.

awakening. The Japanese, who have long known of this phenomenon, call it *kanashibari*, and Western researchers refer to it as "sleep paralysis." About 4% of all people experience it regularly, and 40-60% at least once. Some hear disturbing sounds and incoherent voices. Others hallucinate evil supernatural beings and monstrous creatures. Most find themselves unable to move or speak, and feel a weight on their chest. Also common are sensations of levitation, flying, and passing through spiral tunnels—all with a great sense of dread and terror.

Kanashibari nightmares often involve shadowy demonic creatures, such as the *Dementors* of Harry Potter's world, or the *Ringwraiths* of *Lord of the Rings*. Many such creatures have been identified in myth—such as *Succubi* and *Incubi* who lie upon sleepers and have sex with them, or ugly old hags, goblins and ghosts which squat on a sleeper's chest and choke them. The *Lethifold* is a floating black cloak that envelopes and suffocates its victims. And the fire-eyed black devil-horse we call the *Nightmare* is common to many cultures. Many "alien abduction" experiences may be explainable as Kanashibari.

The best antidote to all types of nightmares is to teach your child to seize control of their dreams, through *Lucid Dreaming*. They can wield spells and powers to combat these monsters of the dark, just as in a video game. In fact, a video game is a very good way to visualize The Dreaming when one is having nightmares!

Another cool thing is to get your child a stuffed doll of a Japanese dream-eater called a *Baku*. According to legend, *Baku* were created by the spare pieces that were left over when the gods finished creating all other animals. They are depicted with an elephant's head, tusks, and trunk, with horns and tiger's claws. A child having a nightmare in Japan will wake up and repeat three times, *"Baku-san, come eat my dream."* The *Baku* will come and devour the bad dream, allowing the child to go back to sleep peacefully. The *Baku* can also be summoned for protection from bad dreams prior to falling asleep at night. It used to be common for Japanese children to keep a *Baku* talisman at their bedside.

Ⱥnti-Ṅightmare spells

Hang a small wreath of gray feathers or a dream-catcher over your child's bed to prevent nightmares and bring restful sleep. A pyramid-shaped crystal under the bed will protect them from psychic attack in their sleep. Hang up a red onion and place mugwort under their pillow to keep away evil spirits. Lay down a circle of salt on the floor surrounding the bed as a barrier. Then set a magick Circle of Protection around their bed each night before they go to sleep, like this:

Stand in the middle of the bedroom and hold up a small mirror, like a makeup mirror, facing outwards, so that the walls of the bedroom are reflected. Turn around *deosil* (clockwise) in a complete circle, and visualize a circular reflective wall spreading outward from the mirror in your hand, as if you are on the inside of a mirrored Christmas tree ornament. As you do this, say:

> *Circles of Light surround thy bed;*
> *All fears of night gone from thy head.*
> *May peaceful dreams come unto thee;*
> *As I do will, so mote it be!*

Another charm against nightmares goes like this:

> *Thou evil thing of darkness born*
> *Of tail and wing and snout and horn,*
> *Fly from thee from now till morn!*
> ~Valerie Worth

(You can teach your children to do this for themselves…)

Art by Oberon Zell.

13. Advice to Parents
How to Raise a Child: 10 Rules from Young Susan Sontag
by Maria Popova

HE SECOND VOLUME OF SUSAN SONTAG'S DIA-ries, *As Consciousness Is Harnessed to Flesh: Journals and Notebooks, 1964-1980*, gives us the celebrated author and thinker's insights on love, writing, censorship, and aphorisms. However, it is in the first installment, *Reborn: Journals and Notebooks, 1947-1963 (public library)*, that the beloved public intellectual coalesces out of a shaky young woman grappling with her place in relation to the world and herself — as we see in her 1957 list of "rules + duties for being 24."

Two years later, in September of 1959, Sontag listed her 10 rules for raising a child. (Their object, Sontag's son David Rieff, edited this very volume.) Underpinning them is a subtle but palpable reverence for the precious gift of "childishness."

1. Be consistent.

2. Don't speak about him to others (e.g., tell funny things) in his presence. (Don't make him self-conscious.)

3. Don't praise him for something I wouldn't always accept as good.

4. Don't reprimand him harshly for something he's been allowed to do.

5. Daily routine: eating, homework, bath, teeth, room, story, bed.

6. Don't allow him to monopolize me when I am with other people.

7. Always speak well of his pop. (No faces, sighs, impatience, etc.)

8. Do not discourage childish fantasies.

9. Make him aware that there is a grown-up world that's none of his business.

10. Don't assume that what I don't like to do (bath, hairwash) he won't like either.

PART III:
The Magickal Child
(age 3-11)

Yesterday a child came out to wonder
Caught a dragonfly inside a jar
Fearful when the sky was full of thunder
And tearful at the falling of a star.

~Joni Mitchell, "The Circle Game"

"Your children are not your children.
They are the sons and daughters of Life's longing for itself.
They come through you but not from you,
And though they are with you, yet they belong not to you.
You may give them your love but not your thoughts,
For they have their own thoughts.
You may house their bodies but not their souls,
For their souls dwell in the house of tomorrow,
Which you cannot visit, not even in your dreams."

~Kahlil Gibran, *The Prophet*

Y dderwen yn cael wedi ei
   thorri;
A fydd hi yn tyfi eto unwaith?
Yn awren mae'r dderwen hon
   ein gwaeth,
I weld ei thardd hi yfori,
I weld ei thardd hi yfori.

The oak was cut;
Will it grow once more?
In this time is the oak our labor,
To see it grow tomorrow,
To see it grow tomorrow.

~Gwydion Pendderwen,
"Can Ceridwen"

14. Raising the Next Generation of Earth-Centered, Spiritually-Aligned Children

Rev. Asherah Allen, C-S.C., Lic. Ac.

For some of us, our rites of passage were made of scratching and clawing with tooth and nail at the bottom of the pit of parental and societal abandonment and neglect, searching for the rope of liberation that would lead us to safety. Many of us were marred by the trauma of caregivers with mental illness, drug or alcohol addiction, and having to survive physical, mental, emotional, or even sexual abuse. We strove to find the rites and rituals to heal our souls as we endeavored to raise ourselves and our children in conscious ways filled with the love and care we did not receive enough of when experiencing our formative years. It's for your benefit, my soul warrior family, that I write this chapter. It's for you, my dear daughter, that I devote with gratitude this writing and my life.

"MAY YOU REMEMBER THAT YOU ARE A TEAM; IT has to work for you both."

My friend whispers in my ear as I feel the warm rose-petal infused water drip down my calves as her strong hands massage my swollen third-trimester feet.

I'm seated in a circle of women. Looking around the room I'm struck by the enormous sense of support I have in this community. Tenderly, with soft music playing, my feet are washed, my hair stroked, as one by one, each woman comes up and offers her blessing for my transition into becoming a mother. Knowing I'll soon be living a life in service to my child, I gratefully take my turn to deeply receive.

When mothers, especially new mothers, come into parenthood without the emotional, financial, spiritual, physical, medical, communal, societal, and family support they need, everyone suffers. In this moment, there is no suffering. I open my hands and let all the love in. One by one, these dear soul sisters press a beautiful, unique bead they have picked out into my hand. I later string these beads on a long necklace and leave it on my birthing altar, gathering power for when I go into labor.

The pain rips down my spine; *back labor, ugh!* I reach for the birthing necklace made at the birthing way ceremony. As I hold each bead, I work my way around the necklace, as I would if I were doing Japa on a Mala, and I'm filled with a strength I couldn't access before. I feel the presence and power of each woman—her words of wisdom and encouragement—and the pain becomes bearable.

My daughter is born, and it's the great stream of divine feminine love and wisdom that nourished me into this moment. I look at the belly cast done a few weeks before my birthing way. As I rock my baby's warm body against my bosom, hearing the slurping of her nursing, I'm transported back to feeling the warm casting material slathered onto my growing breasts and belly, and the sweet songs sung by members of my spiritual community. I felt beautiful, then and now. Without the celebration of my changing body by the women in my life, I wouldn't have felt the expansion of my body temple was beautiful, or nearly as sacred.

I'm filled with tremendous gratitude for the power of ceremony and community to birth new mothers in healing ways that lead to healthy parenting.

Conscious Parenting Ceremonies

Blessing Way—*a celebration ceremony for an expecting mother honoring her journey into motherhood.*

Saining—*a Scots word for consecrating, blessing, or protecting*

Hand to hand and heart to heart, we cast the circle. It's time to present my daughter to the elements, her community, family, and friends. She burbles and coos as we present her to the east. A feather fan is waved about her as a beloved says,

"Open to the power of air, power of clear communication, power of thought, and creativity."

We move to the south. Powers of fire. A candle is danced in front of her eyes and we hear the words,

Open to the power of fire, power of passion, joy, and vision."

We move to the west—the element of water, and she is anointed with water as we hear the words,

"Open to the power of water, power of cleansing, clearing, healing, and blessing."

We move to the north—element of Earth, and a speck of soil is pressed on her tongue as we hear the words,

"Open to the power of Earth, power of the ancestors, of knowledge, and wisdom."

Finally she is held high and presented to Spirit in the power of silence. Her spirit name is said aloud for the first time, a name that will be known to only those gathered here.

At this time, she belongs to us, to the elements, to Earth, and we celebrate her form. When she passes from this world she will be everywhere and become everything. We rejoice and cherish her arrival among her tribe.

First Moon Ceremony—*a celebration to mark the onset of menstruation*

My daughter and I are driving over to a much beloved annual gathering in our community.

"Can we go home for a minute? I have to get something."

"Sure," I say to my daughter. "What did you forget?"

"I didn't forget anything; I just need some pads."

Stammered; I try not to drive the car off the road.

"Of course we can, sweetheart, no problem. Do you have everything you need?"

"Mama, you've been preparing me for this day for years. I'm fine."

As we arrive home and she gets her things, I search the bookshelf quickly for a book on Pagan rituals and rites of passage. *A-ha! Yes, there it is, the chapter on rites of passage for the first moon.* I grab the book, we pile back into the car and are off.

When we arrive, I take a moment to ask my daughter if she'd allow me to conduct a first moon blood ritual for her with women from the community who are present, women who've seen me through the many years of wanting a child, conceiving, birthing, saining and now—gulp—this.

The merchants' area is mercifully full of a vast array of red items, and in no time, we whip together a ritual and decorate a throne draped in red cloth.

As she enters, my daughter is greeted by a room full of these magnificent and powerful women. They circle around her and share wisdom with her as her hair is brushed and she is bedecked with flowers. Her hands and feet are gently washed. The women form a line, standing with legs spread; they form a tunnel and have her crawl through so that she may birth herself into young womanhood. When she arrives out the other end she is led to her throne and it's her time to share her wisdom with us as we listen, share food and drink, and each woman gifts her with a red item to mark her growth.

This is a far cry from my grandmother's first moon. Having never been told of the event, she thought she was bleeding to death. I send the healing of this moment back through my matrilineal lines so that all the women in my family may be healed of the lack of this magic.

Coming of Age Ritual—*a ritual or ceremony of separation marking a time of significant change when a young adult acknowledges the circle of family they came from and begins to develop a circle of support of their own.*

Having written her letter of intent—my daughter is ready to participate in her coming-of-age ritual. She is primed now to become a more active participant in her community, stepping into young adulthood and asserting more of her independence and autonomy. She spends the night alone in the forest, a chance to feel into her journey leading up to this moment and what awaits her on the other side. In the soft light of morning, she is witnessed in her growth and she is led down to hundreds of her community members singing to her as the sun rises, tears coming down their faces as we all remember her in the womb, as a baby, as a toddler, as a pre-teen, as a teen, and now as a young adult stepping into her power. She is so deeply held and honored. She is witnessed fully. I'm filled with pride and wonder at the miracle of the turning of the wheel of life and the healing power of ritual and of spiritual family.

The Ceremony

Many of us were not raised in spiritually nourishing ways, and learning how to do so for our children can be a steep learning curve. One of the things we can do to heal this is to divinely parent ourselves.

I invite you to find a picture of yourself as a baby or a small child. Set aside a space for an altar for this work. Place a soft cushion to sit on in front of the altar. Take a moment to be still and quiet, and tune into your image as a child looking back at you. What does little you need? Is there a negative thought loop, a limiting belief your child-soul believes is damaging or wounding? Write that belief on a piece of paper and place it next to the photo. An example would be, "I'm not worthy." Now write down the opposite of that belief or statement, i.e., "I am worthy," and place that written statement on the other side of the photo and repeat those healing words looking into the eyes of yourself as a child. Do this as a practice daily until it feels like a true statement all the way down in your bones. Once the healing statement feels true, burn the limiting belief or shred it and bury what remains somewhere you never plan to return.

Take time to talk to your child-soul. Tell them what comes to pass in the years ahead. Tell them how deeply they are loved and will be loved.

What was one of your favorite foods as a child? Make that food as an offering to younger you. You may even enjoy eating it with your hands and letting yourself make a joyful mess. Enjoy nourishing your inner child with good food, positive thoughts, and blissful actions. Practice being unconditionally loving toward yourself. This is a lifetime practice, a daily practice. You may keep the photo out on the altar for as long as it feels right and bring it back out whenever you have a need.

In order to parent a child in an Earth-conscious way, we begin by understanding that we're not just on Earth; we *are* the Earth. There is no separation. Teaching our children how to have an intimate relationship with the Earth is teaching them how to have an intimate relationship with themselves. Beginning these teachings at a young age instills in them the comfort of knowing that even when their parents aren't around, they're held in the arms of the great mother, Gaea, the Earth Herself. In Mother Earth, our children can find solace and sustenance whenever they have the need, and we can rest assured, knowing when we're gone, they'll have a force greater than themselves to turn to and have a nourishing and sustained relationship with.

We can introduce our children to the Elements of Earth as a way to foster a lasting healing relationship with the sacred. Playing in the dirt, walking barefoot on the morning dew, squishing mud between the toes, stacking stones, and holding rocks are all ways to engage with the element of Earth. For a sense of belonging, we can tell our children about how the bones of our ancestors, and all life, return to the Earth. We can tell them the history of the place their ancestors are from and what the first religious practices of their indigenous roots were like. By being still and rubbing two stones together, we can listen to the voice of the Earth. Encourage your children to find creative ways to engage with the Earth and watch them grow up to be well-grounded individuals.

The whimsical element of air enjoys much satisfaction from our playful engagement. Gather found feathers with your child and display them in lovely vases as you teach them about each bird. Step outside in the early morning and listen to the wind in the trees and the voice of the winged ones. Teach your children to listen to the voice of the air. Invite your child to join you in dancing with the element of air as you light a stick of incense. As we nourish the capacity to listen, we help raise strong communicators.

With a candle lit at bedtime, we can introduce children to the element of fire. Reading a bedtime story by the light of candle or lighting candles at dinner time helps infuse sacredness into the routine of daily living. We can teach our children to write down a wish they have on the Yule log with a marker and watch the log burn during the longest night of the year.

This ritual builds appreciation for how fire keeps us warm even in the coldest time of year. Cooking our food over an open fire when camping teaches our children about the nourishing aspects of fire. Inviting our children to write down something that is troubling them that they wish to release, and tossing that paper into the fire, teaches them how to let go of what no longer serves them. They can then gaze for a time into the fire inviting the vision of what will take the place of what they released that will now serve them well. Opening our children to the power of fire feeds their passion, vision, and capacity for transforming their lives.

We're born in the waters of the womb. We cry salty tears. Water sustains our lives and cleanses our souls. When our children are in the bath we can teach them how to wash away the stress and strain of the day. When drinking water, we can teach them how water is life for all beings. We can visit our local wells, lakes, springs, and sources of drinking water and, with our children, make an offering of flower petals or water from our home that we've breathed our gratitude into. Many children are fascinated by learning about the ocean and sea creatures. Holding shells up to their ear and inviting them to listen encourages our children to hear the voice of the water. Teaching our children about water helps nourish emotionally intelligent people.

Teaching our children about spirit is simple. We can talk to our children about how all beings have an indwelling spirit, including the four-leggeds, winged ones, two-leggeds, trees, rocks, wind, and streams. When our children are raised knowing all life and manifestations of life are sacred, they have a deep and abiding respect for everyone and everything. We're much less likely as a people to destroy our environment, persecute each other, or harden around mere differences if we understand that all life is sacred and diverse. Understanding the Spirit of the Earth, we raise children who desire to live their lives, if not devote them entirely, to the preservation and healing of the Earth and, therefore of the world.

Thank you for consciously raising your children in the Spirit of the Earth. Thank you for healing yourself of the childhood wounds so that you too may walk in freedom and love as we all deserve. May we all remember the way of the Earth and create peace at the heart of the world.

15. Socialization

By Christine Grace

INY HUMANS KNOW THAT TREES MISS THEIR friends and that the ocean is laughing when pebbles tickle its waves. A baby lying in the grass is fully immersed in the sensory experience of grass and comes to know grass through touch and smell in a way that moves beyond our knowledge of photosynthesis or monoculture. In utero the fetus is entwined not only with its mother or gestational parent but already with a plethora of microbial life. The amniotic fluid was once rain or the ocean or part of a dinosaur's body. Even before we become separate persons, humans are not—cannot be—truly isolated. We are fundamentally, inextricably relational. As children we feel this truth in our very bodies and are naturally inclined to relate to the world as vibrantly alive.

As we grow, we all learn from our relationships with others and learn how to be in relationship with others (individuals and groups) and this, as a layperson like myself might understand it, is socialization. From their earliest days, our children are observing us and learning from us and all the beings surrounding them. (And of course, we are learning from and being shaped by our children in return.) Long before we might begin intentionally teaching the alphabet we have taught our littles a great deal about how to view and exist in the world— from gender roles to cultural identity to how we relate with more-than-human beings. Our children and young people are always learning through direct relationship and using those experiences to create their own developing views and beliefs. This early socialization through the family is a uniquely exciting yet complex topic for those of us embracing an Earth-based path. It is complex because as members of a minority spiritual community, the practices, beliefs and values we want to share with our little ones often stand in contrast to those of the mainstream culture and the corporate generators of mass cultural products. It is exciting because we have an opportunity to rethink socialization from an embodied, animistic perspective.

Much of the time socialization is unplanned and unconscious. We all absorb social norms from individuals, groups, institutions, and the media that surrounds us. We learn how to exist in the world by existing amongst others. However, as Pagan parents (folks who are already breaking some social norms and thinking a bit differently), we have this opportunity to reflect on what we want for our families. As parents following Earth-based paths, there is a big gap between how socialization is discussed in the media, and even by most scholars, and how we might define it. In parenting books, on social media and even chatting with fellow parents, the discussion around socializing children is entirely anthropocentric or focused wholly on human beings to the exclusion of all other living and nonliving beings. That emphasis just doesn't sit right with my own orientation as an animist—a person who believes that the world is alive and everything has a spirit. It doesn't sit right with my own orientation as one who honors the interconnectedness of all these beings on both a magical and an ecological level.

Contemporary US parenting culture encourages an awful lot of angst over the human-to-human slice of a child's total socialization. In contrast, a lens of contemporary animism organically lends itself to understanding socialization in enormous, generous, abundant terms. Our children are moving within webs of interconnection linking them with the whole of the Earth—plants, air, animals, water, soil, landforms, fungi, microbiomes, weather events, geological movements—all of whom have a spiritual being, an agency, an aliveness in themselves. To an animist the world is gloriously alive and we are never isolated; in our very being we are relational, connected. To foster Earth-based socialization is to foster a huge network of conscious, embodied interactions far beyond the human. This helps put intraspecies socialization in its place as one part of socialization, but only one part. And since most of our culture is already engaged with that bit, my interest leans toward the other aspects of socialization.

An animist approach to socialization can help children develop their own unique preferences, values, behaviors and motivations within a broader sphere of mutual influence. This expansive understanding helps to free us from equating socialization with a blind acceptance of human cultural social norms and liberates us in body and mind to find a broader sense of our interrelatedness. I have sometimes found it difficult to hear this way of knowing within my own heart over the cacophony of mainstream culture. But if you're reading this, I suspect you are already leaning into an animist approach to socialization, whether intentionally or intuitively.

Ultimately, you know your children best and are best equipped to guide their early socialization in both human and more-than-human spheres. I have found that in my own parenting journey, the early years were marked with a slow, quiet approach to animist socialization. And as my children have aged, the work has become more explicit as well. My children have become increasingly aware that our family approaches certain things in different ways than many of the families around us. It has become increasingly important for my children to have an identity as a Pagan animist family to hold onto. It's an identity that can be a shield against an assault of rationalist materialism or evangelical Christianity. It is unavoidable that they must grapple with the fact that our family lives in a context where we are the minority. Our ways are often strenuously disapproved of by the majority here in the southern US. Either we're evil or we're laughably illogical. It's difficult to navigate the potential for serious discrimination while also cultivating an open and unassuming heart. But even as they age and the problems they face shift, I still believe it is the small, cozy, day-to-day moments that most profoundly shape socialization. Each time they have an opportunity for direct sensory engagement with the more-than-human world or each time they hear us organically expressing empathy for a plant, we are affirming our children's innately animistic approach to socialization.

Children are born knowing that trees, and even chairs can be hurt. To their parents' annoyance a young child may appear to have more empathy and consideration for a puppy than for his sibling. Given the opportunity, they can lose themselves among tree roots, flowing clouds and the scuttling of tiny beasts in fallen leaves. Just as children have an innate drive to relate with fellow humans, they also have a drive to relate with all of their fellow beings on Earth, and the Earth Herself. This makes our role in parenting simple—we have only to encourage, to amplify, to validate. We have only to create the conditions for more-than-human socialization to unfold and to stand tall.

For example, a four-year-old sees a dead bird in the street. She says, "Oh no, the poor bird!" Her face falls. She feels sorrow with the bird, sensing in an immediate child-like way that it was an individual with a selfhood not very distinct from her own. She has a moment of fear before the car's tire, feels the flutter of wings and the grief of the bird's friends and family. The father says quickly, "Oh don't be silly darling, it's just a bird." But what if he paused and engaged with the care that a death calls for? What if the interaction went something like this:

Child: Oh no, the poor bird! (Her face falls.)
Father: Oh no, the poor bird! (With attention and sincerity)
Child: Daddy, will her sister miss her?
Father: Could be. Maybe her mate, her chicks, and the tree where she had her nest, too.
Child: Can we bury her like Feathers? (The family cat)
Father: Yes, baby. (And they give her a tiny, dignified burial and wish her spirit well on its journey.)

There are so many ways that this interaction could unfold. But what a contrast between a distracted dismissal and empathetic engagement.

Neither father here is doing anything other than what he thinks is right. The first is just trying to move his beloved child away from a painful sensation as quickly as possible and get on with the walk. He is implicitly affirming the mainstream belief that humans stand above and apart from other beings. He is loving and well-intentioned toward his daughter. But oh, what the second father has communicated— that the child's empathetic engagement with a non-human being is legitimate and valuable! That they can be present together with those feelings and sensations! That feeling a duty of care and compassion is right. This is just one tiny example of how the seemingly small moments of parenthood can have a big impact on socialization.

By and large these moments just flow organically when we create space in our lives for them, but it can help to consider some of our deeply held values that we as parents want to make available to our children. In my pursuit of creating magic with these small moments of inter-species socialization, there are a few things that I value and want for my kids:

1) More-than-human agency, vitality and personhood: I want them to experience the beings of this world as having agency, vitality and a kind of personhood, whether the beings in question are human or if they are wildly dissimilar from our species.

2) Embodied knowing and sensory engagement: I want them to participate often in the more-than-human world through their senses, their bodies. There is great value in this immediate and embodied knowing that puts human cognition and analysis in the background.

3) Expansive empathy: I want to preserve and uplift their natural empathy and care for all beings, not just humans.

4) Interconnectedness: I want them to appreciate and be curious about the incredible depth of interconnectedness in which we live and breathe and have our being. This tends to encourage a relational sense of selfhood rather than the fortress-of-human-individuality sense of selfhood more widely lauded in Western culture.

5) Reciprocity and mutuality: I want our relationships to be based on togetherness and immersion with the more-than-human world. I want reciprocity and shared power to shape our relationships with others, not the false and isolating assumption of human dominion.

These are some ideas that have been guiding my parenting, even before I had them written down. They've been growing and developing through the years, they will continue to change, and they may not look exactly like what you value. Even if you have never written out a list before, you've still been socializing your children based on your implicit values. We all do! The first father in the example about the bird was socializing his child based on his implicit belief that humans are separate from the rest of nature, and that we have only a minor and subordinate obligation of care beyond our own species. Try writing down your own Earth-based socialization values. Our brains have been so attuned to written language that the process of shaping your general ideas into words can be incredibly clarifying.

Of course, our children will find their own ways as they grow, and make their own sense of their experiences, in their own unique ways. But since parents do have such a tremendous impact on children, and not only during the earliest years, I want to use my influence based on the above values. I want to give them time to have unstructured social experiences, affirm those diverse experiences and share my own experiences in a way that will allow these understandings to shine through. Here are some ways I find myself trying to do that (however imperfectly):

1) I prioritize creating space and time in our lives for unstructured socialization. My role is primarily to create the conditions (including boundaries) for them to interact authentically with a variety of human and non-human beings. It is incredibly easy to find oneself rushing from activity to activity and devoting all of the family's time to structured "productive" schedules. Allowing time to just be. To be bored. To engage in simple tasks slowly. To just be in the presence of others. To be outdoors. This is not idleness or laziness. This is intentional presence and slowness.

2) I strive to notice and affirm my children's sensory engagement in the more-than-human world. Lying in the tickly grass silently is socialization. Drinking in the warmth of sunlight, gazing into a cat's amber-speckled eyes and feeling the ancient roughness of stone are all socialization. If they choose to speak about their sensory experiences, I will affirm them with interest.

3) I cherish their insights. "My friend was very quiet today" or "the bugs are rushing because they know it's going to rain"

4) I uplift and encourage their empathy for all beings, not just for humans.

5) I strive to set the tone by offering bits of my own experiences. My own moments of empathy—losing myself in the excitement of a gathering storm or looking at a cute mushroom and thinking of the way its mycelium is interrelated with soil mycorrhizae which is related with all of the plants that surrounds us—or whatever bit of wonder and enchantment I might experience.

6) I treat my children's experiences of animist socialization with a generous seriousness and curiosity. I try not to allow the tone of an

indulgent parent chuckling down at a child to enter my voice. Children notice what we treat with seriousness and interest. It is not long before they catch on to the way we "politely" dismiss things we consider childish. It is still surprisingly hard for me not to slip into mainstream ways relating that diminish children's innate tendency toward holistic, animist socialization.

7)   I engage—by myself and with the children—in gestures of gratitude and offering with the more-than-human world.

In a way it is strange to share such a simple list but I believe this is the truth of the core of how I "socialize" my children. Sometimes I have done this consciously and sometimes unconsciously. I hope that by sharing how small and simple these moments are I can also uplift the ways that we are all currently doing a fantastic job of approaching Earth-based socialization. Writing this out has been an exercise in treating my own parenting as if it has some meaning and importance to it and I hope you can feel the deep import of your own work. Sometimes that's hard to feel that but we are truly all making the biggest difference even in the smallest ways.

Each time we slow down and allow unscheduled time; each time we put our senses first and analysis second; each time we take seriously the innate animism of children we are committing a countercultural act. Allowing our understanding of socialization to flow from animism is cozy and domestic, wild and revolutionary. Through the small moments of parenting we help weave the big magic of a cultural shift toward a generous togetherness with the more-than-human world.

References:

1. Abram David. *The Spell of the Sensuous: Perception and Language in a More-Than-Human World.* First Vintage books ed. 1997.

2. Harvey Graham. *Animism: Respecting the Living World.* New York: Columbia University Press. 2006.

Art by Pratima Sarkar, for Song of Gaea *(2021)*

16. Signs Your Child Might Be a Witch

- Your child asks to use the broom to cleanse, I mean clean, their room.
- All your candle holders are missing.
- There is always a steak knife missing.
- Your smallest pan keeps disappearing and reappearing, and always smells like ashes and potpourri.
- Your child now enjoys going to the fabric store with you and they want thread, ribbon and cloth of every color of the rainbow.
- Your child's Christmas and birthday wish lists consist of: a white or black full length bathrobe, blank journal books, window box herb gardens and a box of candles in assorted colors.
- Your child's pillows are now filled with all your potpourri.
- Every full or new moon your child asks to have three friends spend the night; and strangely they are very quiet all night.
- Your child now says "Merry meet again" every morning to you and whenever they leave they say "Merry part".
- Your recipe cards are disappearing and when you do find them you can't make sense of the recipes since they don't require any actual cooking.
- Your child has a new ID bracelet that reads something like "StarWolf" "RavenMoon" or "SunDragon"
- Your child asks you one day for a compass, four pails of paint; blue, green, red, and yellow, so that they can paint their room correctly.
- You ask your child to rake up the autumn leaves in the yard, and they come back with a small stick and a large stick; which you later find to have shiny objects on them and unidentifiable etchings.
- Once a jar gets emptied in your house it ends up in your child's room filled with various objects like pins, nails, hair, honey, broken mirror shards, paper, and soil.
- Your child insists that their first car be the color brown and have a license plate that says BROOM.

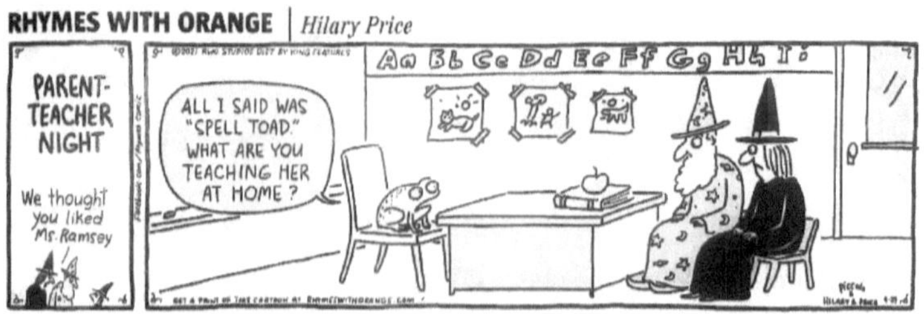

RHYMES WITH ORANGE | *Hilary Price*

17. Superpowers[39]

By Oberon Zell

 WAS NOT BORN INTO A MAGICKAL FAMILY, BUT I was a natural "mageborn," and I was always seeking my magickal heritage. As a young "Wiz-kid," I became quite obsessed with the whole idea of magickal talents and psychic abilities. I read a lot of mythology, fairy tales, science fiction and fantasy, and in those stories, characters often had, like Superman, "powers and abilities far beyond those of mortal men." Long before I found others like myself, or the magickal community, I began studying everything I could find about psychic phenomena. And as I learned about each of those talents that had been catalogued, I began to practice trying to develop them in myself. Since I had no teacher in those days to instruct and train me in the Magickal Arts, I had to make up my own exercises and training programs, and I was much more successful with some than with others. Work with your kids from early on.

A Catalog of Psychic Talents

There are many varieties of psychic talents and phenomena. Almost everyone experiences some of these occasionally in their lives. The more gifted or trained one is, the stronger these abilities may manifest. In many cases, such talents come into effect around the time of puberty, when they may become quite strong. This is the best time to begin an Apprenticeship in Magick, and among Magickal folk, this may be a time for a Rite of Passage.

The scientific method requires systematic observation, study, theories and experiments that can be tested and reproduced. This presents a problem when examining the psi-sciences, as it is difficult to "make" telepathy occur on demand, under controlled circumstances. Psi-abilities are very real but usually manifest best when manifesting organically.

Here is a list of some of the most important Psychic Gifts and Talents. While I've never heard of *anyone* being able to do *all* of them, many people can do one or more—and with your encouragement, your child can learn to do a number of these. I'll offer some exercises that I used to do, and if you practice these with your child, I think you'll be amazed at what you'll be able to do together.

---

[39] Zell, Oberon, *Grimoire for the Apprentice Wizard.* New Page Books, 2004. Pp. 31-32.

- **Empathy**— "Feeling" someone else's emotions, or another's physical pain and/or symptoms. *Empaths* come in two flavors: *receiving* and *projecting*. Receiving empaths "pick up" what others are feeling. When others around you are happy or sad, so are you. Projecting empaths "infect" others with their own emotions. If you're a projecting empath, when you're happy or sad, so is everyone else around you. While essential for compassion and healing, Empathy is important to learn to control, as it is easy for an empath to lose their sense of boundaries— not knowing where you leave off and others begin.

- **Telepathy**— This word means literally "remote feeling," which would seem to make it the same as empathy. But *telepathy* is the word used for direct mind-to-mind communication of thoughts and images, rather than just feelings. Telepathy involves "hearing" the thoughts of others ("mind reading") or being able to project your thoughts to others.

- **Psychokinesis** (SY-ko-kin-EE-sis)— "Mind moving." Moving or influencing objects without touching them physically. This is the most difficult and one of the rarest psi-talents. When it occurs over some distance, it may be called *telekinesis* ("remote motion"). This sometimes spontaneously appears in cases of troubled teens during puberty, in homes with much dissonance or abuse (see *Poltergeist*).

- **Pyrokinesis** (PY-ro-kin-EE-sis)— "Fire moving." Starting or controlling fires by force of mind alone. People who can do this are known as *Firestarters*.

- **Poltergeist** (POL-ter-gyst)— This word means "noisy ghost." It refers to spontaneous *psychokinesis* and mysterious noises that often seem like hauntings. These phenomena are commonly (though not always) associated with adolescents going through major and traumatic psychological changes—especially around sexuality—when psychic powers may rage completely out of control.

- **Healing**— The ability to reduce pain and inflammation, facilitate tissue regeneration and other healing. Usually accomplished by a "laying on of hands."

- **Clairsentience** (klair-SEN-tee-ence)— "Clear awareness." The ability to sense or be aware of things beyond the "normal" range of perception. Each type of "clear sensing" has a name:

- **Clairvoyance**— "Clear vision." The ability to "see" things that are not in sight or cannot be seen. Sometimes this word is used for particularly keen insight.

- **Clairaudience**— "Clear hearing." The ability to "hear" things that are not within hearing range or cannot normally be heard. Also the sensitivity to pick up inner voices or subtle audio input.

- **Clairkinesthesia** (klair-kin-es-THEE-zha)— "Clear touching." The ability to "feel" a sense of physical touch and pressure from nothing present.

- **Clairolfaction**— "Clear smelling." The ability to smell, or be aware of, scents and perfumes that are not physically present, or from other dimensions.

- **Clairgustance**— "Clear tasting." The ability to taste, or be aware of, flavors that are not physically present, or from other dimensions.

- **Psychometry** (sy-KOM-e-tree)— The ability to know the history of a personal object by vibrations and touch. Psychics who work with the police are often *psychometrists* who can "see" a crime or identify a criminal from touching a murder weapon or other associated object. Psychometry is also used by some advanced psychics and healers who have the ability to read disease or physical symptoms in a person's body, even in persons they have never met, by touching an object that has been handled or worn by the person. When reading objects in this way, the psychic often "feels" the symptoms in their own body.

- **Precognition** (pree-kog-NI-shun)— "Fore-knowledge." Knowing or sensing that something is going to happen before it actually comes to pass. This may occur in "True Dreams" or waking Visions. Often the precognitive messages are jumbled, and there is not real clarity of the experience that is to come, just of its "flavor."

- **Déjà vu** (DAY-zha-VOO)— "Already seen." The eerie feeling of having "been here before." A sudden uncanny sense of recognition of a place or events that you have no conscious knowledge of ever having visited or experienced previously. Some instances of *déjà vu* might be the result of "remembering" precognitive dreams. And sometimes people will jokingly say *"Vujà dé!"* to mean "I have never been anywhere even remotely like this before!"

- **Astral Projection**— Traveling "out of the body." This is also called *Transvection.* This may be as in a dream, where one travels to some distant place or dimension. Or it may be an experience of rising out of your body and looking down on it, as often happens in near-death experiences.

- **Dreamwalking**— Entering someone else's dream as a conscious visitor. The dreamer may or may not see and remember the dreamwalker.

- **Teleportation**— "Remote transportation." Disappearing from one place and instantly reappearing somewhere else. The transportation of matter through space by converting it into energy and then re-converting it back into matter at the terminal point, like the transporters in *Star Trek*. This can also manifest as the person's astral body appearing elsewhere.

- **Levitation**— Literally, the opposite of *gravitation,* as in anti-gravity. Lifting yourself or other objects off the ground unsupported by physical means. Levitation is a popular Illusion for performance magicians.

- **Possession**— Entering into someone else's mind, whereby you see and hear through their senses. A possessing entity (whether human or otherwise) may or may not "take over" and control the body of the one possessed—with or without their knowledge. When this is done with animals, it is called "Borrowing."

- **Time Travel**— Projecting your consciousness into the past or future—generally by entering into the mind of someone in that time. You might travel through time with a familiar or totem, or as yourself.

- **Channeling**— Deliberately pulling your own consciousness out of "the driver's seat," and allowing another consciousness to possess and speak through you while you have no awareness. People who do this regularly are called *Mediums* or *Channels.* Some work primarily with spirits of the dead, and some with non-human entities, such as animal spirits or space aliens.

- **Invisibility**— The ability to not be noticed or seen by others. Many call it "cloaking," as in *Star Trek*—or Obi- Wan Kenobi's "These aren't the droids you're looking for!" in *Star Wars.* Another way of becoming invisible is by "sidestepping" in space.

- **Shape Shifting**— Temporarily "becoming" some other person or creature by mimicking their physical appearance, movements, behavior, speech and vocalizations—even to the extent that others may even perceive you as that being. This might include dressing up in an animal costume and walking on all fours, or sitting on your haunches and howling at the moon. Sometimes shape-shifting may be accomplished through possession ("borrowing"), telepathy or empathy—actually "entering into" the subject. *"Were-"* creatures, such as werewolves, are shapeshifters who may or may not be conscious of their alter-form. Those who become animals deliberately may be called *Animorphs* or *Animages.*

- **"The Voice"**— A powerful "tone of command" which elicits instant unthinking compliance from others. The "Bene Gesserit" of *Dune* are an excellent example. This is also called "the Mom Voice." Military officers and police are particularly trained in the use of The Voice.

18. Introductory Psychic Training

by Archonstone[40]

 NID HOFFMAN'S BOOK, *DEVELOP YOUR PSYCHIC Skills,*[41] has many types of games in it. Guessing cards, rocks, pictures, empathy and telepathy of people all are useful.

Mindful meditation.

At this age the quieting of the mind may be easier than adults. Space and time available that is undisturbed is helpful. Otherwise like most adult mindful meditation, where a four square potbelly breath needs to be cultivated. Starting with at least a count of 4 for in breath, hold, out breath, hold and repeat. Judge every thought and emotion. Is it yours, yes or no? If yes, organize it into useful categories. If the boxes are trauma memories they will have to deal with it. Do not let them get buried in neurosis, or disassociate with it. Make sure they get therapy about them. Tarot or kabbalah is a good framework for organizing thoughts. Create their own organizations. What is not your own thoughts and emotions, let them go. If you can answer where they came from acknowledge, so they can gatekeep what they experience. Let the thoughts and emotions go. Use good physical grounding mechanism. Five-point breath, with feet and shoulders width apart, feet pointed slightly inward. Stretch up, bring arms up, palms up, hold onto yourself. Descend down slightly, feel the stretch of the legs rotating outward creating a conduit to release astral junk, palms extending toward the floor on an outbreath.

Bubble breath

When they find a bit of nature that is compatible and uplifting, have them learn to take a full breath in and expand their senses into the environment. Remember it, commune with it. They can invoke in the future to draw from. Breath out and contract, bringing that energy into the body. Take the hands and close them, palm up, bring them close to the body upper abdomen. Let that energy soak into their skin and bones. This is *Wu chi,* shaman or protective chi. Or, bring it, concentrated and circulate it

---

[40] Hegeman, William, *Magic, Mind, Emotion and Body, the Praxis: Magic No Woo, the How and Why Book.* People Embracing Change Tribe, 2021.

[41] Hoffman, Enid, *Develop Your Psychic Skills.* Redfeather, 1997.

in their abdomen between 2nd and 3rd chakra. Visualize and physically circulate and compress it. This is consistent with Tantric Kriya and Taoist Chi Gong practices.

Remote retrospection exercises

Use the imagination, projecting a body of light, and have one view the world around them from different perspectives. Fly, walk, alter ones shape. It is more fun and dynamic that tattwa concentration exercises. Observe from these retrospections and go out into the world and verify the visionary information matches what was observed. Letters in mailbox. Keys on the bureau. Number of Fruit on the bowl. Nests in trees. Cars parked on the road etc. When the data is different, have them take notice of patterns that are different. Are they on other planes, what shows up at what time of day, season, or weather. This is useful for lucid dreaming, astral projection and plane walking.

Intuition, allow your subconscious to give you answers. Follow them up and verify your guesses, with all things, people and places. Guess what people are going to say next.

The biggest thing is:

The Eternal Question: Questions that you feed your subconscious to answer everything anything as they happen. How do you get your internal dialogue to be copartner in the cocreation of relationship to the world. Thoughts and emotions are they yours, can you turn all these questions with a 4 square breath. Can you turn them one with one small hold on your breath. Ideally, stop your breath for a second all these questions and psychic disciplines should light up like hopping on a bicycle. Make all of this second nature, like not thinking about how to drive a bike, but to enjoy the ride.

Remember you are the sole programmer of spirit and your soul.

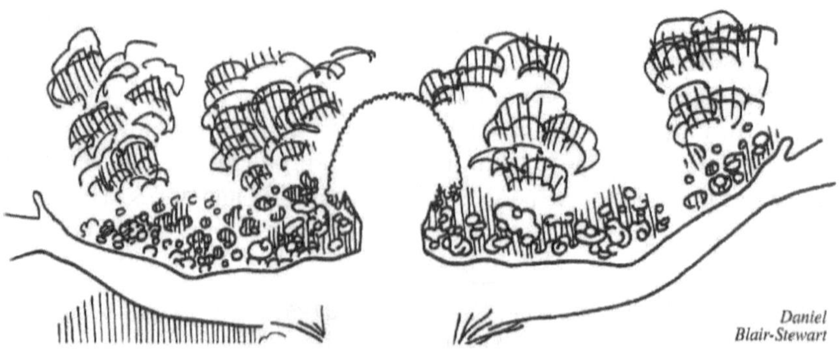

Daniel
Blair-Stewart

19. Psychic Training in the Family

Cat Gina Cole

author of *Psychic Skills for Magic and Witchcraft*

 WAS VERY FORTUNATE TO GROW UP WITH TWO magical adults in my life, my grandma and my mom. In my natal chart I have Aries in my first three houses. To say I was a precocious child is an understatement, but I was a psychic child from early on. I remember talking to fairies when I was four, and projecting myself out of body when I was six, not to mention the wild dreams I had. The greatest gift my mother ever gave me was to tell me I could control my dreams when I was six. And because mom said I could do so I believed her and just did it. It is for this reason I encourage parents to ask their kids about their dreams on a regular basis.

There are many reasons for this. Psychologically it can tell you more about your kids than you will discover any other way. Their dreams can tell you about their fears, their thoughts, their hopes, their hidden talents and so much more. I have found the best way to talk to kids about their dreams is while drawing and coloring with them. This allows them to not feel so on the spot and uncomfortable and you get a peek into what their drawings reveal about them too. Coloring, drawing and talking is one of the best ways to get kids to express things they otherwise do not know how to. This also builds trust and a safe space for them.

Another way my mom used was to run away together. Being the youngest I was home with mom more often while the other kids were in school. When I got bored, I became a pain in the butt, and on occasion one of us would say, I am going to run away! Mom would pack a snack and we would take a walk to a place where it was just the two of us. This was usually the lake behind our home that was close by. We would talk and walk. We would talk while having our snack once we got there and, on the way, home. I was allowed to talk about anything I wanted. She would encourage my imagination by asking what shapes I saw in the clouds or what did I imagined the cats did with their day and other like things.

By doing this by the time I was ten, mom knew my mind and interests pretty well. That is when she began to give me books that aligned with my interests and psychic abilities. Books like *Marco Polo, Kubla Khan, Laub Sang Rampa's, Cave of the Ancients,* Sci fi books, from Issac Asimov, A book on dreams by Edgar Cayce and so on. She would also send me to my grandma's now and then to have a break, I am sure, but I learned much while there.

My time with grandma was always chore oriented, but also psychic and Witchcraft oriented. They had figured out keeping me busy while they talked to me was the best way to reach me. Nowadays most know the best way to teach an ADHD child is to have them do two things at once. But ADHD was not a thing back then, they were just perceptive and attentive.

While in the garden helping grandma or doing housework together, grandma would tell me about the soul and spirit of each thing, the life of it beyond what our eyes could see. This too was a great gift. It gave me the idea there was an unseen world and the idea there was life beyond myself, and others to be considered. The work and chores gave me not just a work ethic, but the idea of service to others.

Another tool my mom or grandma used to help build my psychic talents was to bring out a large tray of small items and say we are going to play a game. They would instruct me to look at each item carefully, and to touch them and take my time to feel them. Then one of them would place those items around the house or have them on her. Throughout the day I would be asked to find an item and instructed to close my eyes and think about the item, see it clearly and let it lead me to it.

Not only did this build my intuition, clairvoyance, and psychometry, but it improved my ability to focus, remember, and concentrate. It also gave me something to keep me busy when I was bored and taught me ways to deal with my restless energy. Once I found the object I would be asked "What is it saying to you, is it telling you a story?" Sometimes the story I would relate back was the made-up ramblings of a kid, which promotes creative thinking. Sometimes I would tell them who it belonged to, or how the energy of it felt. Either way the creative energy and activity was always encouraged.

The method by which mom and grandma encouraged and helped build the skill of telepathy was to tell me that when I "felt or thought" they were thinking of me to believe they were and to check in with them to confirm. I am sure this was a safety thing as we lived in the country, and I would wander far and wide as a kid. But it built a pathway in my system to pay attention when you "feel" or notice someone thinking of you. Later when I was a bit older, they asked me to listen, to see what they were saying and to send a message back to them. Sometimes that message was a visual of where I was and more often than not, that neighbor would get a call, "Is she there? Would you send her home?

Another trick of my mom's was to send the dog for me. She would let my dog out and tell her to go find me. Sure, enough the dog would show up and of course I had to take the dog home where she belonged. Later as my own son became an adult who liked to wander, I would send the crows to find him. Every time he would see a murder of crows fly in and crowing like crazy, he knew it was me and he would either come home or call me.

There are many ways to use psychic and or magical skills with kids that will also build other needed skills. For example, Oberon Zell wrote this amazing book by the name of *Grimoire for the Apprentice Wizard* whose Forword is written by Raymond Buckland himself! This book is like a magical manual for any youth. The table of contents is extensive, allowing a parent to choose the things their child might be interested in or have a natural talent with. There are deeper explanations a parent can use to guide them in the many projects for kids to make. And no this is not a book review. I am describing to you one of the best tools for raising magical kids available to us in our modern time. This book really is a tool filled with skills for parents and kids.

On page 15 of the *Grimoire,* in "Lesson 2: Seeing and Thinking," the reader is encouraged to "close one eye and hold your head still and look at a scene like a room full of people or trees in the woods." This lesson reminds me of one my mom gave me. The idea is to "see without seeing" which is something I write about in my own book *Psychic Skills for Magic and Witchcraft.* My mom would have me look out the sliding glass door and cover my left eye and ask me what I could see, and to take my time. After telling her what I saw, she would have me do the same with my right eye. When done with this (this is where moms "game" differs from Oberon's book) she would have me close my eyes and ask again what I saw. This kind of "game" was actually exercising both sides of the brain, encouraged visual sight strength and perception but went further when asked to close the eyes. The closing of the eyes accessed the conceptual vision of the brain rather than just the visual sight. Having this skill strengthened when I was a kid allowed me to apply critical thinking to many levels of sight. Conceptual thinking skills are just as important to us as linear thinking. Having both allows for the individual to have a larger view of a whole, rather than just one part of it as linear thinking by itself provides.

Another "game" mom and grandma would play with me as a kid was when we were outside. Sometimes she would ask me to close my eyes and ask me if I could feel the Nature around me. "Can you feel the trees, or the air? Are they talking to you?" Other times she would ask me what I could hear, increasing my sense of awareness of things around me sure but also teaching me to be attentive in my conceptual and psychic hearing. It was in these ways I was taught that all skills I had in everyday life, I could also use in the dream world and beyond.

Other simpler things that can be "games" for magical and psychic skills are tear up several colors of construction paper, have the kids help that is the fun part. Then scramble them up and put them in a bag or basket then have the child choose one with their eyes closed. Then ask them to spend time "feeling" the paper with their fingertips. While their eyes are still closed ask them if they can guess what color it is. Wait for a reply encourage them to be open to anything that comes to them, there are no wrong answers.

While out on a walk ask if they saw something you just passed by, ask them the details of it or better yet ask what it felt like to them. My son loved observation games, and he was great at coming up with stories to tell about each thing.

These kinds of games not only build the conceptual part of the brain and valued observation in daily life, but also build visualization and awareness skills needed for psychic skills and magic children may use later in life. Note, these games are of great value in daily life for critical and creative skills for employment and other things. And they are also likely to make your kid a challenge to any teacher or school. Which in turn will create a challenge for the parents.

How to somewhat mitigate these types of challenges also teach your children there are two worlds they walk in. In one world these are the rules and in the other, there are fewer rules and that both are necessary to make a whole. That the two can live easily side by side because there is duality in all things that live in balance with each other. The phrase "As above so below" comes in handy here.

To learn this, some of the things I was shown were to look at a leaf and see that there is both light and shadow on the leaf, the two living in harmony for the benefit of the leaf. After the rain, I might be shown a plant in the garden, one side wet the other dry. This allows the plant to take in the water it needs without getting too much. These kinds of observations usually began with a question from my mom or grandma. Do you know why the leaf is dry on one side, is one example of such a question.

Other creative ways mom and grandma would teach me is through tv movies on any kind of mythology biblical or otherwise. I was encouraged to watch as many of those, and pirate movies as possible. Sometimes we would talk about the movie after but not always. On occasion though I might get asked if I remember the story, for some example they were making or other lesson they wanted me to know. This worked better than trying to get me to sit still long enough to read the book. Their reading me mythology stories at bedtime was another way I learned the stories of the Gods and many other characters.

If you do not know where to start Oberon's book *Grimoire for the Apprentice Wizard* is a great place to start. The adult can read it to a child and make it a bedtime story or a fun project to do for the day. Another good source for bedtime stories is *The Mists of Avalon* by Marion Zimmer Bradley and even her *Darkover* novels. Truth be told most any magical book can be used in this way for children by parents. It is just one of many ways to be creative in raising a magical child and teaching them to think for themselves.

If you are the parent and you have doubts about "teaching" your children about magic, the gods, spiritual or psychic things, remember there are many parents who guide their children's talents and interests in things like music or sports and so on. This is no different if you know this is part of your child and of their interest.

You are just helping them to further develop the skills and understand what they are experiencing. It was of great help to me as a child to have an adult in my life tell me what I was experiencing and that it was real and could be developed as a skill. Having that made me feel ok in the world. I knew it was not just my imagination or something that made me feel odd or like a freak because I was different. It showed me I was like others who did have such skills but also that not everyone does. Once again showing the duality of life.

I get excited when I think of the many ways adults can teach kids and make it fun and nonrestrictive all while building a relationship between them and the natural and etheric worlds. It is my hope that the games and skills shown here reveal how such interaction with kids can teach them very useful skills for daily life while learning skills for a magical life. I encourage all parents to be creative, play games with their kids, ask questions during activities and be open and ready for most anything.

On page 349 of Oberon's *Grimoire,* he states a lesson my family also taught me, *"Bravely explore anything and everything that increases the depth of sensation and the totality of spirit, leading you through empathy into true connection and power. You are a part of the seamless universe as much as your hand is a part of your arm. All of creation is sacred, and thus so are you."*

I think this is a powerful gift to give a child, especially in the world we live in. I know it went a long way in arming me for what was to come in my life with confidence and autonomy. And yes, it is also what made me precocious and difficult for others and even myself at times, and why I say with great love and a smile, that all that I am, is my mother's fault.

20. A Musical Childhood

By Rev. Judith M. Barnett

OR MY ENTIRE LIFE, MUSIC HAS BEEN THE heart-beat of my home. From morning until night, glorious melodies and rhythms have surrounded me like a warm embrace. To me, music isn't just something I hear—it's something I feel, breathe, and experience with every fiber of my being.

Growing up in a home filled with music was a blessing like no other, especially when your father was a talented fiddle player who frequently jammed with his band right in the living room or kitchen. The sounds of laughter, and the lovely melodies of the fiddle, guitar, and piano would fill the air, creating an atmosphere of joy, camaraderie, and a deep appreciation for the power of music.

As a child, I would often sit on the floor, or in my Grandmama's rocking chair, watching in awe as my father and his band mates effortlessly played their instruments, their fingers flying across the strings, and their feet tapping in perfect rhythm. The energy in the room was electric, and I couldn't help but feel a sense of pride knowing that my father was at the center of it all. It was always magical the way music brought people together in our home. Friends, family, and neighbors would gather around, some with their own instruments in hand, eager to join in on the impromptu jam sessions. The living room would transform into a stage, with the furniture pushed aside to make room for the musicians and the makeshift dance floor.

The music they played was a mix of bluegrass, country, traditional folk, and jazz. Daddy had mastered all the genres, even some classical. The fiddle, with its high-pitched, soulful sound, always seemed to take the lead, while the guitar and piano provided the perfect accompaniment. The voices joined in harmonies they created were instruments themselves, and I found myself getting lost in the music, my young mind transported to a world of endless possibilities. I began to understand the stories behind the songs, the emotions they conveyed, and the history they carried. My father would often sit me down and share the tales behind each tune, his eyes sparkling as he recounted the legends of the musicians who came before him, and the life stories of those who sat at his feet, eager to learn. Some of those he taught went on to become famous, but Daddy never dropped names, so I wouldn't either. (Catch me in private someday and I'll fill you in.)

Inspired by my Daddy's talent, I decided to become a musician myself. I was singing on stage with Daddy by age three and started piano lessons when I was six. As I grew older, my appreciation for music only deepened, and I added other instruments to my repertoire. The music we made together became the soundtrack of my childhood, each song a chapter in the story of our lives. The upbeat tunes that filled the air during celebrations, the soft ballads that soothed me to sleep on restless nights, and the lively tunes that had everyone on their feet, dancing until the wee hours of the night. It was during these moments that I truly began to understand that music wasn't just a hobby or a pastime; it was a way of life, a language that connected us all, and a legacy that had been passed down through generations.

But it wasn't just the music itself that made my childhood so special; it was the sense of community and belonging that came with it. Our home became a gathering place for musicians and music lovers alike, a safe haven where creativity and self-expression were not only encouraged but celebrated. I witnessed firsthand the power of music to break down barriers and bring people from all walks of life together. The jam sessions in our living room were a melting pot of cultures, ages, and backgrounds, with each person bringing their own unique style and perspective to the music. It was a beautiful reminder that, despite our differences, we could all find common ground through the universal language of music.

A childhood filled with music was more than fiddle tunes and late-night jam sessions; it was a testament to the enduring power of music to bring people together, to heal, and to inspire. A gift and a legacy that I will cherish forever. Experiencing music as I did shaped me in countless ways, and as I entered adulthood and started a family of my own, I knew that I wanted to pass on that same love and appreciation for music to my children so that they too may experience the magic and joy of growing up in a home where music is not just a part of life, but a way of life.

From the moment they were born, music became an integral part of their lives, just as it had been for me. I would sing to them as I rocked them to sleep, the songs soft and soothing, filled with the same love and tenderness that I had felt from my own father's music. As they grew older, I would play my instruments for them, teaching them the same songs that I had learned as a child, watching with pride as their tiny hands tried to mimic my movements.

We would dance together in the living room, our laughter mixing with the music, creating a symphony of joy that filled our home. I watched as their eyes lit up with each new melody, their young minds absorbing the rhythm and the lyrics, just as I had done so many years ago.

As my children grew older, I encouraged them to explore their own musical interests, to find the instruments and genres that spoke to their hearts. My oldest fell in love with the piano, fingers gliding across the keys with a grace and beauty that took my breath away. My youngest loves music in all its forms. Through music I was able to share with my children the stories of my own childhood, the memories of the jam sessions in my parents' living room, and the lessons I had learned from watching my family and friend. I told them about the sense of community and belonging that music had brought into my life, and how it had the power to break down barriers and bring people together.

As I watched my children grow and develop their own relationships with music, I was filled with a sense of pride and gratitude. Pride in the fact that I had been able to pass on my love of music to them, and gratitude for the fact that music had been such an important part of my own life, shaping me into the person I am today. Now, I watch my very talented grandchild, nieces, and nephews discover that same power for themselves, I am reminded once again of the incredible impact that growing up in a musical household can have on a person's life. I see the same spark in their eyes that I had as a child, the same love and appreciation for the power of music to transform and inspire. I am filled with a sense of peace and contentment, knowing that the legacy of music that began with my father's fiddle so many years ago will continue to live on through the generations, a testament to the enduring power of music to bring joy, love, and connection into our lives. I am filled with a sense of hope and optimism for the future. Because I know that as long as there is music in the world, there will always be a way to connect with one another, to find joy and meaning in even the darkest of times, and to create a legacy of love and appreciation that will endure for generations to come.

The memories of those days are forever etched in my mind, a reminder of a time when life was simpler, and the world seemed a little brighter, all thanks to the power of music. The sound of my father's fiddle, the laughter of the band mates, and the warmth of the community that gathered in our home will always hold a special place in my heart, a testament to the incredible impact that music can have on a young life. I sit here decades later and find myself drawn back to those memories, the melodies of my childhood echoing in my mind. I pick up my old guitar, my fingers finding the familiar chords, and I begin to play, the music transporting me back to those magical nights in our living room. I lose myself in the music, and I am reminded once again of the true joy of being immersed in music—melody and harmonies—and I am filled with a joy that will stay with me forever, a gift that I will always cherish, and a legacy that I will strive to keep alive for future generations.

I look back on those years, I am filled with a deep sense of gratitude for the musical upbringing I was blessed with. The lessons I learned from watching my father and his band—the importance of collaboration, the value of hard work and dedication, and the joy that comes from sharing your passion with others—have stayed with me throughout my life, shaping me into the person I am today.

In the end, living in a home full of music was more than just a childhood filled with lively tunes and late-night jam sessions; it was a foundation upon which I built my entire life. The lessons I learned, the memories I made, and the love of music that I developed have stayed with me throughout the years, guiding me through the ups and downs of life and reminding me of the incredible power of music to heal, inspire, and bring people together.

So fill your home with the uplifting power of music. Expose your children to diverse genres and cultures. Encourage them to explore instruments that ignite their passion. For within those musical notes lies a world of creativity, discipline, and sheer delight that will enrich their lives immeasurably.

For in a musical household, every day is an adventure, every moment is a song waiting to be sung, and every child is free to dance to the rhythm of their own heartbeat. And in a world that can often feel cold and indifferent, there is nothing more beautiful than the warmth of a home filled with love, laughter, and the sweet sound of music.

21. Arts & Crafts

By Oberon Zell

HROUGHOUT MY LIFE, THERE HAS BEEN ONE constant theme—my natural talents and affinities for Arts & Crafts. From the first day I could hold a crayon, I have always had the ability to transfer onto paper anything I could see, dream, remember or imagine. My mother kept a scrapbook of my early art that I still have. I always say that the secret of being an artist is that you start with a blank sheet of paper, and then you put anything you want on it! The same applies, of course, to a block of wood or a lump of clay. It's all yours to shape as you will.

While for my own enjoyment I mostly drew dinosaurs and space-ships, I also did portraits of anyone who asked, and I even drew paint-by-number pictures of horses for the girls in my classes, and cartoons for the school paper. I created the winning design for a big Halloween window painting contest that was featured in the local paper. In college, I learned about oil paints and acrylics, and created a number of paintings in my dorm room—mostly with apocalyptic themes of a nuclear holocaust—a great concern at that time! I gave away or sold all of them, and I have no copies.

I illustrated school programs, posters and publications, and eventually did illustrations for science-fiction fanzines, which were my first professional commissions. And now I illustrate my own books.

I also really got into model-making. First balsa-and-paper airplanes with rubber band motors; then later plastic model kits—which I still enjoy. I particularly focused on spaceships and other science-fiction models, but I also built a lot of planes, anatomy models, and even "Famous Monsters of Filmland." I entered some of these in model contests, and won several trophies. (I still love to build models, and you can read a little more about this in Chapter 26: "Gadgets, Gizmos & Models.")

One year I covered an entire desktop with a model "City of Tomorrow" I built out of shirt cardboard, with futuristic buildings, elevated roads, and even tiny cars and aircraft—all completely my own designs. To enter it into a contest (where it won first prize), my dad had to load the whole desk into a truck!

I eventually turned my hand to woodcarving and clay sculpture, which expanded my art into the 3rd dimension. A major breakthrough came in the mid-'70s, when an artist friend turned me onto Sculpey™, a kind of plastic clay that could be molded, carved, and hardened in a kitchen oven. So I decided to begin my sculpture art at the beginning—with museum replicas of Paleolithic goddess figurines.

When the California Academy of Sciences in San Francisco opened an exhibit of "Ice Age Art," I went down to The City and spent two days sitting on a little folding camp stool in front of the case of ancient goddess figures. I had my box of Sculpey and my clay modeling tools, and I shaped precise replicas, by hand and by eye, of each of the little *matrikas* on display. I managed to buffalo the guards who tried to throw me out ("No photos allowed" says nothing about sculpture...), and I enjoyed the reactions of the people coming to view the exhibit. Many stopped to ask me what I was doing, and I got to speak to them of the Goddess and my devotion to Her service.

From the mid-'80s 'til 2005, I sculpted dozens of altar figurines, wall plaques and jewelry of gods and goddesses, culminating in 1998 with my masterpiece, "The Millennial Gaia." I joined a ceramics club at the local community college, and learned how to make silicon molds to reproduce my little statues in quantity—which we did in our kitchen for years until we got big enough to have production done in factories in Taiwan, China and Thailand. We incorporated a family, business—TheaGenesis LLC—featuring "The Mythic Images Collection," which remains one of my primary financial supports to this very day.

So this long roundabout tale is by way of encouraging you to support and abet your Magickal Child in Arts & Crafts! From their earliest days, keep them well-supplied with pencils, pens, crayons, watercolors, tempera paints—and pads of art paper. Give them Sculpey and Femo, and sculpting tools. If you have room, set aside a special "studio" area with a desk and containers for art supplies. Patronize Arts & Crafts stores, which will often have special classes. Enroll your kids in art classes in school—including painting, ceramics and wood-and-metal shop.

Don't omit soft arts—made from flexible materials like leather, cloth, rubber, or latex. These include sewing (I am a good seamster, and have made many costumes and ritual regalia), fabric art, macrame, tapestry, dying, batik, knitting, embroidery, doll-making, mask-making...

What else? Woodcarving, certainly. Also leatherwork, cabinetry, glass-blowing, metalwork, stained-glass, stonecarving, model-making, laserwork, 3D printing, light sculpture...and new forms of art that have yet to be invented! And culinary arts as well—teach your kids to cook!

Teach your Magickal Children art appreciation. Buy them art books, and take them to art museums and exhibits for inspiration. Explore the amazing crafts at Renaissance Faires and art shows.

And this could be not just another chapter, but an entire library: teach them to appreciate and become adept at cooking as an art form! And if you have enough room in your backyard for a garden, that too would be an excellent artform to pursue with your Magickal Child...

22. All the World's a Stage[42]

By Oberon Zell

 WAS VERY INVOLVED IN THEATRE THROUGHOUT high school and college. As a member of the school's Thesbian Society, I immersed myself in everything from set design, props, costuming, and makeup, to on-stage acting. I regularly got leading roles in school plays, and I remember them each fondly these many years later. I consider my theatrical experience to be one of my most important trainings for my later vocation as a Pagan Priest—especially for large public rituals. And I highly recommend this training to anyone wanting to create and perform rituals and ceremonies.

Due to various serious childhood ailments (in those pre-vaccine days of the 1940s), I acquired a severe speech impediment as a child, and I felt I sounded like an idiot when I tried to speak; this stuttering made me very insecure, shy and withdrawn. A wise school counselor recommended I enroll in speech class, for which I am forever grateful. This got me into debate, public speaking, and eventually theatre—where I found my own social circle of fellow "Beatnik" Thesbians.

Encourage your Magickal Child to get involved in school theatre. They might start out even in kindergarten with little performances with the other children, such as seasonal pageants and sing-alongs. But for older grades there will probably be a drama club—which Magikids will certainly find a very compatible social set, as all the smartest and coolest kids will be there—and many of them will be Pagan!

There is so much more to theatre than the acting. Sure, that's what the audience sees onstage, and the actors do get all the attention and glory. But if you note the credits at the end of every movie, the cast of actors goes by pretty quickly, while the list of backstage support crew that never appear on-screen goes on forever! There is costume and set design and creation, staging, makeup, props, script-writing, casting, choreography (dance and fighting), directing—and for film, there is also camera work, sound, music, film editing, and many, many other jobs. All of these teach valuable skills.

Nearly every community has a local community theatre where plays are performed several times a year. In some places there are summer

---

[42] Zell, Oberon & Morning Glory, *Creating Circles & Ceremonies.* New Page, 2006.

drama camps for kids. Look them up, and take your kids to try out for parts. Some plays (*Treasure Island, Peter Pan, Willy Wonka, Midsummer Night's Dream, James & the Giant Peach, Mary Poppins,* etc.) will have choice roles for kids. And think of all the movies featuring child actors! Even a walk-on or extra role will teach valuable lessons to lend depth and authenticity to eventual adult performances and staging of ceremonies—especially in how to project your voice and energy, and to never turn your back to the audience!

Encourage your children to get together with other neighborhood kids and put on little backyard shows. Help them set up a stage with curtains, and chairs for the parental audience. Help them make costumes and props. There are a number of books available with short scripts for kid plays.[43] Buy them stage magic books and tricks.

Ritual and theatre were originally one. They began around the campfires of our most ancient ancestors, from the time we first learned mastery of this most magickal Element. For our very humanity began with the taming of Fire. All our magick—and all our culture—came first from the Fire. Gathered around our blazing hearths, we sang our first songs, made our first music, danced our first dances, told our first stories, and performed our first plays. These performances recounted the experiences of our lives and adventures for the rest of the clan, enacting, in time, the tales of our ancestors, the mighty deeds of our legendary heroes, the myths of our gods, and the Mysteries of Life, Death, and Rebirth. For hundreds of thousands of years we did this, and only in the past 2,500 years did "theatre" begin to be distinguished from "ritual."

> *If theatre is to be defined as involving the art of acting a part on stage, that is the dramatic impersonation of another character than yourself, we begin with Thespis. A figure of whom we know very little, he won the play competition in honor of the Greek god Dionysus, in 534 BCE. While it is uncertain whether Thespis was a playwright, an actor or a priest, it is his name with which the dramatic arts are associated in our word "Thespian."[44]*

---

[43] https://www.dramanotebook.com/plays-for-kids/; http://www.playscriptsforkids.net/browse-play-scripts-for-kids/free-scripts/

[44] "History of Theatre" http://www.tctwebstage.com/ancient.htm

All Greek drama was dedicated to Dionysos, and performed in the context of sacred rituals in his honor. And for the next 2,000 years after Thespis, the vast majority of Thespian performances continued to enact religious rituals, pageants, and "Mystery Plays." So there is a rich historical lineage and tradition of dramatic ritual, and ritual drama. Good ritual is good theatre. And the motto of both is: *"The Show Must Go On!"*

Read play scripts to learn how to stage and script your rituals dramatically—and how to write them up so they can be easily understood by the performers. Learn how to designate characters, costumes, sets, props, and stage directions. Learn to make ritual implements ("props"): magickal tools, staves, scepters, streamers, etc. Learn to design and create appropriate costumes, such as simple robes and colored tabards for the four directions; as well as masks, wings, tiaras, helms, and headdresses for different spirits and deities, etc. Learn to create dramatic sets, with altars, gateways, henges, ritual fires, tiki torches, banners, etc. Learn special effects to add a flair of drama—such as powders to make the fire flare up in different colors. And develop a good stage voice to reach to the outermost fringes of the largest Circle.

And most important, learn how to *memorize your lines!* Nothing detracts worse from the effect of a ritual than to have the performers carrying around paper scripts, and reading aloud from them! However, for certain formal rituals (such as Handfastings, Initiations, Dedications, Rites of Passage, etc.), it is not untoward to have your script bound into an impressive-looking binder as a *Grimoire* or "Book of Shadows" which will sit open on the Altar as a prop—perhaps even on a stand. An image of a Pentagram or Magick Circle Mandala on the cover will give it a real mystical aura of credibility. After all, magickal rites are often referred to as "Bell, Book, and Candle."

There are many ways that people can be categorized into two groups. One I find relevant is the Performers and the Audience. Most people go through life just being in the Audience—watching the world go by with little or no active involvement or participation. And thus they have little or no effect on what happens. But magickal people get actively involved in working to change the world in positive ways. We're the Performers! And in Life, as in the Theatre, the magick password to get into the show is: *"I'm with the Band!"*

23. Pets and Familiars[45]

By Oberon Zell

FAMILIAR IS AN INDIVIDUAL LIVING ANIMAL WITH whom you are deeply connected and psychically bonded. Your Familiar should be attached to you specifically, and not just a family pet. Usually quiet animals are the best, as these tend to be most receptive to your thoughts. When choosing an animal for a Familiar, keep in mind that you may perform meditations, healings, and magickal rituals that last for some time, so a familiar who will remain still for that time is ideal.

To create a Familiar bond, you should be the primary human being with which your Familiar has close contact. Ideally, you should raise them from infancy, and become their *surrogate* (substitute) mommy—even if you are a boy! You should do all their feeding, cleaning, bathing, medicating, changing their litter box, etc. Perhaps you can even sleep together. More than a pet, or even a companion, your Familiar is your best friend— and you are theirs. When your Familiar dies, it may come to you in your dreams and become a Spirit Familiar to guide and protect you.

The most important clue to sentience in any animal is whether they look you right in the eyes when communicating. Several times a day, you should hold your familiar and gaze deeply into their eyes, building a deep *rapport* (harmony) of love and trust between you. Meditate together, and visualize what you want to say as pictures rather than words. Soon you will begin to communicate by sensing each other's thoughts.

Cats & Dogs

The most popular Familiars, of course, are cats and dogs. There are now 60 million dogs living in American homes, and 70 million cats. Dogs were the very first animals to be domesticated, over 30,000 years ago, and cats were the last, about 4,000 years ago (in Egypt, where they were worshipped). They have been living with people so long that they have become completely

integrated into our human lives. They can be incredibly intelligent, sensitive and psychic, and can bond as deeply as you are willing to go with them. Clearly, these are very special furry people. One of the most satisfying ways to get a Familiar is to go to an animal shelter and rescue a kitten or puppy and give it a home. You will be its hero for life!

---

[45] Zell, Oberon, *Grimoire for the Apprentice Wizard.* New Page Books, 2004. 253-257.

If you get a dog or cat, the most important thing is to have it spayed or neutered, and vaccinated! There are around 40-50 *million* homeless cats roaming the US, and probably half as many dogs. Animal shelters kill over 15 million unwanted dogs and cats *every year.* Only 30% of impounded pets are reclaimed, adopted or rescued. The remaining 70% are destroyed. Many more die from disease, starvation, wild animal attacks and cars. Not neutering a dog or cat is just plain irresponsible.

Rats

Rats make excellent "starting" Familiars for kids, as they are smart, clever, curious and sociable. They also have their own language in their complex colonies, so they are naturally receptive to human communication. And they now come in assorted colors and markings. However, they have a very short lifespan (3-4 years). The best food for rats is Purina® Rat Chow or dry dog chow, but they are omnivorous, and enjoy many other treats—especially right off your plate!

Ferrets

A 2001 census of US pet ownership listed one million ferrets in American homes. These "wascally weasels" are so adorable, curious and fun-loving that most owners have two or more. "Wuzzies" can be litter-box trained, but not as reliably as cats, and they eat cat food. Ferrets have been domesticated for 5,000 years or so, originally for hunting rabbits. In recent years they have become enormously popular in the US. However, as Familiars, ferrets are awfully scatter-brained, excitable and hyperactive—and they have short lifespans.

Bunnies

Bunnies make excellent Familiars for girls in particular, as they are sacred to the Moon-Goddess. Bunnies are quite smart for prey animals, and are social enough to get along well in a household, even with other animals. But unless you are breeding them, you should only have one! It can be kept either in an outside cage, or hutch, or live indoors like a cat or ferret. Your bunny can learn to use a litter-box, but it will chew the bindings off books on low shelves.

They eat mostly alfalfa pellets, but they also enjoy treats and table scraps of garden veggies like carrots and broccoli. Your bunny should not be turned loose in your yard unless it is completely enclosed with a fence that is buried at least a foot into the ground, because bunnies are great tunnelers. If you have a bunny Familiar, you might keep it in your room at night and dream together at the full Moon.

Reptiles

My lifelong fascination with dinosaurs turned my attention towards reptiles at an early age, and I have kept quite a few of them (though we now know dinos were actually related to birds, not lizards). A wide assortment of reptiles can be purchased at any pet store. A 2001 pet census listed *three million* snakes, turtles, and lizards in American homes!

Box turtles are excellent house and yard pets, and no trouble whatsoever. They can live well over 100 years, and they eat most anything, from veggies to bugs (they *love* earthworms!). However, turtles are not particularly bright or sensitive, and I wouldn't recommend them as Familiars.

Bearded Dragons (*pogona*) from Australia make *great* pets and fabulous Familiars! As social lizards, they are intelligent, interactive and cuddly. They will happily ride around on your shoulder all day. They live 10-12 years and some species can grow up to two feet long. If you get a male and female, they will breed in captivity (they lay eggs, but incubation is tricky…). They are omnivorous, and eat veggies, eggs, fruit, grapes, worms, pinkies (baby mice and rats) and bugs (feeder crickets and roaches can be bought at a pet store); get a book on their care, and check out videos.

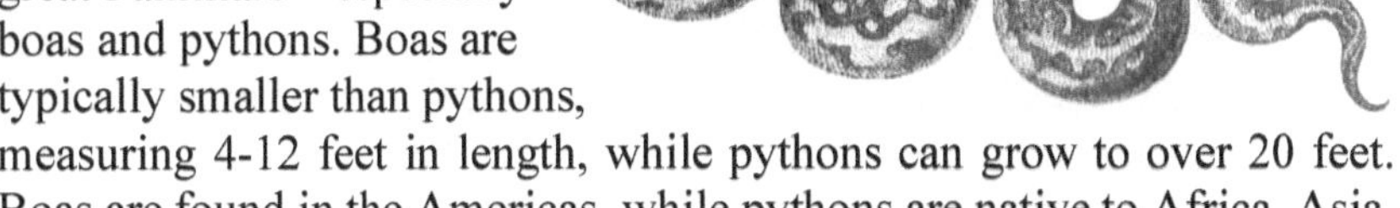

Snakes can make great Familiars—especially boas and pythons. Boas are typically smaller than pythons, measuring 4-12 feet in length, while pythons can grow to over 20 feet. Boas are found in the Americas, while pythons are native to Africa, Asia, and Australia. The green anaconda of South America can grow to 33 feet and weigh 880 pounds! But the biggest ever was *Vasuki Indicus*—a monstrous 50-foot-long snake from India, 47 million years ago!

These giant serpents are the most primitive of snakes, with little spurs on the males where they once had hind legs. Pythons lay eggs, which they incubate, but boas give birth to litters of live babies. Captive boas can live for 20-40 years. Pythons can live even longer, with the record held by a little ball python, at 47½ years!

The roughly 4,000 known snake species vary from venomous sea snakes, giant constrictors and hooded cobras to tiny threadsnakes that burrow to feed on ants and termites. All snakes evolved from a kind of eyeless, earless, legless, worm-like burrowing lizard. They had to reinvent eyes entirely (without lids), as well as other senses unique to them, such as infrared heat receptors and Jacobson's organs for smelling. But they never re-evolved ears, and they have no sense of hearing whatsoever for airborne soundwaves—although they do pick up physical vibrations though their lower jaws. Instead they have acute psychic sensitivity. And a serpent Familiar will happily hang out for hours wrapped around your shoulders.

All snakes are predators (though a few eat eggs…), and they must have whole animals to eat (preferably live). Start with mice, and graduate to rats. (It's best to raise your own.) When they're small, feeding once a week is enough, and once a month when they get big.

If you feel drawn to have a serpent Familiar, I recommend a boa constrictor, as Burmese pythons, while quite sociable, making excellent Familiars, eventually get too big to carry around—up to 16-18 feet!—and require ever-larger prey to eat. Rainbow boas and ball pythons don't get too big—although they do tend to be shy and not very sociable.

Boas and pythons have been captive-bred for many generations, so the best thing to do is find a pet shop that has some babies. Put your hand down into the tank, think loving thoughts, and wait to see if one of the little guys will come to you and crawl up your arm. If one does and then looks you right in the eyes, you've got yourself a Familiar!

But keeping a tropical snake is a really big commitment, and you need to have the right setup to keep them safe and warm (90°F). If they escape from their well-heated *serpentarium* into the outdoors, they can die of exposure. Or, in a tropical state like Florida, thrive to become a menace to local wildlife. Instead, you might want to start with a colorful little corn snake that you can buy from a pet store. Or a harmless garter snake, black snake, or bull snake you may find in your backyard. But these are not very bright or friendly, and so not too good as Familiars.

Birds

Birds will bond very closely with a person—especially if you "imprint" them as hatchlings—and many make excellent Familiars. While most pets and Familiars regard their human as a "mommy," birds will treat their human as a mate. They can be very possessive and jealous of your other friends.

Cockatiels and lorikeets are really smart, and can learn to speak human words. And they can live a *very* long time! I do not recommend, however, getting a parrot, cockatoo or macaw, smart as they are, as these are intensely social birds, and they require constant physical interaction and verbal stimulation to maintain their often-marginal sanity.

Art by Craig R. Miller

Crows, jackdaws and ravens can also be taught to speak a few words, and ravens are now believed to be as smart as dogs. I have never had a crow or raven myself, but I've met some that other magickal people have, and they clearly have a deep bond and Familiar connection with their person. Some states, however, now have laws against keeping any kind of wild bird. Wildlife Rescue can be a wonderful resource.

If you live in the country, some barnyard fowl can make excellent Familiars. When I was young, I had a goose named Gus, whom I raised from a hatchling. Geese are very smart, and can live up to 50 years. But they are *always* an outdoor animal, because they poop constantly all over the place! Gus was utterly devoted to me, and followed me everywhere. Sadly, he froze to death one bitterly cold Winter night, because he wouldn't go into the goose house with the other geese, and insisted on staying outside by the back door.

Owls have long been associated with wisdom and Wizards. Athena, Greek goddess of wisdom, has an owl named Bubo. Harry Potter, of course, has his beautiful snowy owl, Hedwig. Owls are also my very favorite birds. We had a charming great horned owl with a broken wing who lived with us when we worked with Critter Care. I named him Archimedes, after Merlin's owl in *The Sword in the Stone*. Archimedes was a polite, sensible, dignified bird with a keen sense of humor. He was an excellent Familiar for me, but keeping him also entailed having to raise rats to feed him one every night. I do not recommend this to you!

In the US (unlike England), owls are now protected birds, and you can't keep them as pets. However, if you volunteer with a local Wildlife Rescue center, you might get to help heal an injured owl and have the thrill of setting it free back into the wild. Maybe it will fly back into your dreams.

Possums

I think possums make the best pets of all wild animals. Only one kind lives in North America—the original model that has remained unchanged since the days of the dinosaurs. However, many other kinds of possums live in South America, Australia and New Zealand. These are nowhere an endangered species, so if you should come across a baby possum, you  might want to give it a good home. Since the mother carries her babies around in her pouch, and later on her back, by the time you find one apart from its mama, usually in April or May, it's old enough to be on its own. Baby possums are adorable little grey fuzzballs with beady black eyes, whiffly pink noses and ears like black-and-white flower petals.

Get a little pouch to hang around your neck, or carry the baby possum around in your pocket. Possums don't eat very much, and they sleep most of the time. They eat almost anything, but each one has its favorites. They are easily litter-box trained, and very little trouble. A possum is sort of like a retarded cat—not too bright, but very sweet. Having a possum is one step above having a stuffed animal! But sadly, they have too short a lifespan (2-3 years) to be a good long-term Familiar.

Tarantulas

These large, furry and often colorful spiders were among the very first creatures to live on dry land, over 300 million years ago. Back in those days, they were the size of English bulldogs! The females, which are bigger and fatter than the males,  can live up to 25 years. Spiders don't even have a head, much less a brain, and yet they act with an uncanny and deliberate intelligence. To feed, they impale their hollow hypodermic fangs into the body of their prey and inject stomach acids. Then, when the prey's insides are all digested, the spider sucks out the juices through its own straws. Pet tarantulas are usually fed crickets, grubs and pinkie mice.

I have had several tarantulas; my favorite was a Mexican Red-Legged (shown) I named *Kallisti* ("the prettiest"). She learned to recognize me, and would crawl onto my hand when I put it into her terrarium. She would climb up and sit on my shoulder, tucked under my hair, and watch everything with intense interest, holding her front legs up to listen (spiders have their ears—tympanic membranes—in their armpits).

Terrariums and Aquariums

If you have room in your home, you might wish to create a little magickal menagerie of fascinating creatures in glass tanks. The most important thing about keeping any animals, of course, is knowing how to take proper care of them so they will thrive in your hands. Your local pet store will have a whole rack of little booklets on the care and keeping of various types of critters, and you should pick up copies of these for any animals you choose to keep.

Terraria—These are the easiest "starter kits" for small critters. All you need is a large aquarium with a secure screen lid. Measure the dimensions of the bottom, and then go out and cut a piece of natural sod to fit. Cut the sod about 3" thick, and leave room at one end for a 3" deep water pan, at least 6" wide. A square glass baking pan is ideal. Insert a stick and put it against the front of the aquarium so you can see underwater.

In such a terrarium you can keep frogs, toads, newts, turtles, lizards, small snakes and large bugs—all of which you can (and should) find in the wild. Of course, you should be aware that frogs, toads and turtles eat bugs and worms. So if you are particularly fond of any critters, don't put them in the same terrarium with their natural predators!

I recommend having a separate terrarium altogether for interesting bugs. There you can keep beetles, crickets, grasshoppers, spiders, centipedes, millipedes, grubs, worms and caterpiggles. Spiders eat smaller bugs, so you should gather some little insects just for spider food.

When I set up my first terrariums as a boy, I enjoyed going out into the fields and fens searching for little critters to take home and keep. In my insect terrarium, I collected caterpiggles and cocoons, and loved watching the new flutterbys and moths break out and unfold their wings before I released them.

One time I got a praying mantis egg case (which can be ordered through garden stores). Each egg case hatches out about 100 tiny mantids, and I had fun raising these up, feeding them first on fruit flies (easy to do; just leave an overripe banana in your terrarium with a small opening, and soon you'll have plenty!), and later on, crickets. Mantids are cannibalistic, so long before they were grown there were only a few left.

Aquaria—Of course, you can always go the fancy route, with store-bought tropical fish and cute little plastic castles, divers and sunken ships. But my favorite aquariums were ones in which I planted natural water plants and filled with local pond life. I would go down to the marsh with a net and bucket, and catch crayfish, minnows, baby turtles, tadpoles, newts, snails and water bugs. I'd watch tadpoles turn into frogs.

24. Library for the Magikid

By Oberon Zell

HE WORD *LIBRARY* COMES FROM THE LATIN *liber,* meaning "book." If there is one thing that Wizards are famed for, it is our love of knowledge. Hence every Wizard is at heart a librarian and a museum curator—and every Wizard's library is unique. As your children acquire their own books, you should begin thinking of categories for them, and put them on different shelves, or separate them with other objects. My library began as a child when my parents acquired for me the *World Book Encyclopedia* and *Child Craft Library* (1945 edition). Since then, my collection has grown to many thousands of books. Here are some of the main categories in my Library:

1. **Magick**—lore and practice, different traditions, systems of divination, Grimoires, books of shadows, astrology, Tarot, spells, etc.
2. **Science & Nature**—all the sciences, including astronomy, geology, biology, ecology, chemistry, etc. One whole shelf is on Dinosaurs!
3. **Weird Science**—UFOs, unexplained phenomena, mysteries, anomalies, ghosts, cryptozoology, Bigfoot, Loch Ness Monster, etc.
4. **History**—archaeology, timelines, histories of every culture and civilization from the dawn of humanity. Also books on various religions.
5. **Myths & Legends**—stories from every culture and people; gods & goddesses, heroes, epic adventures, creation myths, scriptures, etc.
6. **Fiction**—in my library, this is mostly science fiction and fantasy!
7. **Art books**—all my favorite artists, plus books of photos, cartoons, graphic novels, comics, etc. These are large books, for a large shelf.
8. **References**—various sets of encyclopedias, dictionaries, almanacs, etc., both general and specific. A favorite set is *Man, Myth & Magic.*
9. **DVDs & CD's**—all my favorite movies and music, recordings of TV shows and specials, etc.

At the back of this book, I'll list a few books to get your kids started on their own magickal library. Of course, these are books that are available at the time I'm writing. I'm sure many more will be published by the time you read this! Always check the used book sections of bookstores, junk shops, flea markets, etc. Other good sources for free books are public libraries, which periodically clear old books from their shelves to make way for new ones. Sometimes they'll put out a bin which people can go through and help themselves. You should get your child a library card in any case, and ask your librarian when they're doing their next giveaway.

25. Cabinet of Curiosities: Your Magickal Museum[46]

By Oberon Zell

IZARDS OF OLD WERE FAMED FOR THEIR "CABInets of curiosities." Such collections became the foundations of the world's great Natural History museums, which I love to visit. Take your child to as many as you can!

There are many natural (and unnatural) objects kids can collect. Make a special place for the magical treasures they discover.

For serious collecting, your kids will want to organize and display their collection. Small objects no bigger than chicken eggs can be organized in egg cartons. These work well for collections of rocks, fossils, minerals and crystals. For larger items, they will want glass display cases.

Whatever they are collecting, they should make a nice little identification card for each item. You can buy them little books, such as the *Golden Nature Guides* (my personal favorites) at any bookstore. Then their life becomes one great scavenger hunt, as they search for items for their collection everywhere they go!

Here are a few examples:

Curiosities—really unusual "one of a kind" things are called "Curiosities." In this category, I have things like a meteoric *tectite* from the impact that killed the dinosaurs; a sperm whale tooth; a very realistic shrunken head made of goatskin; cast replicas of a saber-tooth cat and Deinonychus skull; and various little souvenirs and items of local handicraft I've picked up on my travels around the world.

Seashells—these were one of the first things I collected as a boy, the first time I got to go to the seashore. I ended up displaying them on a large Masonite wallboard, running wires through the holes in the board to hold the shells in place.

Flutterbys (Butterflies) & other Insects—when I was a boy at Summer Camp, my mentor, Capt. Bennings, showed me how to make a net and collecting jar for flutterbys, moths and other interesting insects. I made display cases of shallow boxes with glass panes, and developed quite a collection. The "holy grail" of flutterby collectors, however,

---

[46] Zell, Oberon, *Grimoire for the Apprentice Wizard.* New Page Books, 2004. 120-121.

is the elusive and ethereal Luna Moth, which is an unearthly pale green color like the *luciferin* in lightsticks. Finally, after many years of searching, I caught one. I killed it in the cyanide jar, and proudly mounted it in my display case. And so I was absolutely devastated when its luminescent hue soon faded to a sickly straw-color. The Luna Moth, I learned, was a creature of Faery, not meant to be killed and put on display for mortal eyes. And after that I never collected another flutterby.

Rocks & Crystals—in collecting rocks, minerals and gems, you might keep in mind their magickal associations as well as their mineral qualities, and note these on the identifying cards. With nearly 2,000 different minerals on Earth, your kids can keep busy collecting samples for a long time! On the other hand, they might want to specialize, and just collect different kinds of crystals.

Fossils—fossils are a fun thing to collect, especially if you happen to live in some area where there are a lot of them. When I lived in the Midwest, I could often find fossils of *trilobites* and *brachiopods* along riverbanks. Egg cartons were perfect ways to display these. The *Golden Nature Guide to Fossils* is very helpful, with many specimens illustrated.

Skulls—My favorite personal collection consists of dozens of different kinds of skulls of animals and birds that I have cleaned and prepared from road-kills since I was a boy. I find animal skulls to be absolutely fascinating, each with their unique architecture, dentition, and arrangements for the sense organs. When I find a fresh unsquashed road-kill, I carefully cut off the head; then I take it home and plop it into a pot of boiling water. I keep refilling the water, and after a few hours, the flesh and skin falls away from the bones, and I can carefully separate it out after a few rinses in a bowl of clear water.

Soak the skull for a day in hydrogen peroxide, then rinse and clean it. Be especially careful of the front teeth, as these will easily fall out once the flesh of the gums is gone. Glue them in with Krazy glue. Good tools for cleaning skulls are dentist's probes (ask your dentist for used ones he would otherwise throw away) and an old toothbrush. Go over the teeth and skull joints carefully with white glue (wiping it down with a damp sponge), and then glue the two halves of the jaws together (holding them with rubber bands). The final cleaned skull is a very beautiful thing. Collect the whole set!

26. Dragons & Dinosaurs!

By Oberon Zell

ONE OF THE MOST SIGNIFICANT REVELATIONS OF my youth occurred in elementary school when, in the process of reading the *World Book Encyclopedia* volume-by-volume, I turned to the entry on "Dinosaurs," with its two-page spread of Charles's Knight's iconic painting of a Triceratops facing off against a T-rex (Fig. 1). With a thrill that still sends shivers down my spine to recollect, I suddenly realized *Dragons were real!* Just as the stories said, once upon a time, the world really was ruled by huge and mighty reptiles. They lumbered over the land, they churned the seas, and with wings as wide as those of an airplane, they commandeered the air. They were even more immense and diverse than the most imaginative tales had portrayed them…*and they really existed!*

Fig. 1. Triceratops vs Tyrannosaurus-rex by Charles Knight, 1929.
Field Museum of Natural History, Chicago.

From that point on, I became absolutely obsessed with dinosaurs. I learned everything I could about those amazing creatures. I memorized every dino name I could find, and all their statistics: what their Greek names meant, when and where they lived, what they ate, how big they were—like a sports fanatic memorizing statistics of all the players. My parents thought this was all rather amazing, as they couldn't even pronounce most of these names, and they'd ask me to come out at their parties and rattle off dino stats for their guests.

This passion excited by dinosaurs naturally came to extend to other fantastic creatures of long ago, including those of myth and legend. I began hunting for fossils, visiting natural history museums, and collecting dino models when they started being made, which I would carefully paint in realistic colors and install in dioramas (Fig 2).

My library on these subjects grew, as did my collection of models, fossils, animal skulls, artwork, movies, and other memorabilia of the prehistoric and mythical menageries. Today I have perhaps one of the most extensive private collections of miniature dinosaur replicas in existence, going back nearly 70 years. For a few years (2015-2017) I even opened a museum, The Academy of Arcana, in Santa Cruz, CA.

Fig. 2. Dinosaur diorama by OZ.

For 175 million years, dinosaurs ruled the Earth. Mammals had appeared at the same time, in the middle of the Triassic Period, 240 million years ago. Both were warm-blooded. The mammals grew fur for insulation, and the dinos grew feathers. But the little quadrupedal mammals were soon completely outclassed by the dinos, which ran on their hind legs and grew to immense sizes. During all those long aeons, while dinosaurs grew to as much as 100 feet long, weighing up to 100 tons, the biggest mammals were no larger than a house cat. If we think the reassembled fossil skeletons of those prehistoric monsters seem huge to us now, imagine how much more gigantic they would have seemed to our tiny ancestors, who were smaller than a Dragon's little toe!

Dragons completely dominated the lands, the seas, and the air. Sea Dragons grew to the size of modern whales, and flying Dragons were as big as small airplanes. They occupied every environmental niche—except three. No dinosaurs burrowed into the earth; no dinosaurs climbed trees; and very, very few dinosaurs hunted at night.

For the Dragons were not great, sluggish, stupid cold-blooded lizards, as people have assumed for so long. They were active, warm-blooded (and often feathered) members of a Class all their own—*Archosauria*—of which birds are the only surviving members. And as with modern birds, Dragon eyes were mostly designed for day vision, with full-color receptors (called *cones*). Only towards the end of their reign, with the rise of the Raptors, did some of them develop the huge eyes full of ultra-sensitive black-and-white receptors called *rods*, such as we find today in owls and nighthawks. Raptors—by far the most intelligent of all Dragons—were the only ones to be able to hunt at night, like cats and owls do today. What did they hunt? Like owls, they hunted nocturnal mammals. Our ancestors.

The only way mammals managed to survive at all during those 175 million years of Dragon dominion was by occupying those three tiny niches. Some burrowed in the ground, and others came to live in trees. The little rat-like burrowers came out only at night, when the Dragons slept (as all birds except owls and nighthawks still do). In order to be able to see in the dark, they gave up the cones in their eyes almost entirely, and filled their retinas mostly with rods. This is why most modern mammals still don't see in full color—even after the dinosaurs were exterminated by a huge asteroid impact—because almost all later mammals descended from those nocturnal burrowers.

But two kinds of mammals moved into the trees, where the predatory Dragons couldn't reach them. The first of these were the *marsupial* ("pouched") possums—one of the earliest mammalian designs, and still with us virtually unchanged over the past 70 million years. The second were the ancestral *primates* (with opposable thumbs): tree shrews, which later evolved into lemurs, monkeys, apes—and us. Because we lived in trees, neither possums nor primates had to give up color vision for night vision, and we kept both cones *and* rods. Marsupials and primates remain the only mammals today that can see in full-color; and both of us can still see better at night than nearly all birds.

The "raptors" of the *Jurassic Park* movies were actually *Deinonychus*—"terrible claw." As shown in the films, they were human-sized intelligent pack-hunters. And like other pack-hunting predators (dolphins, orcas, wolves, humans…) they would have had language to communicate and coordinate the hunting party. Like humans, they were bipedal, freeing their hands for manipulation, carrying things, and perhaps even wielding tools… And they were feathered. Among paleontologists, I am credited with creating the first model of a feathered dinosaur—a Deinonychus (Fig. 3). Now, 40 years later, I realize I should have put short wing-feathers on the forearms…

*Fig. 3. Feathered Deinonychus model
by Oberon Zell, ©1984.*

To visualize and appreciate how long Dragons ruled the Earth, here's a neat way to demonstrate the time scale with two piles of beans. Take a single bean and place it on a table. This bean will represent a quarter of a million (250 thousand) years, which is how long humans like us *(homo sapiens)* have been on Earth. Then start laying out more beans in another pile, one at a time. It will take 700 of them to represent the 175 *million* years that the world was ruled by Dragons!

At the time of their extermination, the *Deinonychids* were as evolutionarily advanced as humans were perhaps a million years ago. If a giant rock—7½ miles in diameter—hadn't fallen out of the sky 66 million years ago and ended the reign of the Dragons, and they'd had another 66 million years to continue evolving, by this time they would rule the galaxy! Given how far we've come in only one million years, can you imagine where *we'll* be *65 million years* from now? Think about that!

So take every opportunity to visit natural history museums and other museums of all kinds wherever and whenever you get the chance. Even small towns will often have nice museums of local history, and big cities have legendary museums! Turn your children onto dinosaurs, and they as well as you will find enlightenment and inspiration, food for thought and conversation topics for a lifetime!

Fig. 4. "Dino Doomsday" by Oberon Zell & Pratima Sarkar, from Song of Gaea *(2021)*

27. Gizmos, Models & Contraptions

By Oberon Zell

ANY WIZARDS HAVE ALSO BEEN GREAT INVEN-tors, such as Imhotep, Archimedes, Leonardo da Vinci, Ben Franklin and Nicolo Tesla. They also tended to collect interesting and intricate gizmos and artifacts—especially timepieces and instruments for observing and plotting the motions of the heavenly bodies.

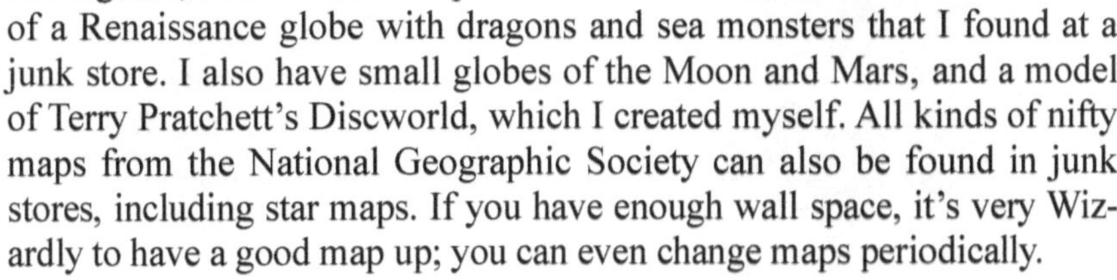

Globes & Maps — Everyone should have at least one globe of the Earth, so you can familiarize yourself with your home planet. In addition to a modern relief globe, I have a small replica of a Renaissance globe with dragons and sea monsters that I found at a junk store. I also have small globes of the Moon and Mars, and a model of Terry Pratchett's Discworld, which I created myself. All kinds of nifty maps from the National Geographic Society can also be found in junk stores, including star maps. If you have enough wall space, it's very Wizardly to have a good map up; you can even change maps periodically.

Sand Timers—Sundials, water clocks, astrolabes, hour candles, and sand timers (often generically called "hourglasses") were all invented ages before mechanical clocks. Of all these, sand timers are still widely available, and remain very useful. I keep several for different lengths of time, and we use them particularly for meetings, giving everyone the same amount of time in which to talk.

Sundials—There are many more possible designs for sundials than the popular garden variety shown here. I have several pocket sundials, and have made larger ones to set up outside. I have a wonderful book full of cutout patterns and designs for many different sundials, including a simple paper Armillary.[47]

---

[47] Adzema, Robert and Jones, Mablen, *The Great Sundial Cutout Book.* Hawthrorne Books, 1978.

Celestial Armillary—This is a clever model of the position of the Earth at various seasons in relation to the constellations of the Zodiac. You see these in many old pictures of Wizards. The Earth is represented as a little ball in the center of a spherical cage with rings representing the equator, tropics of Cancer/Capri-corn, and the Arctic/Antarctic circles. An arrow running through the center points to the North Star. A band marked with the signs of the Zodiac en-circles the cage in the position of the plane of  the ecliptic, and the whole thing can be rotated within a stationary frame marked with the dates of the year. Your kids can make a paper one them-selves from the pattern in *The Great Sundial Cutout Book.*

Orrery—This is a mechanical model of the Solar System, with the Sun in the middle and all the planets (some-times including moons) set up on arms or tracks to move around the Sun in circular orbits. Kids can easily make an Orrery as a mobile, with a gold ball or hanging lightbulb in the middle for the Sun, and painted Styrofoam balls of various sizes rep-resenting the planets hanging by threads from struts of thin bamboo. I made one of these for a science project in school, and it hung from my ceiling for years. The one shown here is a wooden kit from ROKR.[48]

Astrolabe—This is an astronomical instru-ment dating to ancient times. It serves as a star chart and physical model of visible heavenly bodies. In its simplest form it is a metal disc with a pattern of wires, cutouts, and perforations that allows a user to calcu-late astronomical positions precisely. His-torically used by astronomers, it is able to measure the altitude above the horizon of a celestial body, day or night; it can be used to 

---

[48] https://www.robotimeonline.com/collections/rokr

identify stars or planets, to determine local latitude given local time (and vice versa), to survey, or to triangulate. It was used in Classical antiquity, the Islamic Golden Age, the European Middle Ages and the Age of Discovery for all these purposes. This is a great gift for a magikid!

Microscopes, Telescopes, Chemistry Sets, Science Toys, Magic Tricks —These are wonderful things for kids to have, as they encourage explorations of the micro- and macro-universe.

Models—I love to build model kits! I have made countless plastic models over my life—mostly spaceships, but also dinosaurs, armored knights, famous movie monsters, the Time Machine (shown here), Captain Nemo's Nautilus submarine, and transparent anatomy models. Lately I have discovered the wonderful laser-cut mechanical wooden models made by ROKR: clocks, orrerys, music boxes, and other fun kits to punch out and assemble.[49] And there are also little punch-out steel kits made by Metal Earth.[50] And of course, Legos has a wide variety of kits made of interchangeable plastic bricks. I highly recommend visiting your local model shop and picking up whatever strikes your fancy! Another excellent source for sci-fi and fantasy models is Monsters in Motion.[51] In the back of my book, *Companion for the Apprentice Wizard,*[52] I have a number of cut-out paper models you can make, including Leonardo da Vinci's famous ornithopter (shown here all assembled from book).

---

[49] https://www.robotimeonline.com/collections/rokr

[50] www.metalearth.com

[51] www.monstersinmotion.com.

[52] Zell, Oberon, & Faculty of the Grey School of Wizardry, *Companion for the Apprentice Wizard.* New Page, 2006.

Part IV:
Growing Up Magickal
(Adolescence: age 11-18)

Then the child moved ten times round the seasons
Skated over ten clear frozen streams
Words like, "When you're older" must appease him
And promises of someday make his dreams.

…

Sixteen springs and sixteen summers gone now
Cartwheels turn to car wheels through the town
And they tell him, "Take your time, it won't be long now
'Til you drag your feet to slow the circles down."

("The Circle Game" by Joni Mitchell)

Art by Craig R. Miller, from the Wheel of the Year Songbook, *by Gwydion Pendderwen.*

28. Rites of Passage[53]

By Oberon Zell

ITUALS OF TRANSITION AND LIFE CHANGES, called "Rites of Passage," mark significant periods in life, movement between life-stages, and personal transformations. These are rituals of honoring and empowerment. They are a public acknowledgment and recognition of growth. Just as the seasons pass in order, so do the stages of life. The inner and outer worlds mirror each other, so Rites of Passage provide a further link with the Earth and the Cosmos. Rites of Passage include coming of age, marriage or handfasting, handpartings, pregnancy and birth, passage into elderhood, death and rebirth. They can also mark firsts, such as getting your first car, having sex for the first time, casting your first vote, going off to college, renting your first apartment, taking your first trip abroad, getting a new job or a new home…

Birth

When a child is born it is a remarkable event; when a child who is loved by many and nurtured by a whole community is born, it is a miracle. When we gather to name and honor a new baby, we honor life itself. Other terms for this rite are *seining,* or baby blessing. At this time those who will nurture the child are identified: Goddessmothers, Godfathers, parents, siblings and other loved ones who may have a part in the baby's life are recognized before all. We pass the new baby around the Circle, with magickal gifts and blessings for long life, health and happiness: "Live long and prosper…"

Puberty

Centuries ago, the phrase "Coming of Age" meant "of age to marry," but these days we no longer expect people to marry so young. Normally held between the ages of 11-13, modern puberty ceremonies celebrate the onset of adolescence in one's body and mind. From this point begins the exploration of our new and changing bodies. You must learn your own boundaries, likes and dislikes, and about your right to say yes or no when it comes to *your* body. Usually this rite is performed by adult members of the child's own sex, and may involve an initiatory ordeal and the giving of a magickal use-name.

---

[53] Zell, Oberon & Morning Glory, *Creating Circles & Ceremonies: Rituals for All Seasons & Reasons.* New Page, 2006.

Puberty Rites

Rites of Passage for Boys

Traditionally, a boy's Rite of Passage from Childhood into Adolescence occurs at puberty, when he becomes sexually mature. This time, usually around 12-14 years, is marked most visibly by the development of pubic hair, though technically it is said to be indicated by "first seed," or the production of semen.

According to Joseph Campbell, a Boy's Rite of Passage has several phases:

1. Separation from the Mother
2. Isolation and Disorientation
3. Vision Quest
4. The Ordeal
5. Joining the Company of Men
6. The Return

Separation from the Mother

A common way of accomplishing this is by a nighttime "kidnapping," where several men sneak into the boy's bedroom at night, bundle him roughly up in his bedding, being sure to cover his head so he can't see, stuff him into a gunny sack, and carry him off. This should all be conducted in silence on the part of the men, but if the boy cries out, it is appropriate for the mother to come out wailing something like, *"My baby! My baby! Don't take my baby!"*

Isolation and Disorientation

There should follow a period in which the boy is isolated from human contact, while remaining deprived of his normal senses. One way to do this is to stuff him into the (padded) trunk of a car, still in the tied gunny sack, and drive him around for awhile on bumpy, winding country roads. Another way is to place him in a room, blindfolded and tied up, and just leave him there for awhile. Some tribes would place such a boy in a small hole or cave for a period of time, covered over and in total darkness. Some magickal groups use a coffin for this purpose. The idea is to create a sense of both fear and disorientation—and a brush with Death.

Vision Quest

If time and circumstances permit, many tribal societies send a boy out on a Vision Quest or "Walkabout" during this phase. He is taken to some isolated spot, given a few basic tools, such as a knife and fire-making tools, instructed to avoid human contact, and left alone for a period of time which may be as short as a few days or as long as a full lunation. He may be expected to fast entirely, or to eat only what he can find in the wild. His assigned mission on this quest is to make contact with his inner spirit, totems and allies.

The Ordeal

There should be a challenge and a "life-or-death" ordeal of some kind, requiring the candidate to undertake a "leap of faith." It should be something which is really scary to him, but carefully structured by the men to present no real physical danger. For Zack's Rite of Passage, we parked the car near the river after a bumpy ride, took him out of the trunk, stripped and blindfolded him, then walked him down the beach, across the shallows to the other side, then up the far bank to a large rock outcropping with a ledge about 20 feet above the water which was a favorite jumping-off place on our tubing trips. I stayed down below, in the river, which was over ten feet deep at that spot. Still blindfolded, Zack was led to the edge of the rock and told he must jump. He took a long time, standing there, hearing the river flowing far below, but eventually he did jump. As he surfaced, blindfold washed away, I caught him and we all cheered triumphantly, Zack most of all.

Other such "leap of faith" ordeals might even be as extreme as bungee-jumping or parachuting, if they can be done with absolute safety. It could be done off the high dive of a swimming pool. Of course, if a person is blindfolded, he has no way of knowing whether the cliff he is jumping from is 30 feet high or only three feet. A "leap of faith" can be just as effective from a small height as a great one, provided it is done convincingly, involving a long climb upwards and voices coming from far below.

Other types of ordeals may, of course, be equally effective. Emrys had to drum all night, without stopping or losing the beat, for a Walpurgisnacht ritual.

Joining the Company of Men

After successfully passing his Ordeal, the candidate is then welcomed into the men's circle. This might include a sweat lodge ritual or other formal men's ceremony. It might happen as a part of a "Wild Men Weekend," or a FireDance. For Zack, we held a sweat, then brought him into a campfire circle where all the men were masked. We each told stories of how we first became men—our own various "Rites of Passage." For most of us, it was our first sexual experience that was the threshold. This is a time when the young man might be given a new name; a "man name" to replace his "boy name."

The Return

In the morning the young man is returned to his mother. He is proudly introduced to her by his new name, and she is told that *"we took from you a boy, and we return to you a man."*

Rites of First Blood for Girls
by Marylyn Motherbear Scott

Blood rites for girls are bloody hard; *periods* are embarrassing to some girls. In primitive cultures there was a long tradition to the way a first blood was acknowledged and honored, a profound respect for becoming woman and a vessel for bringing in life. It was sacred. A glimpse at this can be seen on the movie video *Where the Spirit Lives*.

Even for the Neo-Pagan community, these rites are new, and it's important that we don't presume what should be done. Out of half a dozen blood rites I attended, I recall only one where the girl seemed to feel relaxed. Every effort should be made to find out what the girl will enjoy and what will make her feel comfortable.

In one ritual of first blood, a lovely circle of females gathered... all ages including some of the girl's peer group. Red, of course, was featured in candles, scarves, and food. As we went around the circle, everyone who cared to share a story, told of their first blood, what happened, how they felt about it, how their mother treated it. Some of these stories were sad, some delightful, some absolutely horrible. Most of them seemed attitudinally antiquated!

The teens and young adults are caught in an intense passage that plays out the struggle of millennia. It's a question of life or death—drug wars, prostitution, aids, pollution, and so on. Teen pregnancy is oddly on the rise, in major denial of what they fear. Are they grabbing at life now because it might be too late, later? Or is it an expression of wanting life now and of hating your own so they make a new body for it?

Rites of Passage are important and will be carried out whether or not the parents and community take a part. Modern rites tend to be created out of the peer group, the "gang," often putting kids at risk. Creating rites consciously, with sensitive intention and honoring our children's steps into the mysteries of living, is a way of telling them they are valued and loved; it helps to create an awareness of who they are for themselves and others so that a positive self-image can emerge.

29. Adventures in Nature[54]

By Oberon Zell

 LOVE TO GO ON ADVENTURES! IN MY 80+ YEARS, I have climbed to the peaks of mountains and dived to the bottom of the sea. I have crawled through narrow passageways of prehistoric painted caves and celebrated total eclipses of the Sun within ancient stone circles. I have hiked through the jungles of Peru, Australia, Guatemala and Costa Rica, wandered amid the giant redwoods of Califia, and swum in clear pools at the base of high mist-shrouded waterfalls in Hawaii. I have walked with Unicorns at Renaissance Faires and swum with Mermaids in a New Guinea lagoon. I have explored ancient ruins of lost civilizations in Europe, the Mediterranean, and the Americas. I have ridden camels and elephants, petted tigers and dolphins, and hung out casually among herds of deer and mobs of kangaroos, scratching them behind their ears.

I have slept out in the high desert and scrambled down into the craters of extinct volcanoes. I have walked the Inca roads, and explored their ancient ruins under the full Moon. I have climbed the Mayan pyramids in Guatemala, and snorkeled through the underground rivers of Xibalba. I have bathed in natural hot springs, and frozen my ass off on an Alaskan glacier. I have combed for shells on beach sands that were black, white and glass. I have kayaked with 10-foot alligators in the Florida Everglades and swum with a 30-foot whale shark in the Coral Sea. And I have trod the paths of the Dead, where bones and skulls were stacked like cordwood by the hundreds of thousands on either side.

All these things and more…I have always regarded Life as a continuing adventure story. And every adventure I have gone on has taught me Lessons.

My most important Teacher has always been Nature Herself. From the time I was a little kid, I have always spent as much time as I could alone out in the woods. I would climb up into trees in the Springtime, and sit so still the birds would get used to me being there, so I could watch them build their nests, lay their eggs, hatch and feed their babies. I would go out into meadows where I saw deer grazing, and sit quietly under a certain tree day after day until they learned to ignore my presence, and would come within a few feet of me. I would climb out of my bedroom

---

[54] Zell, Oberon, & the Grey Council, *Grimoire for the Apprentice Wizard.* New Page, 2004.

window on the nights of the full Moon, and wander among the Children of the Night. And from my mid-30s through early 40s, I lived for eight years in the middle of 5,600 acres of undeveloped land in the Misty Mountains of NorCalifia, with no electricity, radio, TV or telephones, and raised wild animal babies, foraged for wild foods, and experienced the turnings of the seasons from the Earth to the Stars. I consider the foundations of my Wizardry to be rooted in such experiences, and I strongly encourage you and your children to get out into Nature as often as possible. There is only so much you (and they) can learn from books!

Camping

As a boy, I joined the Cub Scouts, and later the Boy Scouts. I also went to Summer Camp for two years. My father was a devoted fisherman, and he loved to take our family on camping trips to remote areas where he could fish undisturbed by tourists or other fishermen. Each of these experiences taught me a great deal about camping out, and I consider these very important lessons, which I would like to encourage you to learn and teach your kids.

If it is possible for you to send your kids to Summer Camp or have them join the Boy Scouts, I urge you to do so. Perhaps you can take family camping trips to National Parks. But staying in a cabin, trailer or RV doesn't count as camping out! If you have any friends who live on a farm, or in the country, see if they would like to hold a campout in their woods. But even if none of these are a possibility for you, maybe you can at least pitch a tent in your backyard this Summer, and let your kids sleep out under the stars.

Water

Some of my best adventures and lessons have been with water, the first Element I really explored, and with which I have had a lifetime love affair. I grew up near a crystal-clear lake, and I rigged up an air pump and hose so I could stay underwater for long periods and watch fish making their little nests in the sandy bottom, and laying their eggs. I have lived my whole life close to water, always having a place nearby where I could swim. To me, swimming seems as easy and as natural as walking.

The River

For eleven years of my life I lived with my family right on the Rushing River (or *Russian River,* as it was called by mundanes…) in NorCalifia. Our backyard was a private beach and swimming hole, with a rope swing dangling from a high tree. Salmon and otters played in the running waters, and friends hung out all the time. At the beginning of each Summer, I would go to a tire store and buy up a bunch of used but airtight big truck inner tubes. On weekends we would gather up a bunch of folks and tubes, take everyone a few miles upstream in trucks, and float down the river back to our place—or sometimes all the way down to Lake Mendocino, where the trucks would be parked to take us home.

Along the way, the experience itself offered so many lessons that I came to think of it as a magickal teaching all its own. There were rapids with white water; deep still pools; giant rocks forming narrow passages; high cliffs to jump from; sandy beaches and gravel bars. Drifting along, arms and legs draped over the sides of the tube, embraced in the arms of the River Nymphs and watching the world go by, has been the most perfect place I have ever known for meditation and reflection. The more times we rode down that river (and, of course, I went far more often than anyone else), the better we would get at navigating it. By coming to know The River, I now *know* rivers, and I can tube, raft, canoe or kayak along them with perfect ease. I have even done serious white-water rafting down world-class rivers in Costa Rica!

Here are some of the best lessons I've learned from the River:

1. The stream of consciousness flows like a river.

Spirit moves like water. It's always seeking to return to The Source, and it always finds its own level. Like water, Spirit can be bottled up, diverted or dammed for a time. But eventually the container will break and water/spirit will flow free and move to continue its passage downstream. Water/spirit diverted will find a way around, and cut new channels to rejoin its course. Dams will one day overflow and be swept away, and the flow will continue. Always towards the Ocean, from whence it came. As water flows ever downwards to merge with the vast Ocean below, Spirit flows ever upwards to merge with the eternal cosmic Ocean above.

2. Go with the flow.

Any time you come to a fork in the river, a big rock in the way, a log jam, an island, or rapids ahead—and you can't see ahead to know which passage to take, the trick is to look at the current. Wherever the current is strongest, there will be a "V" in the water. And all you have to do was steer your tube down the center of the "V." Trusting to the flow, rather than fighting it, you become one with the current, which will carry you around and over all obstacles. But often newbies would try and paddle desperately to avoid the fast water, and they would find themselves getting swept into rocks, logs, and embankments—or just going round and round in a little side eddy and left behind by the rest of us. Just so in life;

the trick is to learn to see the flow of the current, and then steer your course right into the middle of it. The heart of the flow may seem too fast and scary, but it is truly the safest course.

3. You can change the course of mighty rivers with your bare hands.

Every river begins with a tiny stream. If you go far enough back upstream towards the source, the course of that stream can be changed by moving only a few pebbles. Further down, it takes boulders, and far enough along, whole mountains would have to be moved. I've moved and tossed plenty of metaphorical pebbles in my time—and I've diverted tiny streams that have become mighty raging torrents which have carved great canyons and washed away mountains. Consciousness, like water, ultimately cannot be resisted, and through Dark Times (such as are going on as I write), I draw my hope and inspiration from this certainty.

Inner tube trip

Find a river or large stream somewhere you can get to easily, that is suitable for inner tubing in the Summer. You may have to ask around a bit. Not so small that the water doesn't flow, or it's too shallow to float in; and not so big or fast as to be dangerous. Ideal rivers for kayaking are often also good for tubing, as long as there's enough of a current to carry you along. Get some friends—with at least one experienced adult—who'd like to make a day of tubing. Get truck inner tubes, and over-inflate them into the shape of a fat donut. Wear sneakers or good rubber sandals that won't come off in the water. Practice maneuvering in a still pool before you venture into the moving water. If you should capsize, hold onto your tube! You'll need a big pick-up truck to carry yourselves and your tubes to the upstream drop-off place, and then drive down to the other end to pick you up. Start with a short easy trip—maybe a mile or so—and try longer ones as you get better at it. Go with the flow, and become one with the cosmic stream of consciousness…

The Ocean

Around five million years ago, in the Northeast corner of Africa, certain apes took up a life at the seashore. Wading out into deeper water, they learned to walk upright, and swim. Nostrils shifted to point down to keep water out of their noses, and they gained the ability to excrete excess salt through tears and sweat. Like other aquatic mammals, they lost body hair, gained a fatty layer of insulation under the skin, grew webbing between their fingers and toes, and learned to use rocks as tools to crack open shellfish.

And also like other sea mammals, these aquatic apes became more intelligent than their land-bound relatives as pregnant females ingested certain brain-enhancing nutrients (*Docosahexanoic acid* or DHA) richly found in fish. They were our ancestors, from whom we have inherited all of these and more characteristics that separate us not only from the other apes, but also from all other land animals.

We are the children of the great Mother Ocean, the womb of all life, to which our pre-human ancestors once returned, and to which we still feel irresistibly drawn. The plasma of the very blood that courses through our veins is basically seawater, with the same chemical composition as that of the ancient seas from which we first internalized our circulatory systems, over 500 million years ago.

Movements of human populations have traditionally followed water pathways. Whether along a coastline, or along rivers, early settlements are always found near water. It is not difficult to envision early *hominids* (proto-humans), and later true humans, walking, wading and swimming along coastlines and rivers, thus populating the globe. If they were swimmers and divers, it would only serve to drive them on, in the search for food as populations rose and the climate changed.[55]

One important adaptation that had to occur in order for humans to speak is the ability to consciously hold our breath. Other primates don't speak because they are physiologically unable to voluntarily hold their breath. Also, the range of sounds that humans can make is a result of our "descended" larynx. The only other known animals with this feature are the dugong, sea lion and walrus.[56]

The majority of heat loss is through the top of one's head. Hair would have naturally remained on the head, to prevent heat loss, and sunstroke. It has also been suggested that the long hair length on the head may have given babies something to hold onto.

Most of us enjoy the water and beachside. Not only do we swim, but we also boat, waterski, "jetski," raft rivers and surf the waves. We dive both by breath-holding and using SCUBA gear or snorkeling. We play in the water and continue to find food in the water. More than any other ape we are drawn to the sea, in so many ways. It captures our awe and our curiosity—scientifically, spiritually and intellectually. It is the source of legends, myths and dreams. Water has always been a big part of us.[57]

---

[55] Tobias, Phillip V., "Water and Human Evolution," *Dispatches Human Evolution*, Dec. 1998.

[56] Morgan, Elaine, *The Aquatic Ape Hypothesis*, Souvenir Press, 1997.

[57] Friedl, Catherine, "The Role of Water in Human Evolution," March 2000, http://www.wf.carleton.ca/Museum/aquatic/cont.htm

Return to the Sea

If you live anywhere near the ocean, learn to experience its magic and mystery. Go beachcombing and tidepooling, and see what you can find for your collection (but *never* take anything alive from a tide pool!). Become a good sea swimmer, and learn body-surfing (also surfing and boogie-boarding if you're in the right place). Get yourself a good set of ocean fins, a mask and snorkel, and explore the undersea world (*always* with a partner!). If the water is cold in your area, get a wet suit. And for the most complete experience of the ocean, take SCUBA lessons, get certified, and go diving with a group and a professional dive-master.

SCUBA diving is, to me, the ultimate experience, connecting us at once with our entire 500-million-year heritage as creatures of the sea, and also giving us a taste of the weightlessness of outer space, wherein lies our ultimate destiny. There is simply nothing in all the world comparable to the feeling of floating—indeed, "flying"—in perfectly balanced buoyancy far beneath the waves, the surging sea around us at one with the pulsing ocean within our bodies. I even suspect that our love of roller coaster rides, and our universal dreams of flying, reflect our deep memories of weightless life in the sea, and our intuitive reaching towards the heavens.

References:

1. Friedl, Catherine, "The Role of Water in Human Evolution," March 2000, http://www.wf.carleton.ca/Museum/aquatic/cont.htm
2. Morgan, Elaine, *The Aquatic Ape Hypothesis,* Souvenir Press, 1997.
3. Tobias, Phillip V., "Water and Human Evolution," *Dispatches Human Evolution,* Dec. 1998.

30. The Magickal World[58]

By Oberon Zell

YES, THERE REALLY *IS* A WORLD OF MAGICK beyond the boundaries of Mundania. Just over that hill, or inside that forest, or behind those doors, or down that country road, there are magickal people gathering. Women wearing lovely gowns of silk and velvet, corsets and bodices, or beautifully-batiked Balinese saris and sarongs. Fantastic jewelry, armbands, necklaces, rings, anklets and belly-dance belts. Headdresses, tiaras, and pointy Witch hats with wide brims. Men wearing kilts, khitons, leathers, breeches, togas, tunics and jerkins. Helms and headbands with horns and antlers. Everyone wearing long flowing robes and dark swirling capes and cloaks. Faces mysterious behind paint or masks. And even more fantastic dress and costume than can be described...

The Gathering

Come with me to the Gathering...

When you enter the Gathering Place, you are greeted with warm smiles and big hugs. Everyone tells you, *"Welcome Home!"* And you know they mean it, for you feel in your heart that, indeed, you *have* come Home.

Music is playing everywhere, from madrigals to rock; from flutes to drums. Colorful banners flutter from walls, trees, tents and pavilions. Hearty feasts are set, where crowds sit together at large tables, joking, laughing, and sharing stories in between bites. Children of various ages are running through it all in happy "kid packs."

The Gathering by Dirk Dykstra.

Workshops teach mask-making, macramé, belly dance, chants, spells, drum-making,

---

[58] Zell, Oberon, *Grimoire for the Apprentice Wizard.* New Page, 2004. pp. 124-126

weaving, figure-sculpting, story-telling, cloak-making, drumming, healing, Tarot-reading, crystal-gazing, fire-building, yoga, meditation, mead-making, and pretty much anything else imaginable that someone wishes to teach and others wish to learn.

Circle after circle comes together in the fields and groves, the rings of stones, the medicine wheels, and around great trees. Group after group conducts rituals enacting myths and Mysteries as old as Time and as new as Tomorrow. Circles range from silly to solemn, from loud and boisterous to totally silent.

If the Gathering Place is outdoors (as most are, when the weather is pleasant), there will be campfires in the evening, and candles and torches will be lighting paths and shrines. As you walk into a circle of firelight, glowing faces turn to welcome you. Folks will make room around the fire, and pull up a seat for you (it may be just a log…). Someone passes you a chalice or drinking horn, saying, "Never thirst!" Folks are singing songs, or telling jokes and stories. At the big central bonfire, there will definitely be drumming and dancing around the fire—and this could go on all night. At some gatherings, there may even be a midnight fireworks and laser show.

And wherever you go, you are welcomed home.

The Magickal Marketplace

The real-life Magickal Marketplace is more fantastic than "Magic Alley" or any bazaar from the Arabian Nights. The finest craftspeople of the New Renaissance proudly display their best arts and handiworks—all in one place! There are wands, knives, swords, staves and chalices; robes, cloaks, gowns, hats and capes; jewelry, headgear, horns, helmets and chain mail; books, cards, paintings and posters; statues, figurines and dolls of Goddesses, Faeries, Dragons and Unicorns; creatures, crystals, candles and cauldrons; masks, music and magick. You think, "Diagon Alley really exists!" And it's true.

But you don't have to go to a Magickal gathering to shop in the Magickal Marketplace. There is hardly a major city in the English-speaking world today that doesn't have at least one magickal store, and some may be found even in small towns. In Black and Hispanic neighborhoods, they are called *Botanicas* ("herb shops"). You can look these up under "Metaphysical/Occult Stores." Though all these stores are independent, many are interconnected, and most of them carry my books, statues and jewelry.

These metaphysical and occult stores are your best gateway into the Magickal community. Get to know the folks who work there. They will usually have a bulletin board listing events, contacts, and local groups. Many of them offer classes on various magickal topics, and sometimes they will bring in speakers and presenters (I've done a number of guest appearances and book-signings at such stores). Take your kids, because many stores won't let children attend classes or buy materials without the permission of their parents, as they don't want to get into trouble with Mundane parents.

Faires, Festivals & Cons

Here are several events which occur annually in or near many large cities, and which are always attended by many real Magickal folk. These are open to the public, and widely advertised. Once you learn to recognize each other at these events by our dress and jewelry, you'll be able to make many Magickal friends.

Renaissance Faires

"Ren Faires," as we call them, are the most public of these gatherings, being held every weekend over a couple of months, and advertised everywhere. The Ren Faire is sort of like an outdoor theme park set in a fantasy version of "Camelot." The common language spoken at the Faire is *Elizabethan*—the English of Shakespeare. Sometimes there will be elements of historical accuracy, such as having Queen Elizabeth or Henry VIII as the reigning monarch. Unlike the real Middle Ages and Renaissance, however, there'll be no Black Plague or Witch-burnings here!

At the Faire, there will be jousting matches with armored knights battling on horseback with real lances. Bands of Pyrates will fence with swords over looted booty—"Aaarr!"—and will teach you a bit of swordplay, if you wish. Gypsies will be camped in the woods, with gaudily-painted wagons, and will tell your fortune by cards and crystal balls. You might meet Robin Hood, Maid Marian and the green-clad Merry Men and Women of Sherwood Forest. Real Wizards and Witches will be afoot—cleverly disguised as Wizards and Witches of fantasy (but you'll know if you check out their jewelry…).

The Marketplace at the Faire goes on and on—with all that I have described above, and more! Beautiful costumes like those worn by regular Faire-goers can be purchased at specialty boutiques. Exotic foods can be bought at stalls—such as "Toad in the Hole," shepherd's pies, turkey legs, the Queen's buns and the King's nuts. On stages small and large, performers will be acting out side-splitting comedies—and may even bring you on-stage to join them if you stand too close! Strolling minstrels, musicians and magicians provide continuous entertainment, and bawdy wenches in overflowing bodices will turn your head and give you whiplash!

And here's a good tip for you and your family: Don't go to the Ren Faire in mundane clothes, such as jeans and a T-shirt. Dress in your most magickal regalia, or even a simple tunic and leggings. Watch a Shakespeare play or movie, like "Romeo and Juliet," "Midsummer Night's Dream," or "Shakespeare in Love," and learn to speak in Elizabethan. The best way to enjoy the show is to become part of it! The secret password is "I'm with the band." And bring along your best friends.

Celtic Festivals, Ħighland Games, SCA

Renaissance Faires were founded by members of the Society for Creative Anachronism (SCA) which in turn was founded by science-fiction/fantasy author Diana Paxson, in her backyard in Oakland, Califia, on May 1 (Beltane) of 1966. Over the years other Medieval-inspired cultural festivals were created as well, and these have become major annual events in various places around the world. Examples are Celtic Festivals such as the Scottish Highland Games, which feature traditional old-country contests of strength and skill—such as heaving heavy poles and stones. Highly-trained dogs (and maybe pigs) will demonstrate their skills in herding sheep and ducks. There will be live music and traditional folk dancing. Shepherd's pies and *haggis* (my favorite) will be offered to eat. Vendors will be selling jewelry, artwork, hats and many other items. If you have Scotts or Irish ancestry, discover your family *tartan* and buy a scarf or even kilt made in that pattern.

Science Fiction/Fantasy cons

"Con" is short for "convention," and this is what these Gatherings are called when they are held indoors at hotels and convention centers. They are almost always called "Something-con," like "Baycon," "Discon" or "Fantacon." The original model for such events was Science-Fiction & Fantasy ("FS&F") cons, which began in the late 1930s. Nycon 1, the first annual World Science Fiction Convention ("Worldcon"), was held in New York on July 4th weekend, 1939. 200 people attended. Now the attendance at each year's Worldcon (always held over Labor Day weekend; the first weekend in September—in a different city each year throughout the world) is in the thousands!

Favorite FS&F authors are invited as Guests of Honor, and they give talks on-stage, sign books, and hang out in the lounge just like regular folks. Previews, trailers, "making of" and special advance viewings of new movies are shown in the con theater. Displays of props and costumes from famous films fill whole rooms. Art exhibits feature professional art from book covers, posters, calendars and movie mattes, as well as fantastic paintings and sculptures by pros and fans. The "Huckster Room" is where people bring FS&F-related books, comics, toys, art, models, action figures, trading cards and games to sell or trade.

My favorite part of these cons, however, is the Masquerade Ball, where people may have spent many months creating the most amazing costumes, props and makeup. Aliens, monsters, heroes, barbarians, Wizards, astronauts, Elves, Trolls, creatures and characters from stories and movies parade across the stage for hours. Costumes are judged in various categories, and winners become famous. I have won some of these!

However, you don't have to wait 'til the Worldcon comes around to your part of the world to attend a Sci-Fi/Fantasy con. Check with the folks at your local comic book store regarding smaller cons which may be held in your area. In many ways, these are even more fun, as the crowds are not so large that you can't even meet people. Some of these may have a very specific theme—like *Star Trek* or *Star Wars*—and actors from the movies or TV series will make personal appearances (just like in the movie, *Galaxy Quest*). You'll find that many of the folks who attend such cons are Magickal people. Check out their jewelry…

Gaming cons, Comicons and Cosplay

Gaming cons are much like SF&F cons, but with a specific theme around role-playing games, like "Dungeons & Dragons" or "Magic: The Gathering." Such cons feature big tournaments as well as many smaller games. LARP stands for "Live Action Role-Playing," and is lotsa fun! Much trading goes on—of cards, games and miniature figures. Comicons and Cosplay (for "costume") cons are similar—often with themes, such as comics and anime. As with SF&F cons, check with the folks at your local comic book store for when the next one will be in your area.

Pagan Festivals & cons

Large "Pagan Pride Days" are being held annually in ever-more cities around the country. They are held in public parks, are open to everyone, and are lots of fun, with vendors, music, rituals and other activities.

Other Pagan festivals and cons are not generally open to the public, and seldom advertise. The description of "The Gathering" I gave at the beginning of this chapter depicts a typical outdoor Pagan festival—and there are hundreds of these going on every year, all over the world. Ones I've been to range in size from less than a hundred participants to thousands. While most are held outdoors, there are also several Pagan hotel cons held in different cities each year. These are very much family events. However, minors are not admitted without legal guardians.

31. Note to Teachers: You have a Pagan in your classroom!

by Suzanne "Cecylyna" Egbert
November 2, 2000

 STUDENT IN YOUR SCHOOL PRACTICES A RE-ligion with which you may not be familiar. This leaflet is simply to give you information you may need to understand the different experiences this student may share with you, and answer any questions you might have.

What is a Pagan student likely to practice and believe?

Because Pagans generally follow a non-creedal, non-dogmatic spirituality, there may be even more variants between Pagan religious beliefs than there are between denominations of Christianity. The most commonly practiced types of Paganism are Wicca, Asatru, Druidry, or simply Paganism, just as a Christian can be Catholic, Presbyterian, or simply Christian. All of these are somewhat different from each other. Because of this, the following statements may not be true for every Pagan you encounter. However, there are some practices that are generally common among Pagans; the student or his parents will tell you if their practices differ significantly from the following:

A Pagan student will celebrate a nature-based, polytheistic religion

- A Pagan student will honor Divinity as both God and Goddess, sometimes with a feminist emphasis on the Goddess. One effect of this is that the student is likely to treat gender equality as an assumption.
- A Pagan student will celebrate religious ceremonies with small groups on Full Moons and at the beginning and midpoint of each season, rather than with large congregations or at a set weekly schedule. These celebrations are often called 'rituals,' 'circles,' *'esbats'* or *'sabbats,'* and the congregations are called 'covens,' 'groves,' 'hearths,' 'nests' or 'circles.' Some of the items commonly found on the altar in a Pagan ceremony are statues of the Goddess or God, candles, crystals, wands, an *athame* (a dagger used as a symbol and not as a tool with which to

cut), cups, cauldrons, incense, and a five-pointed star called the *pentagram* or *pentacle.*

- A Pagan student may wear a symbol of his or her religion as an item of jewelry. The most common symbol is the pentacle, a five-pointed star in a circle. The misconception of the pentagram as a Satanic symbol is based upon its inverted use by those groups, in the same manner in which devil-worshippers may use the Christian cross inverted. The meaning of the pentacle as worn by Pagans is rooted in the beliefs of the Greek Pythagoreans, for whom the pentagram embodied perfect balance and wisdom; inserting the star in the circle adds the symbol of eternity and unity.

- Other jewelry that may be worn includes Celtic knotwork, crosses, and *triskelions;* Thor's hammer; the *labrys* (a double-headed axe used as a symbol by Greco-Roman worship of Cybele); Goddess figurines; crescent and/or full Moon symbols; the Yin-Yang symbol; or the eye of Horus or horns of Isis from Egyptian mythology.

- A Pagan student will view Divinity as immanent in Nature and humanity, and view all things as interconnected. This often leads to a concern with ecology and the environment, and a fascination with the cycle of life.

- A Pagan student will believe in magic, and may spell it 'magick' to differentiate it from stage illusions. This may include belief in personal energy fields like the Chinese concept of *chi,* and may also include the use of rituals and tools to dramatize and focus positive thinking and visualization techniques. It does not mean that the student is taught that he can wiggle his nose to clean his room, summon spirits or demons, or do anything else that breaks natural laws, though if young, like any child, a Pagan child may pretend these things. It also does not mean that the student is taught to hex or curse; in our ethical structure such actions are believed to rebound on the sender, and therefore are proscribed.

- A Pagan student may believe in reincarnation. It is the most common eschatological belief held among Pagans, but is not universal. However, a Pagan student is unlikely to believe in either Heaven or Hell; she may believe in the Celtic Summerland, a place of rest between incarnations, or Valhalla, a realm of honor in Norse religions.

- A Pagan student may call herself a Witch, a Wiccan, a Pagan or Neo-Pagan, a Goddess-worshipper, a Druid, an Asatruer, or a Heathen. He is unlikely to call himself a *Warlock,* as that is believed to come from the Scottish word for "oathbreaker." And while a Pagan student may or may not be offended by the stereotype, she is likely to quickly inform you that the green-skinned, warty-nosed caricature displayed at Halloween bears no relation to her religion.

A Pagan student will be taught ethics emphasizing both personal freedom and personal responsibility

Pagan ethics allow personal freedom within a framework of personal responsibility. The primary basis for Pagan ethics is the understanding that everything is interconnected, that nothing exists without affecting others, and that every action has a consequence. There is no concept of forgiveness for sin in the Pagan ethical system; the consequences of one's actions must be faced and reparations made as necessary against anyone whom you have harmed.

There are no arbitrary rules about moral issues; instead, every action must be weighed against the awareness of what harm it could cause. Thus, for example, consensual homosexuality would be a null issue morally because it harms no one, but cheating would be wrong because it harms one's self, one's intellect, one's integrity, and takes unfair advantage of the person from whom you are cheating.

The most common forms in which these ethics are stated are the Wiccan Rede, "An it harm none, do as thou wilt," and in the Threefold Law, "Whatsoever you do returns to you threefold."

A Pagan student will hold a paradigm that embraces plurality and inclusivity

Because Pagan religious systems hold that theirs is one way among many, not the only road to Truth, and because Pagans explore a variety of deities among their pantheons, both male and female, a Pagan student will be brought up in an atmosphere that discourages discrimination based on differences such as race or gender, and encourages individuality, self-discovery and independent thought.

A Pagan student is also likely to be taught comparative religions

Most Pagans are adamant about not forcing their beliefs on the child but rather teaching them many spiritual systems and letting the child decide when he is of age. However, a Pagan student is unlikely to have an emotional concept of Heaven, Hell, or salvation as taught by Christian religions, though he may know about them intellectually. And a Pagan student will be taught to respect the sacred texts of other religions, but is unlikely to believe them literally where they conflict with scientific theory or purport to be the only truth.

A Pagan student is likely to enjoy reading, science, and helping professions

Margot Adler, National Public Radio journalist, reported the results of a survey of Pagans in the 1989 edition of her book, *Drawing Down the Moon.* The results showed that the one thing Pagans hold in common despite their differences is a voracious appetite for reading and learning. Pagans also seem to be represented strongly in the computer and health-care fields, so the Pagan child is likely to be computer-literate from an early age.

Despite their sometimes-misunderstood beliefs, Earth-based religions have grown steadily throughout the past few decades, and provide a satisfying spirituality to their practitioners. With the current appreciation of diversity and tolerance, more people now understand that different cultural backgrounds bring perspectives that can be valued instead of feared. It is our hope that as an educator this will provide you with the information you need to be able to facilitate understanding.

32. Boys, Girls & Others

By Haleigh Isbill

"Sweet Mother, I cannot weave—
Slender Aphrodite has overcome me
Withb longing for a girl."
~Sappho, *Sappho: A New Translation of the Complete Works*

My early life was dominated by dogmatic and extreme Christianity. I grew up in a state of fear—the church my mother and I attended was incredibly open about their hatred for homosexuality and sometimes children were kicked out of their houses for being queer and being open. I do not want that for my queer children. I have an asexual teenager, a gender fluid teenager, and a transwoman child.

Contemporary (as of the time of this writing, 2024) political and social issues center around transgenderism and whether transgendered people and drag queens are grooming children to be trans. I fear for my transgendered child's safety, growing up in this "Trans Panic" society. She has, at nine years old, a better understanding of who she is than I do of myself. And she can speak to who she is clearly and concisely. She is a transwoman and a Latina—which is the second highest murder demographic in the United States.[59] I fear for my little girl every day. I fear for all non-conforming children.

This chapter is written as a guide for myself and for you—the Pagan parent.

It is also written as a love letter to my children.

HEN THE AMERICAN PAGAN MOVEMENT BEGAN it was on the forefront of acceptance. Ex-Christians, tired of the dogma and splintered factions and absolutes, came running to a faith that was not only full of colorful gods and goddesses, but was also sort of a DIY (Do It Yourself) that allowed Pagans to build a faith that nurtured and spoke to the individual, allowed for solitary witches to do what feels right for them. No one path is the same, we all have different spiritual needs and Paganism was perfect for creating something that feeds the individual spiritually—

---

59 Westbrook Laurel, "How does race, gender, and sexuality shape the murder of transgender people in the United States?" Work In Progress Sociology, www.wipsociology.org/2023/05/18/how-does-race-gender-and-sexuality-shape-the-murder-of-transgender-people-in-the-united-states/ 5/18/2023. Accessed 2/10/2024.

and yet, covens exist because like-minded people can come together to worship or celebrate Deity while still being true to themselves.

Initiations are rites that bring beginnings, and for today's queer children, resonate with them in a way that nothing else really has. We have few natural initiations—initiation into living, breathing humans begins with birth, and death is initiation into our next forms (whatever they may be). Many of us hold baby showers and funerals to mark these occasions, but we need those rites in between. We need those milestone markers such as birthday parties, *quinceañeras,* weddings, *et cetera...* These are important rituals that mark changes in our lives or celebrate being alive on this plane of existence.

Witches often have additional rites—for women there are initiations into womanhood at menarche and cronings for witches shedding their mother role and moving into being wise women. Men have similar rituals for becoming grown men (sometimes signified as the hunter) and for becoming greybeards or sages—though milestone rituals for men are less common, as women in western Paganism are often at the forefront of creation as a means of rejecting "male" or "patriarchal" faiths. (See chapter 28, "Rites of Passage," for more on these milestones and how to mark them.)

> *"These types of ceremonial initiations are the "launch" of something new; the mark of a personal origin story in which the new initiate is reborn into a new life, often taking a new name in the process."* From Storm Faerywolf, in her article "Initiations and the Queer Craft"

There are initiations into our craft, handfasting for lovers to initiate them into a new togetherness, and death rites to initiate our loved ones into the Afterlife. All beginnings of new chapters are worth celebrating! Many rites and initiations within the Craft are centered on gender. But there is also so much space for the LGBTQ within modern Paganism.

> Amanda Kohr, in her article "Why Queer People Love Witchcraft"—
> *"In a world where **queer people**, particularly queer people of color, are told over and over that their otherness is wrong, it becomes a daily struggle to take one's power back. It requires ritual, affirmation, and community—and witchcraft provides all these things. The magic (or magick) explored and created in witchcraft is more than just casting spells and seeing results; it is about stepping into one's power,*

> *and celebrating identities that society deems too strange to be valid."*[60]

Queer witches can also often feel left out—male and female magick does not always speak to gay, lesbian, genderfluid, non-binary, and transgendered people. But we can change to be more inclusive.

From Keegan, a trans-masculine adult Pagan interviewed March 18, 2024. He says:

My grandmother was Pagan and had a lot of family traditions that I did not realize were Pagan until my teens. She accepted me as trans and even gave me the name Keegan. I lost her when I was sixteen, but I was introduced to Paganism at a young age because of her.

But I drifted away from Paganism because of the extreme genderization. Most modern Pagan traditions are very life cycle binary. Maiden, Mother, Crone/the sacred masculine. I became agnostic with Pagan window dressings. I love the imagery and the Wheel cannot help but turn.

As a queer woman in Paganism, I often find the god/goddess dynamic leaves me feeling left out. I want to feel included, and the next generations want that as well. There is room for all of us! And there are so many of us! As the modern world becomes accepting, more people are stepping out of the closet. Queers have always been there, but now it is so much safer to live authentically. And every time one of us stands up and says who we are, the world becomes a safer place for us all. Let your children be who they are—make space for them to tell you who they are.

Paganism as a religion is on the rise and now is the perfect time to mesh Paganism with the Gender, Relationship, and Sexual Minorities—the GRSM—which also includes those who are intersex (physically and hormonally), and polyamorous persons, as well as relationship anarchists.

So, how do we include people who are gay and do not resonate with male/female dynamics? Non-binary kids or kids whose gender is fluid and changes? How can we be better at making our rites and religion relatable to our queer children?

This can be as simple as having a menarche ceremony for a transwoman witchling when they start hormone therapy, or a ritual to celebrate a transman getting to experience puberty as a man. Some kids may want a ritual that ushers them from one gender to the other. Handfastings can

---

[60] Kohr, Amanda. "Why Queer and LGBTQ People Love Witchcraft" Refinery 29, https://www.refinery29.com/en-us/2020/06/9861310/queer-lgbt-witch-trend 6/17/2020. Accessed 2/10/2024.

be written for two people of the same sex, five people in a polyamorous relationship, or a couple of gender fluid lovers. The possibilities for inclusion are endless and effortless.

Centering rituals on deities that cross gender and sexual boundaries are a wonderful way to bring inclusion to rituals. Dionysus is a gender-fluid deity often shown with both male and female parts. Or Loki who has both fathered children as well as birthed them. Rituals and rites can call upon asexual deities like Hestia and Artemis—who are perpetual virgins. For bisexual or pansexual folx, there is Apollo and Hermes. Athena can be called on to represent lesbians. Even Aphrodite famously put a fire in Sappho's belly for women and while she is mythologically very much a straight Goddess, she is also an ally for her LGBTQ children and for queer kids everywhere. She appears to be polyamorous right along with Zeus, and she gave birth to Hermaphroditus—a deity of intersex folx and effeminate men. This is just a sample of LGBTQ gods. LGBTQ deities exist in so many pantheons and bringing their energy to a ritual or rite can make all the difference for people who are under the GRSM banner.

As differences among people are increasingly accepted and space is given for GRSM folx to be themselves, Abrahamic faiths appear to be doubling down on heteronormative ideology that is harmful to everyone. Parents reject their children and put them on the street, queer children must hide who they are from their patriarchal parents for their own safety, asexual folx are told there is something wrong with them for having no desire for romance or intimacy. Abrahamic and patriarchal extremists do so much harm to society and to themselves; the damage they do is astronomical.

Paganism should be a beacon for everyone, a place of hope and acceptance, a collection of faiths that rejects patriarchy and embraces the different and whose gods move over a seat so the queer deities can also sit at the deific table. Allies like Aphrodite can literally be the difference between life and death for many GRSM kids, teens, and even adults. Accepting them and folding them into our faiths, initiating them into our craft while honoring their queerness, initiating them into queerness itself, can psychologically help our LGBTQ communities live and thrive and change the world to something less patriarchal and more egalitarian.

As parents, it is important to include queer deities and use less gendered rituals as we raise our children. Many people realize that they are gay, transgender, or even polyamorous at an early age. To grow up with representation means that they know they are free to be themselves with their parents and communities.

> From Angelina Greenwood (a non-binary witch and parent), interviewed February 15, 2024: *"Make sure they [queer kids] have a good sense of gender and sexuality to combine with their spiritual sense of self-, so they know their body, they know themselves, and then they know themselves within the greater scheme of things."*

Many queer kids fall into dangerous coping mechanisms if they do not feel supported at home or if they feel adrift in life. We, as parents, need them to know that they are perfect and beautiful and full of magick from the moment of their birth until the moment of their death, and into the beyond. We can instill these ideals in them from an early age and give them a spiritual and emotional shield from bigots.

Build rituals for our children that feed their souls and sense of self and once they've told us parents who they are, believe them and meet them where they are at.

> *"Meeting someone where they are requires breaking free from societal norms and preconceived notions. It means accepting individuals for who they are and where they stand in their journey. By doing so, we can offer genuine support and compassion to those around us. Remember, sometimes all a person needs is someone to hold their hand and walk with them to a better place."* ~Taylor Genter, *The Taylor(ed) Report*[61]

Taylor Genter says that meeting them where they are at is six steps:

1. Actively listen to your children when they are telling you who they are.
2. Pay close attention to their body language and emotions as well as their words.
3. Be aware of your own biases and reject preconceived ideals that might interfere negatively with the relationship you have with your children.
4. Be careful and intentional with your words and body language—when kids tell us who they are, they are also looking at us for any sign of judgment. Repeat their words back at them to show you are listening and understanding—this will also give you all a chance to clarify any misunderstandings.
5. Ask open-ended questions so that they have the space to really communicate and be vulnerable.

---

[61] Genter, Taylor. The Tayor(ed) Report, LinkedIn, https://www.linkedin.com/pulse/meet-them-where-theyre-taylor-genter?trk=news-guest_share-article 7/7/2023. Accessed 2/25/2024.

6. Finally, accept and validate their feelings and identity. Accepting and validating them and allowing your family culture and faith to intertwine with who they are is incredibly important for your child's mental health.[62]

Kids who are queer are at a higher risk for drug use, prostitution, and suicide. Meeting kids where they are at lessens the likelihood of these things happening. Just having loving, accepting parents is literally a life saver. From the Trevor Project:[63]

1. Suicide is the second leading cause of death among young people aged 10-14, and the third leading cause of death among 15-24 year olds (Centers for Disease Control and Prevention, 2022). Lesbian, gay, bi-sexual, transgender, queer, and questioning (LGBTQ+) young people are at significantly increased risk.
2. LGBTQ+ young people are more than four times as likely to attempt suicide than their peers (Johns et al., 2019; Johns et al., 2020).
3. The Trevor Project estimates that more than 1.8 million LGBTQ+ young people (ages 13-24) seriously consider suicide each year in the U.S.—and at least one attempts suicide every 45 seconds.
4. The Trevor Project's 2023 U.S. National Survey on the Mental Health of LGBTQ+ Young People found that 41% of LGBTQ+ young people seriously considered attempting suicide in the past year, including roughly half of transgender and nonbinary youth.

Pagan parents of today have a unique opportunity to raise our children in judgment-free homes, where our children—queer or not—know they are safe to be themselves and their identity reflected back at them through their deities and rites of passage. We can raise children who are accepting of others, who are willing to bring others into the shelter of modern Paganism; so when our babies go out into the world and are bombarded by rigid gender norms, compulsive heteronormativity, transphobia, and patriarchy, that they know there's a safe haven waiting for them when they get home. Let us make the world a safer place for all children to grow into who they are while still being mentally healthy and able to become fully functional adults.

---

[62] IBID
[63] "Facts About Suicide Among LGBTQ+ Young People", The Trevor Project
https://www.thetrevorproject.org/resources/article/facts-about-lgbtq-youth-suicide/
12/15/2021. Accessed 2/25/2024.

33. "The Talk:" All About Sex

By Haleigh Isbill

Introduction

 T CAN BE DIFFICULT TO KNOW WHAT TO SAY TO our young children when they have questions, or how much to tell our older kiddos so they know how to protect themselves and others. Comprehensive Sexuality Education focuses on keeping information as accurate as possible while keeping the language and information age appropriate. Comprehensive Sex Education includes information about relationships, sex and sexuality, anatomy, puberty, and reproductive health.

Data shows that children and adolescents who get a more comprehensive sex education are likely to begin sexual activity at a later age and when they do become sexually active, they are more likely to use safe practices—practices they are likely to carry with them their whole lives. CSE covers consent, preparation for puberty, and self-respect—which also lowers the risks of unsafe practices. Children who get an in-depth view of sex and sexuality and gender are much less likely to experience prostitution, trafficking, violence, and sexual abuse. It is vital that our children have the tools to protect themselves.[64]

Children will be exposed to a lot of information on sex and gender issues through media and the internet. Kids and their friends may have conversations about what they have heard or seen. Without the tools to understand what is true and what is garbage ideology, the discussions are probably more harmful than helpful.

This chapter is broken down into **Birth through Nine Years Old, Nine to Thirteen Years Old, Fourteen Years Old+** and **Sixteen+.** If you have a child who is more mature or feel your child is not ready for the information in the age range given, then go with your gut. You know your child better than outsiders do. The following is simply a guide and hopefully a helpful resource.

"The Talk" is a scary topic for parents—oftentimes adults are uncomfortable discussing sex with their children. Society shows unrealistic

---

[64] World Health Organization, *Comprehensive Sexuality Education*, www.who.int/newsroom/questions-and-answers/item/comprehensive-sexuality-education, 5/18/2023. Accessed 5/10/2024.

depictions of sex in media but also makes discussing sex taboo, which is a disservice to everyone. Adults need to be using age-appropriate information that can de-mystify sex and create healthy conversation on the topic. Parents need to lay a foundation of trust and honesty from the start and make that foundation a habit—communication and trust will (hopefully) become a habit for the youths.

But how to begin? Start here with some general Do's and Don'ts that can do the groundwork needed to keep communication open with your children:

DO provide a safe space for your kids to talk to you about anything, so when they have questions, they are more likely to talk to you rather than asking friends or Google.

DO keep your parent/child relationship open and available for when children want to talk about anything—forge that relationship before questions come up.

DO encourage them to ask questions. Remind them that you are always open to any questions they might have, ask them questions about themselves, and show interest in what they are interested in. Actively listening to your children shows them you care about them.

DO focus on having multiple casual conversations rather than one big "Talk"—and use questions that come up as a catalyst for those small conversations.

DO help them to build appropriate boundaries, even when it comes to asking questions about sex and sexuality. Let them know that everyone has different rules and not to discuss these things with other children as these topics are private and to only discuss with trusted adults.

DO establish other trusted adults with your child. Remind them that they can ask aunts or grandparents or other trusted adults they are close to, including their pediatrician.

DO give your child the space to feel negative emotions and try not to be dismissive of their fears or concerns. It is okay to express hurt or anger or discomfort. These feelings are normal, and everyone feels negatively sometimes.

DON'T use phrases that dismiss their feelings. Phrases like "It's not that bad!" can leave children feeling like their emotions and concerns are dismissed or unimportant. This can lead to children assuming that adults are not interested in how they, the child, feels, which then becomes a barrier to open communication.

DON'T freak out if you see your young children touching themselves. Kids figure out that touching genitals feels good early in life. It is normal for them to touch themselves and getting upset or slapping their hands away can cause feelings of shame which can have a detrimental effect on how they see sex and their bodies going forward. Instead, maybe calmly tell them that touching their genitals is a private thing to do in the bathroom or their bedroom—while also emphasizing that it is a normal thing to do.

DON'T freak out if they catch you having sex. It is okay for kids to know that grownups have sex and be prepared to have one of those small moments later to answer any questions they might have.

DON'T freeze up when questions come. Kids do not always understand how important these topics are and how it can be difficult for parents and other adults to discuss.[65]

Birth–Nine Years Old

Comprehensive Sex Education begins from birth. Lessons of bodily autonomy, consent, and respect for self are some of the best ways to teach your children to protect themselves, grow healthy bodies and boundaries, and create good self-esteem.

Using The Right Words

Children need to know the medical names for their body parts. This gives them the vocabulary to discuss where to avoid touching others or how to describe abuse. Teaching them medical names goes beyond personal safety, however. Learning the correct names and understanding their bodies can teach kids that their whole body is important and minimizes feelings that certain body parts are shameful. It is an effective way to also establish personal boundaries and understand that others have those boundaries, too. That there are places on our bodies that are a beautiful part of what makes us human but should not be touched by others—and that they should not touch other people in those same places.[66]

Saying No, Boundaries, and Consent

Create guidelines for saying "no" and teach your children that the "no" goes both ways. Allow your child to say no to unwanted touch and

---

[65] *How Do I Talk With My Elementary School Aged Child About Sex and Sexuality?* Planned Parenthood. www.plannedparenthood.org/learn/parents/elementary-school/how-do-i-talk-my-elementary-school-aged-child-about-sex-and-sex Accessed 2/20/2024.

[66] *Ibid.* Accessed 2/23/2024.

tell your friends and family that you expect them to honor "no" from your children. Kiddo does not want to kiss or hug Great Aunt Josephine? That is fine! A friend at school does not like hugs? Respect that. Teach them to ask for permission before touching friends and to accept if the other person says no. Our kids deserve to have agency over their bodies (as much as possible) but also need to understand that the agency applies to other bodies as well. This is the start of healthy personal boundaries and respect for the boundaries of others.

Boundaries are good for your child's self-esteem but also for their safety. Teach them to tell a trusted adult if anyone crosses their personal boundaries. Teach kids what places are on their bodies are private and teach them the actual words for those parts of their body. Have conversations about secrets. Which secrets to keep—like what is in the Christmas present for a sibling—and which secrets to tell a trusted adult—like if their friend tells them the friend is experiencing abuse at home. Identifying which secrets are best kept and which are best told to an adult will help children navigate which of their own secrets to keep and which to tell.[67]

Reproduction

Give children broad strokes early on and fill in gaps as they age and have more questions. Give them some anatomy, as already mentioned, and explain that babies are grown in a mother's body and come out of her vagina as infants. In the beginning kids do not really need more information than that. However, if there are additional questions, answer them. Keep calm and talk to them like you would talk to them about anything else.

Sex and Sexuality and Gender

Kids may come to you with questions about the LGBTQ. Maybe your kindergartener has a friend with two mommies, or your third grader has questions about being transgender because a child in their class has just come out as trans. It is best to answer those questions in broad strokes and ask your children how they feel about what you have gone over with them and if any of the conversation applies to your child personally—give them the chance to talk about themselves within a gender identity or sexual orientation framework.

The absolute best advice to give parents of queer children is to be an ally. Be an ally in private and be an ally loudly in public. Make sure that

---

[67] Tatter, Grace. *Consent At Every Age.* Harvard Graduate School of Education, 12/19/2018.

your children know you have their back no matter what and that you are willing to do so out loud for everyone to hear. Some children know they are trans or gay from an incredibly early age, while other kids may not know until the onset of puberty or later, so be careful what you say about others from the start. If you are always an ally, if your children know that you support others who are gay or trans, they are more likely to come to you to talk about themselves. For more in-depth information, see chapter 32: "Boys, Girls, and Others."

Resources

Harvard recommended books about consent for school aged children[68]:

- *My Body! What I Say Goes!* by Jayneen Sanders, illustrated by Anna Hancock
- *Miles Is the Boss of His Body* by Samantha Kurtzman-Counter and Abbie Schiller, illustrated by Valentina Ventimiglia
- *I Said No! A Kid-to-Kid Guide to Keeping Private Parts Private* by Kimberly King and Zack King, illustrated by Sue Rama

Mayo Clinic recommended sex education books for elementary age children[69]:

- *Good Pictures, Bad Pictures: Porn Proofing Today's Young Kids* by Kristen A. Jenson and Gail A. Poyner
- *Don't Hug Doug (He Doesn't Like It)* by Carrie Finison
- *Personal Space Camp* by Julia Cook
- *No Means No!* by Jayneen Sanders
- *What Makes a Baby?* By Cory Silverberg
- *It is NOT the Stork!: A Book About Girls, Boys, Babies, Bodies, Family & Friends* by Robie H. Harris
- *From Diapers to Dating: A Parent's Guide To Raising Sexually Healthy Children—From Infancy to Middle School* by Debra W. Haffner

Nine–Thirteen Years Old

Preteens are a wild time. Children are becoming more independent, they are about to enter, or are entering puberty and there is a lot of talking about sex and relationships with friends—a lot of which might be

---

[68] *Ibid*

[69] Johnstone, Nick. *When To Start Talking About Sexual Health With Your Child: Earlier Than You Think. https://mcpress.mayoclinic.org/parenting/when-to-start-talking-about-sexual-health-with-your-child-earlier-than-you-think/* 9/30/2022. Accessed 2/19/2024.

misleading, inaccurate, and/or harmful information. Having trusted adults already in place can help kids be comfortable enough to ask questions and sort valuable information from garbage.[70]

Remind your kids that even if they are not comfortable discussing these issues with you—their parent—they have other trusted adults they can turn to. Reinforce bodily autonomy, boundaries, and consent—then build on with additional information. Where once you gave a vague reply to an 8-year-old, you would give a more detailed response to a 12-year-old. Just like with young children, be sure to keep an open and honest relationship with your child and be sure to ask them questions and give them space to talk about what they think or feel about sex, sexuality, and gender.

Bodies

Bodies change during puberty and sometimes those changes are awkward or embarrassing. Give your children a healthy body image that can bolster their self-esteem when their bodies get weird. Be careful not to criticize other bodies, including your own. Kids are listening and if they are hearing negative remarks, they are likely to criticize those body issues in themselves and others, which can lead to bullying. The antidote for bullying is accepting that everyone has different bodies, and that all bodies are good bodies. And all bodies change at a different pace than others.[71]

Puberty for Girls

Puberty is not just hair in new places and excessive body odor. It is also when breasts begin to grow, and menstrual cycles begin. Menarche is the onset of menstrual cycles and is often a time that many Pagan families usher their daughters into womanhood. Often this is a time when arousal begins and the vagina starts to lubricate itself, and a time when the body begins to shed its uterine lining every 28 days or so (though the cycle is likely to be erratic in the beginning). The pubescent girl will need to know what and how to use pads/tampons/menstrual cups—how to use them, how to dispose of them, and in the case of menstrual cups, how to clean them. Provide your child with these accoutrements to keep in their backpacks so that if menarche happens suddenly, they already know what to do. Planned Parenthood has an excellent article titled *What's Up With Periods?* That will help you your AFAB (Assigned Female At Birth) child

---

[70] Tatter, Grace. *Op cit.*

[71] *Ibid*

prepare for the oncoming changes.[72] This article covers everything from what to expect during periods to what happens to intersex women in puberty. Transfeminine children will go through puberty in a vastly different way from AFAB children, and this is covered as well.

Puberty for Boys

Boys also have a roller coaster of changes during puberty. Testes begin to grow bigger and sprout pubic hair, penises grow longer, and voices get lower. Erections occur more often and even when the child is not aroused (called spontaneous erections). These erections can be embarrassing, but knowing how to cover them with a pillow or well-placed backpack can save the AMAB (Assigned Male At Birth) child some anxiety and fear of being shamed in public. Now is when kids begin to experience ejaculation as well. Semen production begins somewhere between 12 and 16 years old and ejaculation happens through masturbation and can also happen during sleep (wet dreams). Warning your child that erections and ejaculation happen and are normal and nothing to be embarrassed or feel ashamed about. This is often a time when boys are ushered into manhood by their bodies and sometimes ritually, as Pagan parents do for their daughters at menarche. Unlike a female child who begins a menstrual cycle, it is harder to pinpoint exactly when to perform these rituals for male children. However, if your sons come to you with questions or concerns about their body changes, that would be the time—if the family follows a tradition that includes puberty rites for boys—to perform those rites.

Transgender and Gender Non-Conforming kids

For transgender and non-binary youth, puberty is not only a hormonal and physical roller coaster but can also be very traumatic. Their bodies are growing into the wrong gender, and this can cause depression and anxiety and gender dysphoria. If your preteen is experiencing this, puberty blockers can be there to help! Puberty blockers will not change your child's physical gender, but rather kick the puberty can farther down the road, giving you and your kiddo more time to figure out how best to go through puberty—hormone replacement or natural puberty. This is also a time when these children will want to start expressing themselves in a way that correlates to their gender and parents should respect that. A trans child needs to transition socially—which is to dress like their gender and use the associated pronouns—even if they cannot transition physically.

---

[72] *What's Up With Periods?* Planned Parenthood.
www.plannedparenthood.org/learn/teens/puberty/whats-periods. Accessed 4/24/2024.

Supporting your child's transition is incredibly important for their mental health and will carry them through the storm of hormones and gender dysphoria. Children who feel supported by their parents are much less likely to feel suicidal or turn to prostitution, which is common for trans youth.

Planned Parenthood has a highly informative and extensive article on puberty and middle school, *What Should I Teach My Middle Schooler About Their Body?* The article offers help on what to say to children, how to encourage them, and how to help them build and keep their self-confidence.[73]

Identity

At this age children are starting to understand themselves better, and beginning to understand labels that help tell the world who they are. Kids begin to compare themselves to others and that can affect their self-esteem for good or bad. Ideas about gender or sexual orientation start to form and solidify. This is a time for first crushes and eternally long phone calls with friends. It is also a time when kids need extra love and support as they explore who they are.

Have a good understanding of gender identities and sexual orientations ahead of time so when children have questions, you have answers. When your children tell you who they are, believe them. But do not pressure your kids to confess their sexual orientation or gender identity, and do not tell family and friends your child's orientation or identity unless your child says it is okay—get their consent. Know that both sexual orientation and gender identity can be fluid and children may go through several label changes as they go through puberty. (And even sometimes throughout adulthood) They need to know that you are not going to call any changes a phase and that it is okay for them to experience multiple changes in their identity and orientation. They need to know that you are there no matter what, and even if they are gay/straight/pansexual (liking all forms of gender)/asexual (not being interested in sexual and/or romantic relationships).

Be careful not to push gender stereotypes on your preteens. No telling sons that they need to "man up" or telling girls to be "ladylike" but let them be the best version of themselves without the damage of gender specific expectations. Toxic masculinity is pervasive and hurts boys as well as girls so let your boys know that emotion is perfectly normal for both

---

[73] *What Should I Teach My Middle Schooler About Their body.* Planned Parenthood. www.plannedparenthood.org/learn/parents/middle-school/what-should-i-teach-my-middle-schooler-about-their-body. Accessed 4/24/2024.

men and women to express and encourage them to verbalize and process their feelings.

If your preteen does confide in you that they are transgender or queer, make sure you tell them that you love them for who they are. Use the name and gender pronouns they prefer; learn about their gender and/or sexual orientation so you can understand them better. Be careful what terminology you use and ask friends and family to do the same. Respect your child's choices in who to come out to and help them figure out the best way to come out to others. In the case of a trans child, now is the perfect time to discuss social transition and medical options such as puberty blockers. Take them to community events for other people like them and allow them online communities but teach them how to be safe online, too.

Ask your children about themselves. Do they have crushes? Do they have boyfriends or girlfriends? Are they feeling anxious or depressed? Are they a target of bullying? Do they feel safe at home and at school? Help them figure out how to be themselves while being safe through constant, honest communication.[74]

Reproduction

Give preteens accurate and honest information about sex and pregnancy—give them the facts long before they need them, so your kids are prepared for when situations come up. Talk to them about birth control and STD protection before they are sexually active and set an expectation of responsible choices. You want your kiddo to get this information from you. Studies show that kids who have open and blunt conversation with their parents on sex-related issues are more likely to wait longer to start having sex and when they do start having sex, they are more likely to use protection and safe practices.

Be detailed about pregnancy, biologically how it happens (PIV: penis-in-vagina) and the options for preventing it. Discuss STDs and how to prevent them, as well. These discussions are not permission for your child to have sex but can help kids make good choices when they are ready for intimacy and intercourse.

Be clear about birth control and how it works. Make sure your children know that abstinence is the only 100% way to prevent pregnancy, but do not stop there. Studies have proven over and over that abstinence only education is harmful to teens while also being ineffective. Discuss what the different birth control options are and their efficacy in preventing pregnancy. Talk about how STDs can best be prevented through barrier birth control such as condoms or dental dams. Make sure your kids know

---

[74] Tatter, Grace. *Op cit.*

that people of any gender or sexual orientation can get pregnant from penis-in-vagina sex and that emergency contraception can help prevent pregnancy up to five days after penis-in-vagina sex.

Talk to your kids about options if a pregnancy happens. There are three options—abortion, adoption, and parenting. It is the time to talk to them about the basics of each option and emphasize and that abortion is very safe and common. [75]

Personal Safety

Pregnancy prevention and STD protection are part of being safe, and so is the ability to recognize sexual harassment.

It is imperative that children recognize sexual harassment and what to do about it. Reinforce that nobody should touch them without their consent, and that sexual harassment can also look like being bullied into consenting. Teach them that sexual harassment can come from anywhere— friends, family, school staff, and inside unhealthy romantic relationships. The best protection from harassment is healthy boundaries and being able to say NO. Encourage your preteen to talk to a trusted adult when they feel like they are being pressured or bullied into giving consent. Let them know that it is always okay to say NO. Make sure they know that sexual assault is a crime and never the fault of the victim. [76]

Peer pressure can be intense at this age and giving your preteen the right tools can help them resist peer pressure. Make rules and make sure your kids know that you expect those rules to be followed. Let your child use you as an excuse to resist peer pressure – "Sorry, my mom would kill me" is a classic that is always in style. Help them to be comfortable with saying no in every situation. Saying no is a skill that must be practiced to be firm. Letting your children make decisions that are age-appropriate will give them practice in making good choices, which is as important as being able to say NO. Teach your kids to help their friends resist peer pressure so your child will have solidarity in resisting. Get to know those friends and help them to make good choices, too. If everyone is making good choices and comfortable saying NO, your child is much more likely to follow along, kind of like herd immunity.

Bullying is a major issue for preteens. If your child is being bullied, believe them, and take steps to protect them. Let them know that you love them, tell the school what is happening, and take your child to a therapist

---

[75] *What Should I Teach My Middle Schooler About Pregnancy and Reproduction.* Planned Parenthood. https://www.plannedparenthood.org/learn/parents/middle-school/what-should-i-teach-my-middle-schooler-about-pregnancy-an. Accessed 5/10/2024.

[76] Tatter, Grace. *Op cit.*

who can give them strategies to cope. Recognize the physical symptoms of a bullied child—being afraid to go places, no longer wanting to go out and be social, getting regular headaches and stomach aches, and being down on themselves. Stay involved with your child. That open and honest foundation you laid their whole lives up to this point will help them feel safe to keep you informed.

Giving your children respect for themselves and showing them empathy at home will teach them to expect that behavior from others as well. Be a good example, model the behaviors you expect from your kids and make sure they know you expect the same in return. This can inoculate them against whatever bullies try to use to bully your child.

Along with protecting themselves from peer pressure and sexual harassment from people in their everyday life, kids these days need to protect themselves online. Basics of online safety include not sharing personal details like their home address or full name online, not sharing pictures of themselves, and assuming everything said and shared online is public—because it is. There can be real life consequences for what is shared online. Let your kids know that if they think they may have messed up their online safety, that you are there to help them. Make sure they know to come to you right away—even if they think they will get in trouble—and you will help them.

Abuse happens and your kids need to know how to recognize abuse. You and your child need to know what steps to take when abuse happens. If your child comes to you and says that someone is abusing them, take them seriously. Stay calm and make sure they know you are on their side. Ask them what happened and let them know you are glad they came to you. Then report the abuse. Contact law enforcement, child protective services, or a children's advocacy group immediately. Find who to report to in your local area. If the abuse is physical, contact their doctor. Doctors can recommend the next steps and take evidence for potential investigations.

After abuse, get your child mental health help. Healing can take a long time and a mental health care professional knows what steps to take to heal your child emotionally and mentally healthy.[77]

Resources
- AMAZE.org—the website and YouTube channel have valuable information and are perfect for you to watch with your child.
- *Great Relationships and Sex Education* by Alice Hoyle and Ester McGreeney is a fantastic guide for parents and educators.

---

[77] *Ibid.*

- Planned Parenthood—PlannedParenthood.org has incredibly detailed information for parents on how to manage situations as they come up and what your child needs to know to make the best choices for themselves. The essays provide references and videos that help really drive the lessons home.

Fourteen Years Old+

Bodies

Puberty is still raging, and bodies are still changing until about 16 years old. Every child develops at a different pace, and some may feel that they are running behind their friends and classmates. They may suffer some depression or anxiety about their bodies causing low self-esteem.

Helping your child have good self-esteem and a healthy body image is vital for their happiness but also their health. Teens who feel good about how they look are more likely to take care of themselves physically. Planned Parenthood has some great points on how to help you help your child love themselves:

- Do not compare your teen's looks to anyone else's—even if you are saying your teen looks better. That sends the message that it is okay to compare themselves to other people.
- Try not to complain about your own looks in front of them.
- Compliment how they look—but do not let that be the only thing you compliment them about.
- Congratulate them on hard work, strength, kindness, or other good qualities you want them to be proud of.
- When you talk about diet or exercise, focus on health instead of attractiveness.
- Remind them that most of the images we see of models and celebrities are heavily edited and not real.
- Take pride in your heritage. How your teen feels about their race or ethnicity can be an important influence on their self-esteem and body image. For example, research shows that young teens who are proud of being African American or Latino tend to feel good about themselves. Help them find good role models. Recognize special cultural traditions, qualities, and values. Involve them in activities that will help them learn about their family history and culture[78]

---

[78] *What Should I Teach My High School Aged Teen About Their Body? Op cit.* Accessed 5/10/2024.

Identity

Kids are still figuring out who they are—it is a process that takes years and years. Sexual orientation and gender identity are ideas that are common these days, so children are finding themselves earlier than when our society forced queer people to be secretive. Because conversations often revolve around these ideas, your teens are getting information about being LGBTQ from all kinds of sources—their friends, their friends' parents, YouTube influencers, their religious leaders, etc. It is important that you talk about your child's gender identity and sexual orientation with them. They need to know that you are going to love them no matter what, and being queer is not a defect.

It can be difficult accepting that your child is part of the LGBTQ. The bullying and hateful rhetoric that queer children and teens encounter, the gender dysphoria that can cause mental distress. There is a lot of heartbreak and struggle coming for the queer child thanks to society at large and you as parents of LGBTQ kids may fear that some bigot, spurred on by trans panic and homophobia, is going to harm or even kill their children. You may also experience sadness for the life of comfortable heteronormativity you expected for them. The fear and sadness are real and normal and having a therapist who is certified in these areas can help you work through the emotions, give you good coping strategies, and explain the next steps to take in case something does happen.

It is important to keep the lines of communication open with your teens. Do not assume you know your child's sexual orientation or gender identity. If you suspect your child fits into the LGBTQ, look for chances to bring it up. Make sure your child knows that you are supportive of queer people being themselves and that you are going to respect your child no matter where on the gender and sexual spectrums.

If you, yourself are lesbian, gay, bi, or queer, talk about your own process of coming out and your own experiences within the community—which can help your child to feel like they are not alone, even if they are questioning where they fit into these labels.

If your child comes out to you make sure they know you love them, that you are going to use the terminology and pronouns they choose for themselves, and that you do not think it is a phase. Be the type of person they would want to come out to. Do not pressure them to come out – to you or to anyone – but be willing to help them figure out how to come out to others, as well.

It is normal to struggle with your child being queer and it is important that you give yourself time to process but makes sure your kid knows that you are going to love them and that you just need a bit to adjust to the idea.

Reproduction

Even if you do not want your teen to be having sex, you should be talking to them about safe sex, pregnancy prevention, and emergency contraception. Give them the information they may not need immediately so that when the situation arises, they already know what to do. Take them to the doctor, talk openly, remind them that you love them no matter what.

Talk to your queer and transgender kids about birth control and disease prevention, too. Make sure they know how to have safe sex no matter what gender anyone involved with them is.

Personal Safety

Now is when most teens start having more serious relationships, they need those healthy boundaries and the confidence to say NO more than ever. Now is when they put into practice the lessons you have spent their entire life imparting to them. They will have heartbreaks and joys, but knowing their own worth and knowing that it is okay to say NO will help them make good choices and give them the tools to recognize abuse.

Ages 16+

Chances are your teen has stopped physically changing by 16 years old. Not always, but generally. Children that have not finished developing by this age may feel embarrassed and may be subject to bullying. Their self-esteem may be impacted, and their body image may take a toll. While the physical changes from puberty have mostly finished by age 16, emotions are still running high and even if their body has finished developing, their brain will not fully develop until they are about 25 years old. Talk to your children about their developmental pace, ask them open-ended questions that provide them with the opportunity to give detailed responses, use that foundation of communication to help you help your teen. If your child is experiencing upset at being "behind" take them to a therapist who can help them deal with their negative emotions or feelings of shame for not being as far along as your kids feel they should be.

Accept that your teen may be sexually active. The average age of first sexual experience is eighteen, but your teen may fall onto either side of that number. Make sure they have the tools to prevent pregnancy and STDs as previously discussed—and make sure they know you are a safe person to come to if anything happens. That trust you have been cultivating for almost two decades will serve you well here. Talk to your therapist if you need help processing the idea that your child is sexually active. Sex is a normal part of life for most people, this includes your children.

If pregnancy occurs, the Planned Parenthood website has excellent articles on how to help your pregnant or parenting teen. Accidents happen, kids mess up, and your kids will need you no matter what choice they make once pregnant. You have already given them the options and now it is time to support them through the situation and accept whatever path they choose for themselves. Making good choices can be difficult and you can guide them through tricky situations if your child trusts you and knows they can come to you with any issues.

If you find yourself struggling, a good therapist can help you figure out how to adjust and how to continue to be someone your children will go to with concerns or questions about what they are experiencing without causing you discomfort or awkwardness.

In conclusion

You have been building a good relationship with your children their whole lives and hopefully they will apply the ideals of healthy relationships that you have instilled in them to all their relationships, romantic or otherwise. Hopefully, the boundaries you have taught them to cultivate will continue to be strong and sensible. Hopefully, they make good choices that set them up for success in relationships, in love, and in life at large.

34. Religion

By Oberon Zell

 ELIGION IS A TRICKSY SUBJECT TO WRITE ABOUT. In countries dominated by the monotheistic faiths (Christianity, Islam, Judaism) most people grow up in families and communities that either practice some particular religion, or (generally in rebellion) none at all. Either way, the dominant paradigm is that of *monotheism*—One God; One True Right and Only Way (all others are false and thus evil). Even declared atheists disbelieve in the same singular God that the devout worship!

There are an estimated 10,000 distinct religions worldwide,[79] though nearly all of them have regionally based, relatively small followings. Four religions—Christianity, Islam, Hinduism and Buddhism—account for over 77% of the world's population, and 92% of the world either follows one of those four religions or identifies as nonreligious, meaning that the remaining 9,000+ faiths account for only 8% of the population combined. The "religiously unaffiliated" demographic includes those who do not identify with any particular religion, atheists and agnostics, although many in that demographic still hold various religious beliefs.[80]

Some churches (specifically fundamentalists and evangelicals) are adamant about compelling their children to accept their particular religious dogma, and punish them severely if they dare to question it in any way. Their primary values are obedience, blind faith, and believing what they are told to believe—regardless of whether it makes any sense. Such religions should properly be considered *cults,* with all the negative connotations of that term. They commonly foster abuse—verbal, psychological, physical and even sexual. And after having dogma forced down their throats from infancy, it is very difficult for their children to grow up with any inclination or ability for critical thinking.

Therefore it is essential that you—my future parents—do not attempt to *force* any religion or dogma (even Pagan) down my childish throat. But that does not mean avoiding the subject entirely. Introduce me to various religions in your neighborhood. Make the rounds of local church services

---

[79] African Studies Association; University of Michigan (2005). *History in Africa.* Vol. 32. p. 119.

[80] *"Religiously Unaffiliated." The Global Religious Landscape. Pew Research Center*: Religion & Public Life. 18 Dec. 2012.

and Sunday schools, and discuss with me the different perspectives of these. Attend interfaith events—take me along—and get to know the respective clergy on a personal basis of mutual respect (if they are willing—which many will be). From my current perspective, of course, I hope you will also introduce me to Paganism, which I hope you will embrace. But if you don't, I'll probably find it on my own…

Today, owing to their experience with the aforesaid abusive churches and cults, many people are so turned off by the very concept of religion that they reject it entirely, proclaiming themselves to be "spiritual" rather than "religious." People confuse religion with "churchianity."

I think this is a sad thing. Spirituality is a personal matter—one's own relation with the sacred, the Divine. It has to do with a personal practice, prayers, devotions, small rituals… But *religion* is what we do in community with others of like mind and heart. And we need that! Religion does not *have* to be dogmatic or abusive—nor should it be.

The word *religion* literally means "re-linking" or "re-connecting." *Religiō* (Latin) is derived from *religare*: *re* ("again") + *ligare* ("bind" or "connect"). Julius Caesar used *religiō* to mean "obligation of an oath" when discussing captured soldiers making an oath to their captors.[81] Roman naturalist Pliny the Elder used the term *religiō* to describe the apparent respect given by elephants to the night sky.[82] Cicero used *religiō* as being related to *cultum deorum* (worship of the gods).[83]

A religion is a body of sacred myths, metaphors, observances and practices in a cultural context, which are designed to connect (re-connect) humanity with Divinity and heal the rift between dichotomized aspects of existence. We observe that the great dilemma and tragic *anomie*[84] of present-day civilization seems at its root to be the alienation caused by splitting apart humanity and Nature, matter and Spirit, light and dark, man and woman, good and evil, Heaven and Earth, sacred and profane. Religions are supposed to *heal* that rift. How are they doing?

---

[81] Caesar, Julius (2007). *"Civil Wars – Book 1." The Works of Julius Caesar: Parallel English and Latin.* Translated by McDevitte, W.A.; Bohn, W.S. Forgotten Books. pp. 377–378.

[82] Pliny the Elder. "Elephants; Their Capacity." *The Natural History, Book VIII.* Tufts University.

[83] Cicero, *De natura deorum.* Book II, Section 8.

[84] The concept of *anomie* in sociology can be defined as a state of normlessness, disorder, or confusion in a society when the standard norms and values are weak or unclear. This lack of social or ethical standards can lead to disconnection, deviance, and social instability among individuals. French sociologist Emile Durkheim introduced it and later expanded it by others like Robert K. Merton. www.simplypsychology.org/anomie.html. Accessed 2/28/2024.

Comparison of Major Religions

Here's a rough general comparison of the five major religions of the world—Christianity, Islam, Hinduism, Buddhism and Judaism:

Christianity[85]

The Christian faith centers on beliefs regarding the birth, life, death and resurrection of Jesus Christ. There are more than 200 Christian denominations in the US and a staggering 45,000 globally, with a total of 2.5 billion adherents. These comprise 31.6% of the world's population, in two main divisions, Catholic and Protestant, which range from the benign (Unity, Quakers, Unitarian-Universalists…) to the malignant (Fudamentalists, Evangelicals, Dominionists, Roman Catholics, cults…). There are also outliers such as Amish, Mormons and Christian Scientists. Each of these considers all the others to be heresies, and the history of Christianity is bloodstained with brutal efforts to exterminate the competition. But they all pretty much agree on the following:

Origin: Founding Prophet, Jesus (Yeshua) of Nazareth (4 BCE-29 CE), believed to be the Son of God and "The Messiah." Following of 12 Apostles. Three years of preaching terminated by execution for blasphemy and sedition. Primary proponent, Paul/Saul of Tarsus (5-65 CE), who coined the terms "Christ, "Christians" and "Christianity."

History: Founded in Jerusalem upon crucifixion of Jesus in 29 CE. Established in Rome by Peter and spread by Paul throughout the Roman Empire. Dispersed after Romans destroyed Jerusalem in 70. In 313 Emperor Constantine lifted the ban on Christianity with the Edict of Milan. In 380, Roman Emperor Theodosius I declared Catholicism the state religion of the Empire, with the Bishop of Rome (the Pope), as the head of the Roman Catholic Church. In 1054, the "Great Schism" split Christianity into Eastern Orthodox and Roman Catholic churches. Crusades to capture Jerusalem (1095-1254). "The Burning Times" (1227-1736). In 1517 Martin Luther initiated the Protestant Reformation in Germany.

Theology: Monotheism: a solitary male Deity, simply called "God"—creator and ruler of the cosmos. Also his son, Jesus, and "the Holy Spirit" (the Trinity); and in Catholicism, Jesus' mother, Mary, and an array of ascended Saints—along with a vast host of Heavenly Angels and Infernal Demons. The antagonist, or anti-God, Satan, also plays a powerful role.

---

[85] Editors, History.com, "Christianity," Updated 8/3/2021; Original: 10/14/2017. www.history.com/topics/religion/christianity

Christians believe God sent his only son, Jesus, as the *Messiah,* to save the world. They believe Jesus was crucified on a cross as a sacrifice for the forgiveness of sins and was resurrected three days after his death before ascending to heaven. Christians believe that Jesus will return to Earth in the "Second Coming" to rule the world for 1,000 years.

Some of the main themes that Jesus taught include: love God; you *are* God; love your neighbor as yourself; love your enemies and forgive those who have wronged you; repent of your sins; do as you would be done by (the Golden Rule); don't be hypocritical; don't judge others; help the less fortunate; and the Kingdom of Heaven is within you.

Sacred Scripture: *Holy Bible. Old Testament* (Jewish), 39 books. *New Testament* (Christian), 27 books, of which the earliest written were the letters of Paul. The first four books—*Matthew, Mark, Luke* and *John*—are known as the *Gospels* ("good news"). Composed sometime between 70-100 CE, these provide accounts of the life and death of Jesus. A final book is *Revelations*—bizarre visions of the end of the world.

Special Practice: Communion—sharing of bread and wine, symbolizing Christ's body and blood, shed in sacrifice to redeem humanity.

Purpose: Personal salvation from "original sin" (disobedience of the mythical progenitors Adam and Eve in eating the forbidden fruit of the Tree of Knowledge of Good & Evil in the Garden of Eden).

Afterlife: Those who believe in Jesus and are favored by God's grace are "saved," and go on to eternal bliss in Heaven; everyone else is condemned to suffer eternal torment in Hell. Catholics have an interim realm called *Limbo* where they await Judgement Day.

Islam[86]

The word *Islam* means "submission" (to the will of God—*Allāh*). Numbering more than two billion, Muslims comprise 25.8% of the world's population, and make up a majority in 49 countries—particularly in the Middle East, Africa and Indonesia. Islam is the world's fastest growing major religion, projected to be the world's largest by the end of this century, due to the relatively young age and high fertility rate of Muslims. Islam is divided into two main branches, *Sunnis* (85-90%) and *Shias* (10-15%). A third tiny branch is called *Ibadism* (~0.08%). There is bitter rivalry among

---

[86] Editors, History.com, "Islam," Updated 10/23/2023; original 1/5/2018. www.history.com/topics/religion/islam

them, and bloody efforts to exterminate each other, as well as rival religions, such as Hindus, Jews and Christians. But they all agree on the following:

Origin: Founding Prophet, Mohammed (570-632 CE), Arabia.

History: In 610 CE Muhammad retreated to a cave near Mecca, where he received the first revelation of the *Quran* from the angel Gabriel. In 622, Muhammad performed the *Hijra* ("emigration") to Medina where he established his authority. By the time he died in 632 (at age 62) Muhammed had united the tribes of Arabia into a single religious polity. However, after his death, bitter wars of succession raged for centuries, and continue to this day. From the 8th-13th centuries, the Islamic Golden Age was a period of scientific, economic and cultural flourishing far surpassing Europe, which was in its Dark Ages, under Church dominion.

Theology: Monotheism (a solitary male Deity, called *Allāh*—creator and ruler of the cosmos). Angels were created to worship God and also to serve in other specific duties such as communicating revelations from God, recording every person's actions, and taking a person's soul at the time of death. Also *Shaitan*—the Moslem version of *Satan,* the Tempter.

Sacred Scripture: The *Quran,* considered to be the verbatim word of Allāh and the unaltered, final revelation. Muslims also believe in previous revelations, such as the *Tawrat* (the Torah), the *Zabur* (Psalms), and the *Injil* (Gospel). Abraham, Moses and Jesus are considered prophets.

Purpose: Islam teaches that everything in the universe was brought into being by God's command, and that the purpose of existence is to worship God/Allāh.

Special Practices: Muslims must pray five times a day, facing Mecca. A pilgrimage to the *Kaaba* (a black meteorite in Mecca), called the "*ḥajj*" is to be done at least once a lifetime by every Muslim with the means to do so during the month of *Dhu al-Hijjah.* Genital mutilation on girls.

Afterlife: There will be a "Final Judgment" wherein the righteous will be eternally rewarded in a heavenly paradise (*jannah*) and the unrighteous will be eternally punished in hell (*jahannam*).

Hinduism[87]

Hinduism is the world's oldest recognized religion, with roots and customs dating back more than 4,000 years. 94% of the world's Hindus live in India.

---

[87] Editors, History.com, "Hinduism," Updated 1/16/2023; original 10/6/2017. www.history.com/topics/religion/hinduism

With 1.2 billion adherents, Hindus comprise 15.1% of the world's population. There are four major sects of Hinduism: *Shaivism, Vaishnava, Shaktism* and *Smarta,* as well as many smaller sects.

Origin: Unlike other religions, Hinduism has no single founder but is instead a fusion of various beliefs over centuries.

History: Around 1500 BCE, the Indo-Aryan people migrated to the Indus Valley, and their language and culture blended with that of the local indigenous people. The "Vedic Period," when the *Vedas* were composed, lasted from about 1500-500 BCE. The Epic, Puranic and Classic Periods took place between 500 BCE-500 CE. The Hindu Medieval Period lasted from about 500-1500 CE.

Theology: Polytheistic, with hundreds of Gods and Goddesses under a primary Trinity of *Brahma* (Creator), *Vishnu* (Preserver) and *Shiva* (Destroyer). Other important deities include *Devi*—the goddess who fights to restore dharma; *Krishna*—god of compassion and love; *Lakshmi*—goddess of wealth and purity; *Saraswati*—goddess of learning; *Kali*—goddess of time; *Ganesha*—elephant god who overcomes obstacles.

Sacred Scripture: The *Vedas* (composed c. 1500 BCE). These are the *Rig Veda, Samaveda, Yajurveda* and *Atharvaveda.* The *Upanishads,* the *Bhagavad Gita,* 18 *Puranas, Ramayana* and *Mahabharata* are also considered important sacred texts in Hinduism.

Purpose: All living creatures have a soul *(atman),* and all are emanations of the supreme cosmic soul of Brahma. Hindus strive to follow the *dharma,* a code of living emphasizing good conduct and morality. The goal is to achieve *moksha,* or salvation, which ends the cycle of rebirths to become part of the absolute soul.

Special Practices: *Puja* (worship). The giving of offerings, such as flowers or oils, to a god or goddess. Many annual festivals. Also, many Hindus make pilgrimages to temples and other sacred sites in India.

Afterlife: Hindus believe in the doctrines of *samsara* (the continuous cycle of life, death, and reincarnation) and *karma* (the universal law of cause and effect).

Buddhism[88]

Buddhism ("enlightenment") was founded more than 2,500 years ago in India. With an estimated 500

---

[88] Editors, History.com, "Buddhism," Updated 9/5/2023; Original: 10/12/ 2017. www.history.com/topics/religion/buddhism

million to one billion followers, Buddhists comprise 6.6% of the world's population. Buddhism has historically been most prominent in East and Southeast Asia, but its influence is growing throughout the West. Today, many forms of Buddhism exist around the world. These include: *Theravada* (Thailand, Sri Lanka, Cambodia, Laos, Burma); *Mahayana* (China, Japan, Taiwan, Korea, Singapore, Vietnam); *Tibetan* (Tibet, Nepal, Mongolia, Bhutan, Russia, northern India); *Zen* ("meditation"); *Nirvana* ("blowing out").

Origin: Founder, Siddhārtha Gautama (the Buddha—"Enlightened One"). (563-483 BCE), born in Nepal.

History: Born as a prince into a wealthy family, Gautama was moved by seeing suffering in the world. After six years of seeking, he found enlightenment while meditating under a Bodhi tree. He spent the rest of his life teaching others how to achieve this spiritual state. After Gautama died his teachings developed into Buddhism. In the 3rd century BCE, the Mauryan Indian emperor Ashoka the Great made Buddhism the state religion of India. Over the next few centuries, the thoughts and philosophies of Buddhists spread widely throughout Asia and became diverse.

Theology: As a non-theistic faith with no deity to worship, Buddhism is often described as a philosophy or moral code rather than an organized religion.

Sacred Scripture: The Buddha's most essential teachings (*dharma*) are known as "The Four Noble Truths." These are: The Truth of suffering (*dukkha*); The Truth of the cause of suffering (*samudaya*); The Truth of the end of suffering (*nirhodha*); The Truth of the Eightfold Path that frees us from suffering (*magga*).

Some of the most important sacred texts are: *Tipitaka,* thought to be the earliest collection of Buddhist writings. *Sutras:* There are more than 2,000 sutras, which are sacred teachings embraced mainly by Mahayana Buddhists. *Book of the Dead:* This Tibetan text describes the stages of death in detail, and the passage through the *Bardos.*

Purpose: Followers of Buddhism focus on achieving "enlightenment"— a state of inner peace and wisdom. Upon reaching this spiritual echelon they attain *nirvana.* The ultimate goal is to no longer reincarnate. Really!

Special Practices: Followers of Buddhism can worship in temples or in their own homes. Buddhist monks, or *bhikkhus,* follow a strict code of conduct, which includes celibacy. *Vesak* is an annual festival commemorating Buddha's birth, enlightenment and death.

Afterlife: As in Hinduism, Buddhists embrace the concepts of karma (the law of cause and effect) and reincarnation (the continuous cycle of rebirth).

Judaism[89]

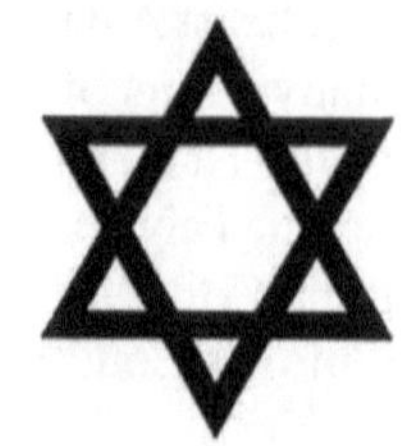

Jews comprise 0.2% of the world's population, about 14 million people. Their influence is far greater than these numbers would suggest, however, as Judaism is the original Abrahamic parent religion of both Christianity and Islam. Most Jews today live in the US and Israel. There are several catgories in Judaism, which include: *Orthodox Judaism,* a diverse sect that includes several subgroups, including *Hasidic Jews.* There is also *Reform Judaism, Conservative, Reconstructionist* and *Humanistic Judaism.*

Origin: According to the *Torah,* God first revealed himself to a Hebrew man named Abraham who became the founder of Judaism.

History: In 1628 BCE, more than 1,000 years after Abraham, the prophet Moses led the Israelites out of Egypt (the *Exodus*) where they had been enslaved for centuries. God revealed his laws, the Ten Commandments, to Moses at Mt Sinai. 40 years later, they invaded Palestine, setting up a Jewish kingdom. Around 1000 BCE King David ruled the Jewish people. His son Solomon built the first holy Temple in Jerusalem, which became the central place of worship for Jews. The kingdom fell apart around 931 BCE and the Jewish people split into two groups: Israel in the North and Judah in the South. In 587 BCE the Babylonians destroyed the first Temple and sent many Jews into exile. A second Temple was built in about 516 BCE but was later destroyed by the Romans in 70 CE, scattering the Jewish people in the *Diaspora* ("scattering"). Throughout history, Jewish people have been persecuted for their religious beliefs. In 1948, in compensation for the Holocaust, by edict of the United Nations Israel officially became an independent Jewish nation.

Theology: Monotheism. Jews believe in one God, named *Yahweh,* who revealed himself through ancient prophets, including Abraham, Isaac, Jacob, Moses, Solomon and others. Jews believe that Yahweh made a special covenant with Abraham and that he and his descendants are "Chosen People" destined to create a great nation. Most Jews believe that their Messiah hasn't yet come—but will one day.

---

[89] Editors, History.com, "Judaism," Updated 8/11/2023; Original: 1/5/2018. www.history.com/topics/religion/judaism

Sacred Scripture: The Jewish sacred text is called the *Tanakh* or the "Hebrew Bible." It includes the same books as the Old Testament in the Christian Bible, but they're arranged in a slightly different order. Around 200 CE, scholars compiled the *Mishnah*—a text that describes and explains the Jewish code of law that was previously orally communicated.

Purpose: Observing the Laws.

Special Practices: Circumcision of all males. No graven images. Worship in religious centers known as *synagogues*. Leaders are called *rabbis* ("teachers"). Celebration of several important days and events in history: *Passover, Rosh Hashanah, Yom Kippur, High Holy Days, Hanukkah, Purim.* From sunset on Friday until sunset on Saturday, *Shabbat* is observed as a day of rest and prayer for Jews, with special ceremonies.

Afterlife: No official dogma. Many believe the soul continues to the afterlife and receives judgment. Some anticipate a resurrection in the Messianic Age—a time known as the "world to come."

Minor Religions

Taoists/Confucians/Chinese traditional religionists comprise 394 million people—5.6% of the world's population:

Confucianism is a system of thought and behavior variously described as a tradition, philosophy, religion, theory of government, or way of life. Confucianism developed from teachings of the Chinese philosopher Confucius (551-479 BCE), during a time referred to as the "Hundred Schools of Thought." His sayings comprise *The Anelects*.

Taoism is variously characterized as both a philosophy and a religion. Taoism emphasizes living in harmony with the *Tao*—the impersonal, enigmatic process of transformation ultimately underlying reality. Despite the popularity of its great classics the *I Ching* and the *Tao Te Ching*, the practice of Taoism has not spread widely. Nonetheless, Taoist ideas and symbols such as *taijitu* have become popular throughout the world through *tai chi, qigong,* and various martial arts.

Sikhism is a monotheistic and panentheistic religion: There exists only one God, who is simultaneously within and all-encompassing. Sikhs comprise 26 million people—0.3% of the world's population. The Sikh homeland is the Punjab state, in India, where Sikhs make up approximately 58% of the population. The basis of Sikhism lies in the teachings of Guru Nanak (1469-1539) and his successors. Sikh ethics emphasize the congruence between spiritual development and everyday moral conduct: *"Truth is the highest virtue, but higher still is truthful living."*

Jainism is an ancient Indian religion that traces its spiritual ideas and history through the succession of 24 *tirthankaras* (supreme preachers of *Dharma)*, with the first believed to have lived millions of years ago, to the 24th *tirthankara* Mahgavira, around 600 BCE. The three main pillars of Jainism are *ahiṃsā* (non-violence), *anekāntavāda* (non-absolutism), and *aparigraha* (asceticism). The function of souls is to help one another. Jainism has around 4.5 million followers (0.05% of the world's population), who reside mostly in India.

Shinto is Japan's indigenous Nature religion, with 4 million adherents—0.05% of the world's population. There is no founder or central authority, with much diversity of belief and practice. Polytheistic and animistic, Shinto revolves around supernatural spirit entities called *kami*, which are believed to inhabit all things, including forces of Nature and prominent landscape locations. *Kami* veneration has been traced back to Japan's Yayoi period, 300 BCE-300 CE.

Zoroastrianism is an Iranian religion based on the teachings of the Iranian prophet *Zoroaster,* also known as *Zarathustra*. About 1000 BCE he founded a monotheistic religion with a dualistic cosmology, predicting the ultimate triumph of good over evil. Zoroastrians worship a supreme benevolent deity of wisdom, *Ahura Mazda*; opposed to Ahura Mazda is *Angra Mainyu,* the adversary of all things good. The world's current Zoroastrian population is estimated at 110,000-120,000 people, with the majority residing in India, Iran, and North America; their number is thought to be declining.

Paganism

Generally ignored in religious surveys, modern Paganism is a revival and reconstruction of ancient Nature religions adapted for the modern world. It is a religion of the living Earth—a theological motif especially appropriate to the Aquarian Age, as Christianity was the dominant religion of the Piscean Age.

The most universal conception of Deity among all Pagans—modern and ancient—is Mother Earth/Mother Nature: *Gaea, Hertha, Terra, Akna, Prithvi, Hòutŭ, Papa, Danu, Ninhursag, Pachamama...* Modern Pagans view humanity as a functional organ within the greater organism of all Life, rather than as something special created separate and "above" the rest of the natural world. Pagans seek not to conquer Nature, but to harmonize and integrate with Her. Paganism should be regarded as "Green Religion," just as we have "Green Politics" and "Green Technology."

The word "Pagan" derives from the Latin *Paganus,* meaning peasant or country dweller. A term of derision among Christians, it has long been used by anthropologists to designate the indigenous folk religions of particular regions and peoples, and by classical scholars to refer to the great ancient pre-Christian civilizations of the Mediterranean area (as in the phrase, "Pagan splendor," often used in reference to Classical Greece). Indeed, the term is commonly applied to all polytheistic non-Abrahamic religions. Paganism is the ancestral religion of all humanity.

Modern Pagans include people identifying as Christo-Pagans, Judeo-Pagans, Buddheo-Pagans, Atheo-Pagans, Witches, Heathens, Hellenes, Khemetics, Druids, Celts, Baltics, Hindus, American Indians, Africans, Polynesians, and countless other cultural and ethnic Traditions.

The basic commitment of modern Paganism is to the re-integration or re-linking of people with ourselves, our fellow humans, and with the whole of living Nature around us. Pagans create no artificial demarcation between the sacred and the secular. To a Pagan, religion is ultimately a whole way of life, not just some acts performed once a week in an authorized ritual. In this sense, Paganism *is* religion; the foundation, ground and source of all we may term "religious" *and* "spiritual."

The liturgical cycle of Paganism revolves around the Wheel of the Year. Rather than commemorating historical events, or the births and deaths of prophets and saints, Pagans throughout the world are united in celebrating the seasons of the natural year: Solstices, Equinoxes, and the cross-quarters between them. These are (dates variable) Ostara (3/21), Beltane (5/1), Litha (6/21), Lughnasdh (8/1), Mabon (9/21), Samhain (11/1) Yule (12/21) and Imbolc (2/1). Many celebrate the phases of the moon.

Paganism is re-emerging today because natural religion is a spontaneous evocation of the spirit of Life, and will inevitably find expression in human cultures. The practices of the ancient Pagans occurred during a different era in culture, when we lived closer to the land and were more directly connected with farming and hunting. Much of what was practiced in those days has been lost, due to millennia of persecutions, from the onset of the Iron Age, through the Inquisition and Witch-burnings, to the present day. We are "remembering and inventing" together.

35. More Magickal Exercises for Teens[90]

By Oberon Zell

 T'S NEVER REALLY TOO EARLY TO START MAGickal training with your Magickal Child. Just pay close attention, and you will know when they are ready for particular lessons. Here are a few from my personal experience:

When I was a boy, I used to practice memorizing the layout of spaces, such as the interior of my house, a stretch of sidewalk, or a familiar part of the woods. Then, while holding that image firmly in my mind, as if it were a map, I would close my eyes and walk through the space, "seeing" and navigating it according to my memory.

As I came to where I visualized various objects should be, I would stop and reach out to touch them. If they weren't where I expected them to be, I would open my eyes, go back to my starting point, and begin over. This was one of my earliest exercises in *visualization,* an essential magickal skill. I recommend you try it...

Here are a few more exercises to practice that will help you develop some of the psychic talents described previously. Don't try these all at once; you don't even have to do all of them. But if you are interested in learning how to do some of these things, and if you have any natural Gifts in these areas, these exercises will help you.

And remember, the more you practice, the better you'll become! Grey Council member Jeff "Magnus" McBride, who is a renowned professional Conjurer in Las Vegas, has a particularly awesome trick with cards that he has practiced every single day for over fifty years. As you might imagine, he's become *very* good at it!

I am phrasing these exercises for the child, but the whole idea here is for you, as the parent, to work together with your Magickal Child, and you both will develop your skills!

Body Control

Take every opportunity to practice body control in your everyday life. If you feel tired, force yourself to go on just a little longer before resting. If you feel hungry, don't eat for an extra half hour. If you feel thirsty, don't drink for awhile. Practice walking a balance beam. Take gymnastics. Do

---

[90] Zell, Oberon, *Grimoire for the Apprentice Wizard.* New Page Books, 2004. Pp. 32-38.

handstands, somersaults and backflips. Learn to juggle balls and spin fire. Become a good dancer.

When I was a boy in school, I would practice holding my breath, using the big clock on the wall to time myself. I practiced constantly, and eventually I got so I could go four minutes without breathing. As I was still growing at the time, these exercises increased my lung capacity tremendously. 50 years later, I could still swim underwater the entire length of an Olympic-size swimming pool, and I could stay down for longer than anybody else when diving for abalone off the Califia Coast.

Another kind of body control is mastering your facial muscles. As a boy, I practiced for hours in front of mirror to learn how to raise and lower my eyebrows independently, wiggle my ears, dilate my nostrils, achieve certain emotional expressions, etc. All good actors practice in this way, and you should, too.

Meditation

Meditation is the most important foundational skill to learn, as it will help you to be able to do many other things. I'm sure you have seen Masters meditating in movies, especially those involving martial arts. What you are trying to do in meditation is to completely "center" yourself into a still and focused place where you are perfectly balanced and in tune with your body and your surroundings. From this center point, you will then be able to move in any direction in mind and body—even through time and between dimensions.

Sit or lie in a comfortable position and relax your body completely. Then observe yourself carefully to note any muscles which start to become restless. Allow such muscles to consciously relax and do the same for any other groups of muscles—but don't fall asleep! Complete and total relaxation is your goal. Use a timer, starting off with five minutes the first day, then increase your meditation period another five minutes each day until you can completely relax for half an hour.

Seeing & Reading Auras

When you have become skilled at meditation and visualization, you will be ready to learn to see *Auras*.

Auras are the fields of *biomagnetic energy* which emanate from and envelop all living things. Like the Earth Herself, each of us is a living field generator. Since we're not spinning on our axis like the Earth, our field poles are not generated by rotation, but are more like those of a magnet. One pole, called the *Crown Chakra*, is at the top of our heads, right at the juncture of the three large skull bones (frontal and parietals) that come together there (when we are babies, this point is actually an open hole!). The opposite pole—called the *Root Chakra*—is at the base of our spine, right at the tip of our tailbone.

Just like the Earth's *magnetosphere,* with its Van Allen Belts, our Auras form several layers, based on energy levels. The first layer, extending about an inch out from our skin, is called the *Etheric Body.* Because it is the densest layer, it is also the easiest to learn to see. The next layer is called the *Astral Body*, and it extends another several inches further. Beyond the Astral body are the *Mental* and *Spiritual* bodies. These are very high-energy and elastic, and their limits can vary under differing circumstances.

Perhaps you know of the *Aurora Borealis,* or "Northern Lights" that fill the skies of northern countries with brilliant, shimmering ethereal "curtains," "spears," and dancing "flames" of rainbow-colored light. Around the South Pole, these are called *Aurora Australis,* or "Southern Lights." These awe-inspiring displays are caused by the ionization (stripping away the electrons) of particles from the Solar Wind as they are sucked into the circular "event horizons" of the Earth's magnetic field around the magnetic poles. This is just like what happens inside a fluorescent light, including a "black light."

Your Etheric Body, then, is equivalent to the Earth's Auroras. And if you learn how to look for it, can be just as visible. Here's how to see auras:

Ⅲagickal Exercise: Seeing Auras

Have a friend sit in front of a blank wall or curtain—something tan, beige or off-white is best. Have the lighting be low, with the light source out of your view (a few candles can work well). Sit about ten feet back, settle yourself into a light meditative state, and stare blankly at your friend's "third eye"—right between the eyebrows. As you do so, open your eyes wide and let them go into a soft focus, as if you are actually focusing on a spot about half-way between you. (You may find this easier to do by hanging a white thread from the ceiling at this distance, and focusing on it.) Breathe smoothly and maintain your off-focus. After a bit, you will begin to see a clear light outlining your friend's head, as if they were glowing softly. But if you shift your focus to try and see it clearer, it will disappear. The trick is to not look directly *at* the aura, but rather catch it at the edges of your vision.

(The aura around the head is called the *Nimbus;* around the whole body it is called the *Aureole.*)

Practice this awhile until you can do it easily. Then try the same thing under differing lighting, different backgrounds, and with different people. Eventually, you will be able to see auras around anyone—in school, on the bus, in restaurants and theatres. And when you can see auras around people, you will be able to see them also around pets, plants, and especially trees (which have enormous auras!).

> **NOTE:** *Don't feel bad if you simply cannot manage to "see" these auras, no matter how much you try. Just as some people are color-blind, or tone-deaf (as I am), we may develop some senses more strongly than others. After all, what we sense and experience really occurs in our brains, not actually in our eyes, ears, etc. Just as the Marvel hero Daredevil, although blind to sight, developed sonar hearing in compensation, you may find that you can sense auras in other ways—"feeling" them, perhaps, or "hearing" a hum around people...*

What you will have learned to perceive in this way is the Etheric aura. As your perceptions improve, you can also learn to detect the energy that radiates into the Astral Body and beyond. You may be able to see it flowing, ebbing, wavering and shimmering like the Earth's Aurora. With practice, you may become able to see colors, which can indicate a person's emotional or physical condition. Any state of the individual's being causes reactions in the aura. Emotional states will primarily affect the color. Physical conditions not only affect color, but also cause peculiarities in the patterns of the aura, such as ragged edges or holes over injuries or sore spots. Learning to see these patterns will be of great use if you become a Healer.

> **NOTE:** *Seeing the colors of auras takes considerably more skill than merely perceiving a glowing light around someone. And such colors, when they are perceived, will be very individual to the perceiver. You and a friend may both learn to see aura colors, but they may seem to be different to each of you. This is normal. With time and practice, you will learn your own system of what these colors mean to you.*

Magickal Exercises:
Controlling your Aura

Seeing the auras of others is a passive exercise. Now here are some exercises for you to actively expand and contract your own aura.

Hold your hand out in front of you, back towards you and fingers spread wide, as if you were pushing something away. Use the same technique you have just learned to see the aura of your hand and fingers. Now start breathing intensely, rapidly in and out, through your nose. Without changing your position, tense your muscles, and stare at your aura as if your eyes could emit laser beams. As if you are turning up a burner on the stove, focus your intention on "pumping up" your aura, so that it seems to "burn" brighter and brighter. Visualize the auras lengthening from your fingertips, extending like the flames of a blowtorch as you level your hand and point your fingers away. Then, when you have extended them as far as you can, suck in a deep breath, and retract them back to the normal glow as you slowly close your fingers into a loose fist. Practice this over and over.

If you have friends to work with, you should each take turns practicing pumping up, extending and retracting your auras while the other watches. This will help each of you learn to both see and control your auras.

Tractor Beams and Repulsor Beams: When you have practiced this technique enough to get good at it, you will be ready to try projecting psychic *tractor beams* and *repulsor beams*, like in *Star Trek*. It's just a matter of extending and retracting your aura. As you forcefully extend it, use it to push against (repulse) anything before it. And as you retract it, use it to suck in (attract) stuff in the same way. Also, for practice, try just reaching out with your aura and "tapping" someone on the shoulder; see if you can get them to turn around!

Here are my favorite aura exercises:

Candle flames: Light a candle in a darkened room, and practice using your auric tractor and repulsor beams to affect the flame. Make it flicker, flare up, or die down. As you get better at this, keep moving the candle further and further away from you, until you can affect the flame from across the room.

Smoke-Weaving: I attend quite a few gatherings and drum circles where the campfire is the center of all activity. Around such campfires, the smoke can often become a problem as it drifts into our faces. When the smoke begins to drift to my side of the fire, I use both hands to weave and shape it away from me, and to direct it straight up. To do this, I spread all my fingers, extending their auras. Like a potter shaping clay on a wheel into a tall vase, I wave my finger auras against each wisp of smoke, brushing, patting, smoothing and redirecting its flow. This can become like dancing. And I have a policy about this: anytime anyone notices what I'm doing, and asks me about it, I show them how. Most people, I've found, can learn this fairly easily.

Cloud-Busting: Large-scale weather-working should not be done casually, as there can be unforeseen consequences. But I've found that small-scale cloud-busting is pretty harmless, so I will explain it here. If it's a cloudy day and you'd like it to clear up, say, for a picnic, the first thing is to find some little patch of blue sky somewhere (this is called "sailor's breeches")—or even a place where the cloud cover seems a bit less solid. Reach toward that weak spot in the clouds with both hands, and visualize extending your aura as far as you can in a long repulsor beam. It may take years of practice to be able to reach it all the way up to the clouds, but it can be done. Hold your hands back-to-back, fingers extended, then "pry" the clouds apart as if they were piles of cotton right in front of you. As the clouds open, and the blue patch becomes larger, just keep pushing the edges of the opening wider until the sun shines through.

Shields up! You can also learn to "harden" the outer shell of your auric field into a psychic shield. This is done in pretty much the same way as projecting an auric repulsor field. But instead of making it into a single tight beam, move your hands, palms flattened and fingers spread wide, up, down, and all around your body at arms' length, while visualizing that you are shaping and pressing against the inside of an impenetrable "Teflon-coated" shell all around yourself. Like the Earth's Van Allen Belts, this shell will protect you from any incoming psychic energy—and it can even be developed into a "cloaking field" to make you invisible.

Cloaking: Psychic invisibility does not mean that you can stand in the middle of a room jumping up and down and waving your arms and no one can see or photograph you. Being invisible means that you become so inconspicuous that people simply do not notice that you are there at all. Their gaze will pass right over you, sliding off your aura like it was Teflon, or reflected elsewhere as a mirror. Afterwards, they will not remember your having been present. In addition to "hardening" your auric shell into a cloaking field, there are two opposite tricks of invisibility that Wizards use; both involve your *gaze*.

The first works best with total strangers, as on the street or in a crowd. In this trick, you gaze intently at the other person, locking eyes briefly with them. Usually they will blink and look elsewhere almost instantly just to avoid your gaze. And as soon as they do, drop your eyes and turn away, and you will become invisible to them. They simply will have erased you from their mind.

The second trick of invisibility is just the opposite, though it also works best in a crowd—like at a party. If there is someone who knows you whom you don't want to see you, the most important thing is to not let them catch your eye. Look anywhere else, but avoid looking at them, or even closely enough where they can see your eyes. With your cloaking field up, you can slip right past them and they'll never notice you were there. When I do this, I say very quietly, *"These aren't the Druids you're looking for."*

Psychokinesis

When I was a boy, I read about people who could move things around by the power of their minds (called *psychokinesis*) and I determined that I was going to learn to do this too. I practiced over and over with flipping coins and tossing dice. I would hold the coin or die with the face I wanted up, and stare hard at it until that face was burned into my mind. I always chose the "head" on the coin, and the six on the die. Then, I would hold that image focused in my mind, and repeat the word "heads" or "sixes" silently to myself as I tossed the coin or die. Eventually, over several years, I got quite good at this. So good, in fact, that my younger brother and sister refused to toss a coin or play any games involving dice with me! They insisted I "cheated." But I'd practiced long and hard to develop this skill, just like my brother practiced shooting baskets.

However, there is great wisdom in the Hogwarts prohibition against using Magick around Muggles—especially to gain an advantage over them. If you do, they may come to resent you, and make life difficult for you. This sort of behavior has gotten people burned at the stake! For many beginners, the impulse to "be powerful" often interferes with ever getting a true handle on what power actually is, and how to use it wisely or well. Never forget the super-hero's credo: "With great power comes great responsibility." (Stan Lee—*Spider Man*)

ῌagickal Exercises: Psychokinesis

Here are a few more little exercises you can try to develop your psychokinetic abilities. Remember, practice is everything!

Spinners: Spinners are very easily made. Take a small piece of paper, about two inches square, and fold it in half both ways, so it is only one inch square. Then unfold it and refold it diagonally from corner-to-corner both ways. Open it out and re-shape it along the folds with the diagonal folds high and the cross folds low, like the picture.

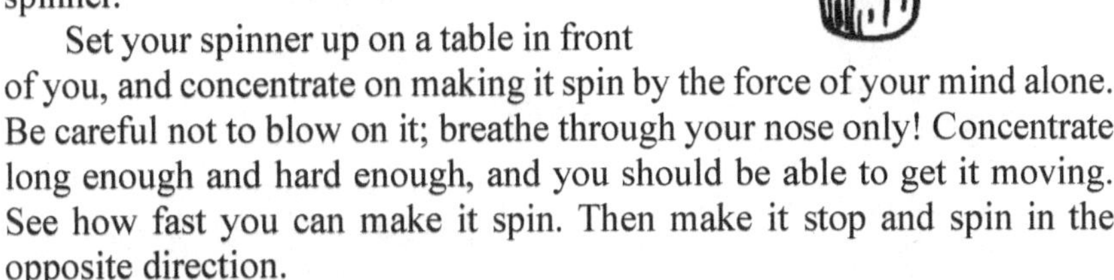

Now get a bottle with a cork in it (like a wine bottle) and stick a sewing needle eye-end into the cork, with the point up. Balance your folded paper on the point of the needle so it spins freely. This is your spinner.

Set your spinner up on a table in front of you, and concentrate on making it spin by the force of your mind alone. Be careful not to blow on it; breathe through your nose only! Concentrate long enough and hard enough, and you should be able to get it moving. See how fast you can make it spin. Then make it stop and spin in the opposite direction.

Candles: Just as above in the aura exercises, light a candle and try to make it flicker, flare up, or die down by the power of your mind alone. This is the basis of *Pyrokinesis* ("fire-moving"). Some few who become highly skilled at this can actually light a fire this way!

Plasma Generators: These are high-voltage generators used to create electrical sparks. *Plasma*—which consists of ionized gas (in which the atoms have been stripped of electrons)—is the fourth *state* of matter (the other three being solid, liquid and gas). This is the same stuff as in the Earth's auroras and the Sun's *corona.* Plasma generators are used in plasma balls—those clear globes that house little electrical storms and are often found in trendy gadget stores like Spenser's. I highly recommend getting one of these things—they are both very cool Wizard balls (like a *Palantir*), and useful devices for developing and honing your psychic skills. Make sure the one you get has a sliding scale for variable settings.

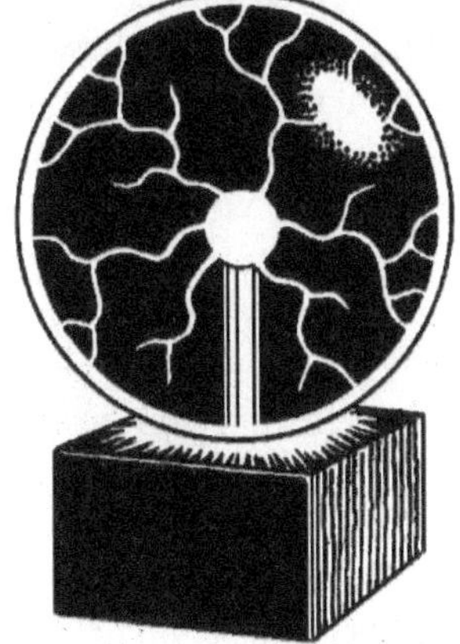

In a darkened room, set your plasma ball on a table, at a low enough setting that there are no lightning bolts—just a faint glowing cloud of sparkling octarene-colored plasma. Now bring one finger slowly up to the glass until a single electrical bolt arcs from the generator to the glass. This will indicate that you have the right setting.

The exercise here is to focus your attention on the plasma ball to make electrical bolts come towards you over a distance. Hold your face about a foot from the plasma ball, keep your hands out of the way, and "think" a bolt of lightning into hitting the glass aimed straight for your "3rd eye" (the center of your forehead). See how often you can call these bolts forth to you. Now the really fun part of this exercise is when you get someone else to sit on the opposite side and do exactly the same thing. You can have a little contest to see who can bring the most bolts to their side!

When you touch the glass with a finger, or the palm of your hand, you will notice a radiance around it, like an aurora. This is called a *Kirlian field,* and is a kind of way of making part of your aura visible—the way iron filings make a magnetic field visible.

Tubiflex worms: *Tubiflex worms* (also called "sludge worms") are commonly sold in pet shops as live food for tropical fish. These tiny thin worms are red because their blood, 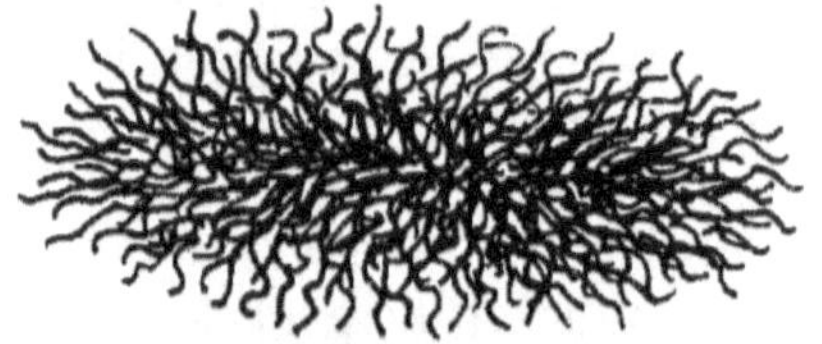 like that of mammals, contains iron-rich hemoglobin. Because hemoglobin can hold more oxygen than the body fluids of most pond animals, tubiflex worms can live in water that does not have much oxygen. Tubiflex worms live packed together in a mass, make tubes in the mud, and spend all their time eating muck with their heads stuck in the bottom of the pond and their tails waving above in the water. If part of a worm is eaten or broken off, it can regrow that part.

Buy an once or so of live tubiflex worms at your neighborhood pet store, and dump them into a round, shallow glass bowl of water, like a punchbowl. Don't use city water, as it will be treated with chemicals that will harm the worms. Well water is fine, as is bottled water or (best) pond water. The worms will stick together in a single squirming mass.

Because of the high concentration of iron in their blood, tubliflex worms are particularly sensitive to electromagnetic fields. Try moving a magnet around the outside of the bowl, and watch how the worms react. You will find you can affect them with the magnet, just as if the worms were iron filings. But this squirmy-wormy mass can also be manipulated psychically! Concentrate on the mass of worms, just as with the plasma, and form it into a ball, a donut, a cross, a star—even send out tentacles and extensions in different directions. You will be amazed at how responsive the worms can be to your thoughts.

> **NOTE:** *If you want to keep your tubiflex worms more than a few days, you will need to provide them some food. They don't eat much. A ½ teaspoon of muck from a fish or duck pond, a horse trough, a fish tank, or even a bit of garden dirt will serve. And when you are done with your worms, you should release them into a pond—or feed them to your fish.*

Telepathy & Clairvoyance

It is very difficult to read a human mind. Most humans are thinking about so many things at any given moment that it is almost impossible to pick out one stream in the flood.

Animal minds are different. Far less cluttered. Carnivore minds are easiest of all, especially before meals. Colors don't exist in the mental world, but, if they did, a hungry carnivore mind would be hot and purple and sharp as an arrow. And herbivore minds are simple, too—coiled silver springs, poised for flight.

An ant has an easy mind to read. There's just one stream of big simple thoughts: Carry, carry, Bite, Get Into The Sandwiches, Carry, Eat. Something like a dog is more complicated—a dog can be thinking several thoughts at the same time.

But a human mind is a great sullen lightning-filled cloud of thoughts, all of them occupying a finite amount of brain processing time. Finding whatever the owner thinks *they're thinking in the middle of the smog of prejudices, memories, worries, hopes and fears is almost impossible.*

But enough people thinking much the same thing can *be heard...*[91]

The first Gift I discovered as a child was that of Telepathy. I could often "hear" voices in my head—most commonly, the thoughts behind conversations. Sometimes when people were talking to me I could not even distinguish what was coming from their mouth, or what was coming from their minds. When I was very young, before starting school, I lived in a big Victorian house with my mother, my aunt, and my grandmother. My grandfather had died right about the time I was conceived (in fact, I was really him reincarnated), and my father was in the South Pacific fighting World War II. So my whole world revolved around these three women. And I heard their thoughts just as clearly as their words. But I had no way of knowing there was anything unusual in this; I thought everybody communicated this way.

One night, after I had gone upstairs to bed, I woke up with my head full of noisy voices. I got out of bed and crept to the stairwell, where I saw that the big living room was full of people; my folks were having a

---

[91] Pratchett, Terry, *Witches Abroad;* HarperTorch, 1991. pp. 150-51; 186-97.

party. I had never heard so many voices all talking at once, and it seemed overwhelmingly loud to me. So I cried out, "Be *QUIET!*" And as all heads turned to me there on the stairs, behind the banister, I saw that all their mouths had stopped moving. But their voices seemed even louder than before; I was still hearing their thoughts! I clapped my hands over my ears, ran upstairs to my bed, and hid under the covers. Eventually I was able to sleep. And when I woke, I no longer heard people's thoughts as voices in my head.

Over the years, I sometimes had brief "flashes" of spontaneous telepathic communication—especially in romantic situations. But something in my mind had acted to protect me, and "shut off" that open gateway that had allowed the thoughts of others to just come pouring uncontrollably into my head.

As a teenager, I heard about scientific experiments in telepathy that were being conducted by the Rhine Institute at Duke University. Remembering my earlier experiences, I set out to duplicate these experiments to recover my childhood talent.

Ṁagickal Exercises: Telepathy & Clairvoyance

Thought transference actually occurs more commonly than most people realize. How many times have you found yourself talking with someone, and one or the other of you will say: "That's just what I was about to say!" Or you'll be thinking or talking about someone, and the phone rings, and it's them. My late wife, Morning Glory—who was a famous Witch and Enchantress—and I often heard ourselves saying the exact same words at the exact same moment from opposite sides of a crowded room. And people would go: "Wooo—stereo Zells!"

Two of the experiments developed by the Rhine Institute are fairly easy to do, and I recommend you try them with your child. If you do them often enough, your performance will improve with practice.

Zener cards: Zener Cards were developed in the late 1920s through a collaboration of Dr. Karl Zener (Duke University) and J.B. Rhine (Harvard). Zener Cards are well suited to developing and experimenting with psychic skills. They are like psychic exercise equipment. There are five different standard symbols in a deck of Zener Cards, and five cards of each symbol for a total of 25 cards per deck. To make your own set, copy these cards onto card stock and cut them out. Make 5 sets. You will also need to make recording charts, numbered 1-25, with two spaces after each number: one for the sender, and one for the receiver.

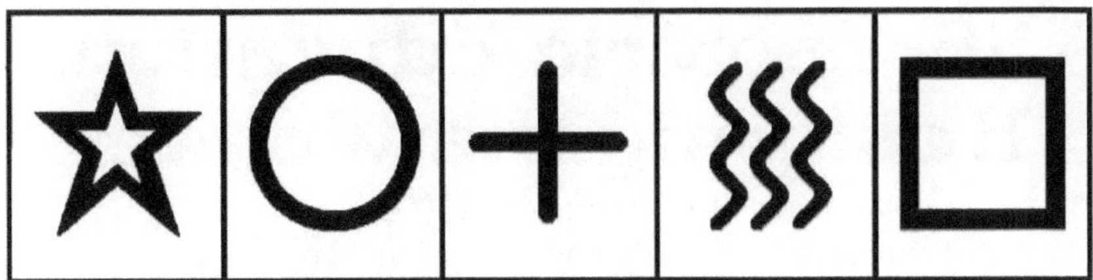

Sit in a quiet room out of direct view of your partner. One of you (the sender) shuffles the deck and focuses on each card for a few moments, writing it down on the chart. The other person (the receiver) says which symbol they sense the sender is focusing on. The sender should then right that response next to the first. The sender should not tell the receiver whether they are right or wrong. Do this little exercise often, and keep records. Over time, you may find that one of you is a better sender and the other a better receiver.

"Far-Seeing" Drawings: In a similar manner to using Zener cards, try transmitting drawings by telepathy. Laboratory experiments using this technique were called "Far-Seeing," and they were used to train spies! To do this, you and your friend should be in separate rooms or even separate houses (you can keep in touch by phone or computer). Each of you should be sitting at a desk, in a quiet room, with a pad of drawing paper and pencil or charcoal. One of you (the sender) will draw a simple picture of anything you want (tree, house, person, animal, whatever…). Draw it with your *left hand*, and concentrate strongly on the image as you draw it. At the same time, the other person (the receiver) should relax, close their eyes, and allow an image to form in their mind. Then, after a few moments, the receiver should draw whatever they think of—also with their left hand. Then you should take turns and switch. Later, compare notes and see how close you've come; you might be surprised! As with all these exercises, practice will improve your performance.

Songs: A similar exercise can be done with songs. To do this you really do need to be in separate houses. As with the drawings, the sender should think of a catchy popular tune, chant or jingle known to both of you, and start singing it. The best kind are those ones you just can't get out of your head (they're called "Pepsis" because they're used for advertising). Then the receiver opens their mind to let the song in—and after awhile you check with each other and see how you did.

36. Esoteric Education: Restoring the Wonder

By Oberon Zell (2005)
Founder & first Headmaster, Grey School of Wizardry

*"With the explosion of information especially, a transformation
of publishing and information distribution that compares only to
the invention of the printing press, one is tempted to wonder
how long it will take for the people to realize how bad a deal
public education really is. In the near future, people will see that
the failing pubic school system can easily be replaced with a
more customized, and far less-expensive system of learning."*
~Eric Garris, "The Internet vs. the State"[92]

NCE, NOT TOO LONG AGO…EDUCATION WAS CON-
sidered a rare privilege to be earned or granted, a goal to
achieve, a dream to fulfill. Schools were seen as reposito-
ries of esoteric knowledge that would unlock the keys to
the universe, and the secrets to success. Scholars were held
in the highest esteem by all members of society. What we take for granted
today was once considered a cherished opportunity to be strived for at any
cost. Consider this: less than a century ago, women in traditional Eastern
European Jewish culture (which prides itself on education and scholar-
ship) were not even allowed to learn how to read! And many women today
in traditional Moslem and Hindu societies are still not allowed the "lux-
ury" of literacy. Indeed, throughout most of human history, education—
even the basic ability to read—was limited to a small and privileged class
of literati. Now, at least in America, it is available to everyone, and anyone.

Did you know that 60% of American high school graduates cannot
find their own country on an unmarked globe of the world? These same
graduates believe that cave men lived with dinosaurs! In fact, according
to the National Science Foundation, one in five American adults thinks
the sun revolves around the Earth![93] Indeed, there is a deliberate anti-in-
tellectual and anti-educational current running through our entire country,
which is even influencing the outcome of national elections. Pop Culture

---

[92] From a talk delivered at the Burton S. Blumert Conference on Gold, Freedom, and
Peace. Nov. 2, 2005. http://www.lewrockwell.com/orig/garris3.html

[93] Jacoby, Susan, "Dumbing Down of America," *Santa Rosa Press-Democrat*, Feb. 24,
2008.

has long supported disdain for education. How did a terminally depressing song—"The Wall," by Pink Floyd, with the droning refrain, *"We don't need no education"*—become the hit of a decade, and the theme song of an entire generation?

I have always had an obsessive love of learning. I want to know everything! As soon as I learned to read, at about age two, I began to devour every book and magazine in the house. When I visited friends, I'd spend my time just reading the books on their shelves. My reading compulsion even extended to the fine print on cereal boxes! The first time I saw the inside of a library, I was agonizingly torn between sheer delight at the vast number of books available to me, and utter dismay at the realization that I could never possibly read all of them. My own personal library today has several thousand treasured volumes—many of them dog-eared from frequent consultation. When I'm not actually writing, I'm usually reading.

Unlike many of my friends when I was growing up, I passionately loved school. I could hardly wait 'til summer vacation ended and I could return to classes, armed with fresh questions for my teachers from my summer of reading everything I could get my hands on about everything that interested me.

When I wasn't actually in class, I spent as much time as possible in the public library, and was on a first-name basis with the librarian, who would always set aside for me new arrivals in my favorite subjects. In high school, I served as a teacher's assistant in biology, edited the school literary journal, published a student newspaper, was very active in the Latin and chess clubs, and had a major role in every school play. And I continued most of these activities and involvements all through college.

I have spent most of my life in learning and teaching. When in college I read A.S. Neil's *Summerhill*, B.F. Skinner's *Walden Two*, and learned of Maria Montessori's schools. After receiving a BA from Westminster College in Pre-Med, Psychology, Sociology and Anthropology, I shifted my interests to Developmental Psychology and Education, entering the graduate program in Clinical Psychology at Washington University, and earning a Teacher's Certificate at Harris Teacher's College. My first post-graduate job was with the newly-launched Head Start program and the Human Development Corporation, and I served as a public school teacher and school & family counselor for several decades.

Student Attitudes

Oprah Winfrey said this about why she chose to build a new school in South Africa rather that in the US: *"I became so frustrated with visiting inner-city schools that I just stopped going. The sense that you need to learn just isn't there. If you ask the kids what they want or need, they will say an iPod or some sneakers.* "[94]

From my own observations growing up in public schools, college and university, and from working many years as a teacher, one simple fact became overwhelmingly clear at all levels: Most students hated school! They only attended because it was compulsory. They did everything they could to get out of actually studying, from watching TV and not doing homework as kids, to partying all night in college. Their interests centered around their friends and relationships, not around actually learning anything. Many of them barely scraped by, some by cheating (often in elaborately creative ways), and many simply dropped out as soon as they could.

So what was wrong with all these U.S. schools? How is it possible that generations of students could come away from classes in history, science, geography, literature, foreign languages, and mathematics feeling bored out of their skulls—believing that these were terminally dull subjects with no relevance whatsoever to anything they considered important in life? How could such fascinating studies as natural history, evolution, astronomy, cosmology, geology, archaeology, paleontology, anthropology, psychology, sociology, biology, and all those other wonderful "logies" fail to engage the interest of young minds—even in the passionate era of the '60s?

How can students and their families sit idly by, unprotesting, as "controversial" books and essential topics of study are systematically removed from their school libraries and classrooms by illiterate religious fundamentalists and corrupt politicians?

In lamenting the sorry state of our public schools, and the many failures in our American educational system, analysts have blamed just about everything—television, video games, teachers, parents, the home, society, politics, lack of funding, and "the younger generation." And all of these may indeed be factors. But few seem to have considered that perhaps the entire concept of education as it is presented today may be fundamentally at fault.

And I think this is the core of the problem. School and education is no longer viewed by students, or the public, as something special, something to aspire to. Learning is seen more as a distasteful and onerous drudgery, akin to working in a factory (as in that Pink Floyd song). Something one *must* do, perhaps, but hardly as something one would *want* to do. This is clearly, an untenable situation for public education.

---

[94] *Newsweek,* Jan. 8. 2007.

Harry Potter and the X-Men

And then (drum roll) along came Harry Potter! After numerous rejections by short-sighted publishers who couldn't imagine any reader interested in stories taking place in a school, Scholastic Inc. had the good sense to publish J.K. Rowling's delightful Harry Potter series. And the rest is history. The Harry Potter books became the biggest-selling books of all time. With seven novels and eight movies, and more toys, games, clothes, ancillary books, theme parks and other tie-ins and spin-offs than you can wave a wand at, Harry Potter is the greatest literary phenomenon ever known!

And here's the most important thing: These books are being most eagerly read by *kids!* Clearly something is happening here, and understanding it may be the key to an entirely new concept in education.

Every kid (and many adults as well!) who reads Harry Potter wishes more than anything that they could attend Hogwarts School of Witchcraft and Wizardry. The very fact of its exclusivity makes it irresistible, to say nothing of the lure and wonder of forbidden and arcane knowledge it promises. Magic and Mysteries, spellcraft and sorcery, hidden history, secret societies, wands and wortcunning, bedknobs and broomsticks, bell, book, and candle, things that go bump in the night…everything that the mundane ("muggle," in Rowling's parlance) world doesn't know about, or believe in. Hogwarts epitomizes all the reasons why Halloween is the most popular holiday of the year for many kids and grown-ups. Embracing the dark, rather than fearing it, is exhilarating and liberating!

Consider also the enduring popularity of the *X-Men* comics, Marvel's best-selling series—which began publishing in 1962, and spawned an on-going animated TV series and several feature-length movies. As with the Harry Potter stories, the X-Men saga centers around a very special school for mutant misfits with various uncanny abilities and powers: "Professor Charles Xavier's School for Gifted Children."

Mystique

Young people find the lure of secret societies and esoteric associations irresistible. They yearn to be on the "inside" of an exclusive group, to access forbidden knowledge and arcane secrets unknown to their parents and their contemporaries. "Knowledge is power," they know, and "with great power comes great responsibility." The enormous appeal of the classical "Hero's Quest" in literature and films bespeaks its intense relevance to every adolescent. They identify with Harry Potter; Frodo Baggins; Luke Skywalker; Dorothy Gale; Peter Parker, Billy Batson—and every other young hero and heroine of every story, as they discover who they truly are, and what they are truly here for. For the Quest is always and ultimately to discover one's own life mission and destiny.

And every Hero's Quest story begins with a wise mentor figure—the "Wizard"—imparting crucial knowledge to the young hero that he or she must know in order to fulfill their destiny. And this is where the idea of a very special and exclusive school of mystical knowledge and arcane wisdom enters the picture.

> One of the most learned men of all time, Confucius (551-479 BCE), became the first private teacher in history. Such was his reputation that people sought him out to teach their sons. Confucius took any student eager to learn, and along with the regular subjects, taught his personal wisdoms on developing responsibility and moral character through discipline.
>
> In ancient Greece, (long acknowledged as the seat of philosophy and wisdom), the value of educating their children was recognized very early on, with some households engaging their own teachers. Through the first centuries CE, Roman families often had educated slaves to teach their children.[95]

The first known school of *philosophy* (meaning "love of wisdom") was Plato's Academy in Athens, founded in 385 BCE. Plato was Socrates' greatest student. Later, in 335 BCE, Aristotle opened his "Peripatetic" philosophical school at the Athens Lyceum. More "Mystery Schools" were later founded by Pythagoras and other great philosophers.

In fact, all early schools and academies were really exclusive "Mystery Schools," and in that very mystique lay their appeal.

> In the Middle Ages, the Roman Catholic Church took charge of teaching the sons of nobility, entrusting that charge to monasteries or specially designated learning "centres." Many of these centres evolved into the distinguished learning institutions of today, including Cambridge University, whose first college, St. Peter's, was founded in 1284.
>
> With the establishment of higher learning in the early 1700s, the curriculum of college preparatory and universities broadened considerably. However not all things were equal inside the schoolroom. In 1749, Ben Franklin's concept of an academy of learning consisted of an English school and a Classical school. The Latin master had a title, and the English master had none. The Latin master made twice the salary, and the English master had twice the students.

---

[95] Teaching Through the Ages: http://historyeducationinfo.com/edu1.htm

> High school, originally known as "terminal" school, came into existence in 1821, in Boston, for boys 12 years and older. Once more, law entered the educational fray, dictating that towns of over 500 families must have a high school with the prescribed curriculum. Towns with over 4,000 inhabitants were required to teach Latin and Greek, as well as other extra subjects.
>
> Agriculture boarding schools enjoyed a very brief existence in the 1820s and 30s, having been established in the country to fulfill the needs of "idle and morally exposed" children from the city.
>
> At the beginning of the 20th century, parents and the general public began to demand more practical and useful curriculums, and in so doing, may have helped elevate teaching to a respectable profession.[96]

Unfortunately, this demand and trend towards a universal education diluted the mystique of learning itself. When a thing is available to everyone and mandated by law, it ceases to be regarded as something special; it becomes "common." What is needed today, I believe, is to restore the wonder and mystique that once surrounded the very idea of education.

The *Grimoire* and the Grey School

In 2002, I convened the Grey Council—an assembly of two dozen respected and learned mages and sages, elders and teachers. Council members follow many different paths, but all hope to spark the imagination, beauty, and power of the minds of seekers everywhere. We worked together over the year 2003 to weave our best lessons into the *Grimoire for the Apprentice Wizard*[97]. It was specifically designed for all the Harry Potter readers who might want to seek further, and explore the genuine "Wisdom of the Ages," as once taught in the ancient Mystery Schools, and imbedded in traditional "Classical Education" into more recent times. For *wizard* literally means "wise one," and wizardry is, pure and simply, wisdom. Much like the term *philosopher* means "lover of wisdom." And it certainly seems that the present world could use a great deal more wisdom!

The *Grimoire,* however, was only the first phase of a long-range Vision to make available the Wisdom of the Ages for a new generation and a new Millennium. It is both an essential handbook of Apprentice-level Wizardry (like the *Boy Scout Handbook*) and a basic textbook for a full seven-year academic curriculum of Wizardly studies. Thus, its lessons begin very simply and become more complex as students advance.

---

[96] Teaching Through the Ages; *op cit.*
[97] New Page Books, 2004

The book was an instant success, encouraging our publishers, New Page Books, to commission several sequels and spin-offs, of which five have since been published. The next phase of the Vision was to establish an on-line School of Wizardry to serve as a larger context for the *Grimoire* and wisdom teachings, and where all the readers whose appetites had been whetted could go for further study.

And so, on August 1, 2004, the Grey School of Wizardry opened its virtual doors. Designed for students of all ages over 11, the Grey School provides an extensive seven "year-level" program of studies, at an Apprenticeship level. Graduates are certified as "Journeyman Wizards."

The Grey School was incorporated as a non-profit educational institution in the State of California on March 14, 2005. We received our 501(c)(3) Federal tax exemption as an educational and charitable organization on Sept. 20, 2007, effective retroactively to March 14, 2005.

Curriculum

Taking the *Grimoire*'s basic curriculum as a starting point, the Grey School of Wizardry offers additional classes, lessons and practical exercises, links to other websites with specialized materials, etc., and many color graphics and images which could not be reproduced in the printed book. Class materials and interactive lessons are designed and taught by highly-qualified faculty members and lectors. Over 500 classes are currently available [as of 2024], in 16 Departments, and new ones are being added continually.

Courses offered in the Grey School provide a grounded classical education in history, mythology, geography, mathematics, literature, natural history, general science, astronomy, chemistry, physics, zoology, botany, and even Latin—with Greek to be offered shortly. The performing arts are included as well, with classes in poetry, music, theater, and illusion. The wonderful thing is, with the mystique of enrolling in a magickal "School of Wizardry," our students are eagerly studying all these subjects which would bore them to tears if they were taking them in a mundane public school!

The Ḟuture

As Oprah Winfrey said about her new school for impoverished girls in South Africa: *"I understand that many in the school system and out feel that I'm going overboard, and that's fine. This is what I want to do. I wanted to take girls with that 'It' quality, and give them an opportunity to make a difference in the world."*[98]

---

[98] *Newsweek,* Jan. 8. 2007.

And this is what we want to do with the Grey School of Wizardry—to find students of all ages who have unique potential that has not been addressed by their experiences in public schools, and give them the inspiration and information that will enable them to go out and make a real difference in the world. This is true education. For the difference between wisdom and stupidity is really all about considering the consequences—"unto the seventh generation," as the Hopi proverb says.

In closing, here's what one of our students had to say about the Grey School Vision:

Just Imagine...
By Stacy, Prefect of the Society of the Four Winds

...years from now: Over a hundred have graduated to Journeymen Wizard, and another thousand Apprentices continue in training. The pendants we wear are no longer merely logos of the school we attend, but the symbol of our Order. And our symbol is not just recognizable to those whom we call brother and sister, but to the greater world, both Magickal and Mundane. We are respected as honored and reliable sources of wisdom, guidance and hope to the communities we live in. We are recognized in congress, the military, in covens and conclaves, and through our deeds we are recognized as an organization devoted to helping influence the evolution of the world.

Addendum by OZ: On Nov. 26, 2022, I formally passed the torch and mantle of Headmaster to my esteemed protégé, Nicholas Kingsley. The Grey School now has a physical campus at 123 Poultney St., Whitehall, NY 12887. www.GreySchool.com

Part V:
Messages in a Bottle

The Stolen Child

Where dips the rocky highland
Of Sleuth Wood in the lake,
There lies a leafy island
Where flapping herons wake
The drowsy water rats;
There we've hid our faery vats,
Full of berrys
And of reddest stolen cherries.
Come away, O human child!
To the waters and the wild
With a faery, hand in hand,
For the world's more full of weeping than you can understand.

Where the wave of moonlight glosses
The dim gray sands with light,
Far off by furthest Rosses
We foot it all the night,
Weaving olden dances
Mingling hands and mingling glances
Till the moon has taken flight;
To and fro we leap
And chase the frothy bubbles,
While the world is full of troubles
And anxious in its sleep.
Come away, O human child!
To the waters and the wild
With a faery, hand in hand,
For the world's more full of weeping than you can understand.

Where the wandering water gushes
From the hills above Glen-Car,
In pools among the rushes

That scarce could bathe a star,
We seek for slumbering trout
And whispering in their ears
Give them unquiet dreams;
Leaning softly out
From ferns that drop their tears
Over the young streams.
Come away, O human child!
To the waters and the wild
With a faery, hand in hand,
For the world's more full of weeping than you can understand.

Away with us he's going,
The solemn-eyed:
He'll hear no more the lowing
Of the calves on the warm hillside
Or the kettle on the hob
Sing peace into his breast,
Or see the brown mice bob
Round and round the oatmeal chest.
For he comes, the human child,
To the waters and the wild
With a faery, hand in hand,
For the world's more full of weeping than he can understand.

("The Stolen Child" by William Butler Yeats, 1865-1939)

Art by Craig R. Miller, from the Wheel of the Year Songbook, *by Gwydion Pendderwen.*

37. Letter to the Future from 1921 to 2021[99]

by Glyn Williams (2021)

ECENTLY A TIME-CAPSULE WAS OPENED IN Dundee, Scotland. It contained (amongst other things) a letter from 1921 addressed to the world of today, written by a young woman, Annie Kier Lamont, a telephone clerk. It was surprising just how uncannily accurate her view of the future was.

You who read this may do so with a great wonder that life was so different in 1921 to what it is in 2021.

Dear Future Readers,

I cannot visualise what changes will have taken place in 100 years, but, that the changes will be vast and far-reaching there is absolutely no doubt whatever.

It is my intention then to give you, my reader, a brief description of the Post Office telegraph clerk as he, and she, are today in this year 1921.

In order to do so, I shall divide my article into two headings: business and social life. And so – 'business first' – is that still the motto of the business world of 2021? I wonder!

The Telegraphist then is a government servant, certainly, but he – (and she) are the lowest paid of their class despite the fact that they are supposed to have a definite and good status in the social world. At present, our salaries are increased owing to the 'war bonuses' fought for, through the Union of Post Office Workers, but, as the cost of living goes down, our salaries will also diminish with the result that, in a few months, we shall probably be back at our pre-war salaries, which were admittedly totally inadequate. The pre-war salary of a woman telegraphist before the war was £1. 14/- per week, and the maximum for a man £2. 16/- per week. Even with the pre-war cost of living it was a struggle for a Telegraphist to bring up a family and educate them properly.

What the future holds for us God alone knows, as the whole economic system of the country is absolutely in chaos.

---

99 Williams, Glyn, https://www.quora.com/ (accessed 4/27/2023)

Armageddon

In my opinion, the whole economic system must be changed before a definite constructive programme can be entered into. This last war was to 'end war'. Never was there such a futile hope, and I predict another and ghastlier armageddon before many years have fled.

However, I'm departing from the subject of my article. With regard to the daily routine of telegraph life, we are, of course, all 'hand Telegraphists' – by which I mean that the absolute 'machine' telegraphy has not yet been introduced. We have the 'creed', the 'gell' and 'Baudot' installed in the larger offices, but the morse key still holds supreme in all offices in the United Kingdom.

*Wireless telegraphy, while making most marvellous progress, is, I believe, still in its infancy, and possibly, in **your** day, even that wonderful discovery will have been superseded by something even more startling and revolutionary.*

*It can plainly be noted too, that Telephony is fast ousting Telegraphy, and may, indeed, be the cause of its ultimate decay, as many business firms prefer to phone direct to their business confreres, and so save the delay of a reply by Telegraphy. One of our **great** grievances is, that **we get no half holiday**, although the Government compels **all** business firms to give their employees a half holiday. How truly like a Government, to be so thoroughly inconsistent. ...*

We have a Union of Post Office workers which fights our battles for us, but, like most other Trades Unions to-day, it is in a very parlous state.

It adopted a 'Strike Policy', as a consequence of which half the membership resigned – which promptly made the Executive Council of the Union fling the Strike Fund overboard, and, though I have great faith in the Union, and have served on its Committees for many years, I am doubtful as to the wisdom of such a volte face – but perhaps you no longer have Trade Unions, and will smile superciliously at my anxiety as to its future.

With regard to the social side of our life, the Dundee Telegraph branch, as a whole, is a thoroughly go-ahead staff and the men take a great interest in sport – golf being prime favourite, while the women are not far behind, and golf and play tennis and swim. ...

In the winter, we go to Lectures, Concerts, and as many theatres as we can afford, while Classes on various subjects are well attended.'

Voting rights

The vote has been granted to women within the last few years, and we are very keen about voting, and indeed, most of the women *in **this** office are very anxious to see Winston Churchill turned out of his seat (Dundee) at the next general election.*

Mrs Winterbotham and Lady Astor are our only representatives in Parliament at present, but we hope there will be a lady premier before 2021.'

Changing world

Living in this extraordinary, ever-changing world as we do to-day, just recovering from the horrors of a most bloody war, with disaster in Ireland, strife in India, and great and terrible discontent at home, our views of many things are naturally changing with the swift moving events of a terrible epoch.

Though our lives apparently go on in the same routine, we are fully and deeply conscious that life in 1921 is fraught with terrible things, and that every day shows new and terrible possibilities springing up from the soil of a ruined civilisation.'

Looking ahead

What does the future hold for the Telegraph Clerk – and the whole world?

***You** know the answer to that question, you who read this, and, I wonder if the millennium has really come in your day, if happiness and peace has at last come to the ravished nations of the world, or whether **you** too are straining tired eyes towards the future and saying: 'What next?'*

It seems to me that the progress of civilisation is no progress at all while we devote all the gifts of science to slay our fellow creature, and that no permanent good can ever be achieved if we forget the "divine" in man.

But surely the world will learn its lesson one day – the great lesson that the things of this world are as naught, while the things of the "spirit" are everlasting.

Let us hope that Browning's beautiful words will come true and that we will 'emerge one day.

~ Annie Kier Lamont

I found this letter quite moving. I was saddened to hear that the writer, whose voice cuts through time with such clarity, took her own life several years later. But perhaps by now Annie has reincarnated, and may even now be reading her letter of so long ago!

And it is in this spirit that we offer the following "messages in a bottle."

38. Ugly Duckling

By Oberon Zell

I WAS A WEIRD KID. Indeed, as in the song, I am my own grandpa!

My mother's father was born in 1875, and he came of age in the 60-year Cultural Renaissance Cycle of the "Golden Dawn" (the 1900's). He died at home of coronary thrombosis on Nov. 25, 1941, just a year before I was born (on Nov. 30, 1942). He was 66, and his room was made over into my nursery. My first memory in this incarnation is of awakening in my familiar room, and there was my familiar family gathered around me. I looked up at them, and they were all looking at me kind of funny. I tried to say something, but I could not articulate. Getting more and more upset, finally I raised my hands in front of my face; and they were little, tiny baby hands.

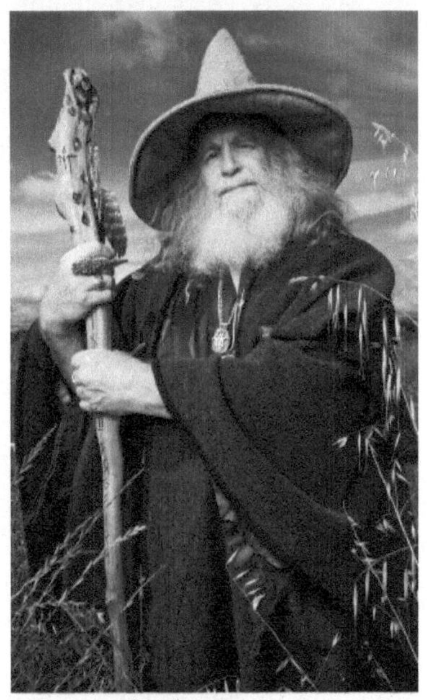

I freaked out and started screaming. I had awakened in the very same room that I had died in. It was a direct transmigration, straight from one life into the next one. Obviously there was a time gap of a full year, but I had no memory of any of that. It was like I had gone to sleep the night before, and I awakened the next morning with the same people around me.

As I became more verbal as a child, they would often tell me "That's just the kind of thing your grandfather used to say!" From the time that I was able to talk I always felt that I was somehow older, wiser, and more mature than they were. I never could quite get it that I was the child, and they were the adults. It always felt the other way around to me.

Backing up a bit…

When the Japanese bombed Pearl Harbor on Dec. 1, 1941 ("A Day that will live in infamy"), my father-to-be joined the Marines to go fight in the South Pacific. But like so many other young enlistees, he wanted to engender a progeny before he went off to war—perhaps never to return. So, I was born on Nov. 30, 1942. For my first three years the only people in my universe were my mother, my grandmother, and my maiden aunt (who never married). So, my whole life revolved around the Maiden, the Mother, and the Crone—the Triple Goddess of Celtic lore.

My early years were haunted by recurrent nightmares of dying. I remembered time and time again in my dreams the sensation of dying. It was like falling down a well. The world got smaller and smaller until it disappeared. Sometimes I would even get that feeling when I was awake, and I would have to kind of blink and shake myself.

I was very telepathic. A lot of the time I heard people's thoughts as clearly as words. And I just took that for granted as perfectly natural. They did not have to speak directly in order for me to understand them. I did not distinguish between spoken words and articulated thoughts.

When I was very small my parents got me a set of the wonderful *ChildCraft* books (1945 edition), which were put out for kids by the *Worldbook Encyclopedia.* There were 15 of them, each on different themes. My favorite was the one on world mythology. The very first things I read were Roman versions of the Greek myths, long before *Dick and Jane* or anything else. I will never forget reading about "Pluto and Proserpine" (Greek Hades & Persephone) as children.

These stories introduced me to many important concepts, one of them being that there were multiple deities, whole pantheons of interesting Gods and Goddesses. So, I did not start off with the assumption that there was only one God; I started off with the assumption that there were many deities worshipped among many peoples.

Later, when I was old enough to go to Sunday school and learned about Christianity, it was not like, "this is the only God." I read the Bible as mythology—just like the legends of Jason, Heracles, Odysseus, King Arthur, Robin Hood, and all the other stories I had been reading. The Bible was just one more story, about one more God—the jealous and vengeful God of the Jews. And I was not Jewish, so it was not the story of *my* People.

After three years on active duty in the South Pacific, my father came home from the war in 1945. We moved into a not-quite-finished house in Clark's Green, PA, where I really came into my identity. Upstairs I had my own room and my own desk. My dad and I were very close—he used to tell me wonderful bedtime stories. He would say, "What do you want to hear about tonight?"

And I would reply, "How did the giraffe get such a long neck?" And he would make up a marvelous story along the lines of Rudyard Kipling's "Just-So" tales.

There were woods and fields all around us that I used to spend much of my childhood time exploring. I would go hang out with the animals. I would merge so totally with the place that the wild critters came to accept me. I would just sit at the base of a tree for hours and hours 'til the deer would come and graze right next to me without being alarmed. I would climb up into the branches during the bird nesting season and just sit and watch them lay their eggs and raise their babies. And they would not be disturbed by me. Those were very happy times.

My lifelong interest in magick and Wizardry was ignited when I first read stories of magick as a child—such as in fairy tales and the Greek myths. In particular, I was deeply imprinted by the animated Disney movies featuring magickal characters.

Disney's *Fantasia* in particular (which came out in 1940—two years before I was born) had a huge impact on me. Of course, I loved the whole "Rite of Spring" evolution sequence, with the dinosaurs. But it was the "Pastorale" that really captured my soul. The final scene, when Nyx draws an indigo veil of night like a diamond—dusted blanket across the Arcadian sky, and we see a thin crescent of the new moon which, as we zoom in, resolves into Diana drawing her bow and releasing a meteoric arrow…well, that arrow plunged straight into my heart, where it has lodged ever since!

I did not have any social sense at all as a kid. Not with people, anyway. I got along great with animals, but I never really formed close friendships with other kids—especially boys. I just did not understand them—or trust them. And this was reciprocal; I was like a "pink monkey." I always liked hanging out with girls more than boys. They were nicer and more interesting, and they did not want to pick fights with me. I understood them better—and I still do.

Eventually I came to understand myself through the fable of the "Ugly Duckling." I was a changeling, a cuckoo, a "stranger in a strange land," born into a family that was not of my own kind—whatever that might be (and I had no idea). It was not until I grew up and went off to college that I discovered others like me; the same "species," as it were. And from that point my focus turned to seeking out such scattered kin—my People—and gathering them together into a clan of our own. I claimed a name for such as we—"Pagans"—and founded a global Pagan community. And the rest is Mystery…

Now, from this distant vantage point of 80 years, as I look back on my childhood and younger life of this incarnation, I realize I was often not a very nice kid. I was arrogant and contemptuous towards other kids, a real little shit. I wielded my superior intellect as a weapon. I was probably "on the spectrum" in my lack of empathy and compassion, and well deserved the negative response I often received. With your guidance, I intend to be better next time around…

To my future parents

Dear Mom(s) and/or Dad(s),

This is a message in a bottle. I am writing to you across the abyss of time with these suggestions for how to raise a kid like me. First off, I recommend you see the movie, *Little Buddha* (1993). It will help you to get a sense of this reincarnation paradigm, and how it works. In particular, sometimes an individual soul may get dispersed into several new incarnations, rather than only one…

You will certainly be wondering how you can recognize me in the next incarnation. The best clues will be in the things that naturally interest me, as I expect them to carry over from this life to my next, with you. I will assuredly retain my passionate fascination with all things magickal and mysterious. I will be obsessively interested in dinosaurs, cosmology, space travel, Nature, evolution, mythology, history, Gods and Goddesses. I will turn my attention to mysteries of the distant past as well as visions of the distant future yet to be. I will love science—fiction. I will want to create artwork and build models—which I will be good at. And all in all, I will no doubt be a weird kid!

Ḣow to Ṙaise me:

First off, and most essential, if I am a boy again this time around, DO NOT HAVE ME CIRCUMCISED! I cannot emphasize this enough. Circumcision is an unforgivable betrayal to an innocent baby, with lifelong consequences; do not do it to me!

Secondly, Momma, nurse me at your breast. I did not have this last time around, and I missed it my whole life. Hold me; cuddle me; sleep with me. Give me lots of naked body contact as a baby.

As soon as I can talk, encourage me to talk about my former life memories, and record these for future reference. They will soon fade.

If I have childhood nightmares, consider that these may be memories of my death in my former life. Encourage me to talk about them and draw pictures.

When I speak of having mystical dreams, visions, experiences, see faeries, etc., encourage me. Never dismiss my accounts of mystic/magickal experiences.

Buy my *Song of Gaea* children's book (2022) and read it to me as a bedtime story from my earliest age. Introduce me to Rudyard Kipling's *Jungle Book* and *Just So Stories.*

Practice psychic exercises with me: telepathy, clairvoyance, psychokinesis, smoke-weaving, weather-working…

Encourage me to set up and work with my own personal altar. Buy me a Millennial Gaia statue for it.

Teach me how to swim, dive, climb trees, fish, ride a bicycle, ice skate and roller skate, shoot a bow and arrow, use tools, dance, sing, play musical instruments…enroll me in martial arts.

Teach me how to play chess and poker.

Enroll me in school drama (acting, directing, makeup, set design, costuming…), and attend my performances.

Introduce me to dinosaurs via books, TV shows, documentaries, and movies). I will want to collect dino models; indulge me.

Take me on camping trips, hikes, explorations; sign me up for Scouting to learn woodcraft, campcraft, and wilderness survival skills.

Take me on family road trips to national parks and roadside attractions. Take me to natural history museums—especially ones with dinosaurs! Take me to theme parks like Disneyland and Universal Studios.

Take me to Renaissance Faires, Celtic festivals, Pagan festivals, Dickens Fairs, Comicons, historical reenactments, and other costume experiences. Go in appropriate costume.

Encourage my curiosity. If I ask questions to which you do not know the answer, say, "I do not know. Let us find out." Then teach me how to do research and experiments.

Encourage my interests in Nature and wild things. Allow me to keep terrariums and aquariums of various small critters. Allow me to keep weird pets—rats, snakes, lizards (esp. bearded dragons), tarantulas, ant farm, etc. Let me catch tadpoles and watch them develop into frogs. Let me bring in caterpiggles and hatch out moth and flutterby cocoons. Hatch a praying mantis egg case in a terrarium…

For my 11th birthday, present me with the *Grimoire for the Apprentice Wizard* (2004) and *Companion for the Apprentice Wizard* (2006), and enroll me in the Grey School of Wizardry.

Introduce me to science fiction via Robert Heinlein's juveniles (in chronological order—see Appendix).

Introduce me to Terry Pratchett's *Tiffany Aching* series—one for my birthday every year, starting at age 11 with *The Wee Free Men* (2003).

Introduce me to J.K. Rowling's *Harry Potter* books and movies— one for my birthday every year, starting at age 11, with *Harry Potter and the Philosopher's Stone* (1997).

And of course, J.R.R. Tolkein books and movies!

Turn me on to superhero movies and comics. Keep those comics safe—someday they will be worth a lot of money to collectors!

Buy me educational science kits, toys, models and experiments (chemistry set, crystal garden, microscope, telescope, astrolabe, orrery, computer, virtual reality gear, 3-D printer, drone, etc. etc.).

Buy me a junior stage magician's set of illusions and tricks to perform. Give me little magic tricks as presents. Encourage me to put on shows. Take me to magic shows and other live theatre performances.

Teach/encourage me to learn all kinds of arts & crafts, including sewing, woodworking, knitting, drawing, painting, sculpture, ceramics… Get me all sorts of art supplies: drawing paper, colored pens and pencils, paints, easel, light table, electronic art programs and setups…

Buy me model kits of things I like and encourage me to build and paint models—plastic, wood and metal.

And most important, teach me love (*"That condition in which another person's happiness is essential to your own."* ~R.A. Heinlein). Teach me honesty and integrity by your own example. Teach me to be kind to others. Teach me fairness, compassion, and empathy. Teach me to find joy in serving others, and making them happy. Teach me to be a good person, and do the Right Thing, no matter what. Raise me to be a Hero.

Advice to my future self:

Do as you would be done by. Remember, how others treat you is up to them. How you treat others is up to you.

Be friendly, courteous, and kind to others. Do not be a dick.

Do not be arrogant. You may be the smartest person in the room, but do not show off and make others feel less than. Do not use your superior intellect against them or lord it over them. People will hate you for it.

Practice compassionate humility. Build up others. Praise your opponents. Spread positive rumors, not negative ones. People will appreciate that, and you will gain a positive reputation, which is a powerful thing.

Remember the Three Rules of Wizardry:
1. Always take credit/responsibility.
2. Reputation is power.
3. With great power comes great responsibility.

Learn to read facial expressions and body language. Study this; it is important!

Spend hours in front of a mirror practicing facial expressions, such as raising eyebrows singly.

Look people in the eyes. Talk less and listen to what others have to say; you do not have to agree but refrain from trying to make them wrong.

Avoid arguing. When talking with people you disagree with, avoid turning it into a debate. Instead, look for something the other person says that you can agree with, and make that the subject of your discussion.

Question authorities! Seek out people who know stuff, ask them questions, and learn from them. Apprentice yourself to wise teachers.

The world is full of wonder; explore everything!

39. Wednesday's Child

By Haleigh Isbill

Salted Memories
I got tears on my glasses,
I changed them out for my spare pair.
Now I've gotten tears on those glasses too.
Cleaning the tears off feels too hard.
But if I don't, I can't see—
There's just so many tears on the lenses.
And so, I'm crying because I've cried so much.
~Haleigh K. Isbill

 WAS BORN ON A WEDNESDAY…
I was born in Southern California. My parents were married. I had an older brother. I had two sets of loving grandparents. My mom worked a mid—level government job. My dad did construction. We lived in a house.

Not long before I was born, my elder brother suddenly stopped being able to do things he could do before. It was a genetic disorder that was degenerative, and his case was severe. This turned my mom into a religious fanatic. As parents, we do tend to blame ourselves when something goes wrong and so she went looking for absolution and hope.

My mom became a born—again, fundamentalist Baptist a year to the day before my birth. A more superstitious person might have found my birth, exactly a year later to the day, to be auspicious. But I was born full of magic, I was fey, and I could not change that. The Independent, Born—Again Baptist that my birth should have heralded never existed. I struggled with trying to be the Christian my mom wanted, but never managed it.

When I was four, my parents bought a houseboat, and my brother was moved into my paternal grandmother's house. I got to commune with the sea every day, and it rocked me to sleep every night. Dad read CS Lewis and Tolkien to me; mom read the Bible. Bedtime stories took me away to far off lands and I learned how to use stories to escape. I also learned to love magic and the Earth.

One morning when I was five, I woke up and my mom was gone. My dad got me ready for school. While attempting to braid my hair, he told me my mom would be picking me up and that my mom and I would spend the rest of the week with family friends.

It was the last time I saw the boat.

It was also when my mom taught me to make nest eggs.

My brother passed away when I was eight, my mom moved me to another state and another church, but the church was more extreme than the last. My mom remarried—a narcissist who emotionally abused me, my mom, and his two sons. My mom was not okay—between mourning a son and being the main victim of a narcissist, that should be expected. They were an unstable and terrifying pair.

My dad remarried, too. My stepmom was a fellow addict, and they fed each other's disease. My summers saw a lot of drug dens and occasionally sleeping under bridges or on random people's couches. My dad and stepmom would get into physical fights—and they were pretty evenly matched. They eventually moved to a new state, got a house, and continued to make each other miserable. Both died in my twenties from complications of Hepatitis C they had gotten from sharing needles. Another unstable, but somehow less terrifying pair.

I was a sensitive and fanciful child. I wanted to be a princess and to be loved, hugged, and allowed to grow and blossom. I needed sunshine, candy, unicorns, and rainbows. But who I was did not fit in with my mom's religious beliefs—magical anything was ***right out***. I was fey in a place that was not safe for fey. Who I was had always been fine with my dad, even encouraged. My dad handed me The Eyes of the Dragon by Stephen King, Game of Thrones by George RR Martin, and Melanie Rawn's Exiles series. *These* places were safe for me, and much more welcome than my realities.

I was alone—I was not much liked by the church kids because I was not one of them with their narcissist god and smug self—righteousness. I was a weird religious kid with none of the normal cultural markers to fit in with the rest of the world. I was lonely and I had books.

And I had Gaea.

I had never seen a ritual before, but when I was about 10 years old, I began to make circles of salt and water in my bedroom. I would sit on the floor, light a candle, and imagine myself as a tree, my roots going down through the foundation of the house and into the earth. I dug deep and I felt a love I did not understand. Gaea loved me, held me in her earthen arms and hugged me with her breezes. She gave me tethers in a wild and tumultuous life when I did not even know tethers were a thing. This has been a lifelong communion.

My mom found my books on Paganism, my tarot cards, and my Harry Potter books when I was twelve. She accused me of bringing demons into her house, burned my things, and beat me ('spare the rod, spoil the child' garbage). I was not trying to bring in demons, I was trying to tether myself in a perpetually wind—tossed childhood.

I was stirring, burning, sacred. And I was rejected for being different.

Thanks to my dad, I dove into books full of magic that would carry me off to fantasy lands where beavers talk, or wizards take an unexpected expedition with a troupe of dwarves and a hobbit. I lived in Narnia, Bag End, Darkover, and anywhere that was not where I currently was. I got to be that princess and hug a unicorn and follow a rainbow to far off places. I lived through fiction and imagination. These are the places I really grew up. Aboard the Enterprise, on the back of a luck dragon, or in a goblin market. I took vacations in Wonderland and spent holidays in Charles Dickens London.

My morals came from authors and from books; my ability to connect with reality came from the Earth Herself, from being rooted in Her. I survived my childhood, not unscathed, but survived—kept breathing by written word and love for nature.

Resilience is not real.

We hear the phrase "children are resilient" but it is a lie adults tell themselves to cope with decisions they must make.

So here is my advice to my future parents:

Please be kind to me.

I am fragile, sensitive, and naive. Harsh words are enough to crush me, I will not need those wooden spoons my previous mother used. I want to be good; I constantly strive to be good—so all I need is to know where I went wrong, and I will correct myself. No cruelty required.

Please protect me.

This life took me to dangerous places as a child, and while I was lucky that I was not permanently physically hurt, I was still surrounded by violence and instability. I got left alone with cousins who molested me. I went to a church that taught me that my queerness is sin, and I should hate myself. My brother's death was not the only one I experienced when young—but there was no therapy, no lesson in how to cope. I was told to pray for Jesus to heal my hurts. By the time I hit puberty, I had already attempted suicide twice. Please protect me from religious extremists who want me to live a life of misery to have a life of plenty in death. Please, please keep me safe. Do not let me live this life again. I do not want to have to survive this again.

Please get me therapy.

Kids are not resilient! Bad things happen in everyone's life, but we are not born with the knowledge of how to cope with bad times. Trauma in childhood revisits us in adulthood in unexpected ways. My current incarnation has Complex PTSD and fibromyalgia because kids are not resilient. I seemed fine, but I swallowed all my trauma, and I am paying for that now. Please give me the tools to not internalize and please do not praise me for seeming to be "handling things so well!" when I should not have had to manage any of it at all.

Please give me room to explore myself.

This incarnation is pansexual, and I was aware of it at age 7—but my mom was telling me how gross bisexual people were at the time. I grew up knowing that if I came out, I might be kicked out by my mom as other queer kids at the church were. My dad knew and accepted me, no matter what, and he is the reason I had space to figure myself out—for 10 weeks a year while coping with drug addicts and extreme poverty. I was beaten by my mother for exploring other religions. Please do not raise me in a death cult. My growth was stunted but the clouds of a church I could never be part of.

Please love me unconditionally.

My dad in this incarnation loved me unconditionally. My mom hardly speaks to me because I am in a closed triad marriage, I am openly pansexual, one of my kids is trans, and I am a published Pagan editor and author. Feels like her love and time are conditional and even at almost forty, it still hurts! I feel unwanted and ignored. But my dad loved me no matter what happened, and even if I were the antithesis of everything he believed, I knew he would still love me the same. He would be proud of who I am and who my kids are. Please love me like he did. Please love me even if I am not what you were hoping I would be, even if my lifestyle is incompatible with your personal beliefs. There is a phrase I use with my own kids. I tell them that I love them *no matter what, and even if.* There is nothing they can do to lose my love and support and I tell them that. Every day at least once.

To Ϻy Future Self

The Rainy Day
By Henry Wadsworth Longfellow

The day is cold, and dark, and dreary;
It rains, and the wind is never weary;
The vine still clings to the mouldering wall,
But at every gust the dead leaves fall,
And the day is dark and dreary.

My life is cold, and dark, and dreary;
It rains, and the wind is never weary;
My thoughts still cling to the mouldering Past,

But the hopes of youth fall thick in the blast,
And the days are dark and dreary.

Be still, sad heart! and cease repining;
Behind the clouds is the sun still shining;
Thy fate is the common fate of all,
Into each life some rain must fall,
Some days must be dark and dreary.

Girl, shit is gonna be hard. You are going to take everything hard—but do not swallow that pain and confusion, do not internalize it. Embrace your emotional sensitivity. I do not know what is coming at you, but as Longfellow said, "Into each life, some rain must fall". Find the tools to help you be resilient because you are not. None of us start out resilient and hopefully you will not need to be but be prepared just in case.

Read books! They will carry you off to incredible places and you will learn so much about everything from them. Read, read, read! Fantasy and Sci—Fi, History and Geography, Philosophy, and religion. Learn everything you can, and question all of it. Think critically.

Trust yourself. Ignore anyone telling you otherwise. You know when things are not right—you get that little queasy, fluttery feeling that warns you—trust it every time. You have many past lives that you may not be able to access, but they are still passing down wisdom and warning to you. Pay attention!

RUN. You will know when. Do not freeze, do not fawn—flee. There are so many people out there who will want to possess you, control you, tell you who you are, and hurt you when you try to have agency. Tell them to fuck off and leave them behind. Real love does not hurt—and I do not mean just romantic love. I mean any love. Family, friendships, and deities can be problematic, and you do not owe them anything.

Let yourself bloom. Feel the Earth, revel in the change of seasons, cast spells. This is who you are. Commune with Gaea, grow gardens, take deep breaths, keep goats.

Let yourself grieve. This incarnation is marked by grief and death—so many loved ones left too soon and in this next incarnation, if this happens, do not let yourself think that knowing and loving you is a curse. You are only cursing yourself. Rather, let yourself feel the hurt and be available to do things that feel meaningful to you and the lost loved ones. Reconnect with them through shared experiences and little moments of quiet.

Be intolerant of intolerance. This is the only way for us to grow as a species. Fight against gatekeeping and hate and bigotry. Fight loudly.

Participate in direct actions to end these things. Protest the unfair and do your best to stop systemic abuse everywhere you find it. Be open minded but think critically. And help others. Never forget to help others.

Finally, love yourself. You are a beautiful soul made of stardust, carbon, and whimsy. Embrace that whimsy, be proud of it, revel in it. You are incredible and you will forget that sometimes, but you are. Do not let what others say about you or to you affect that. Do not let the world crush you under cynicism and normalcy.

Oh, and do not be born on a Wednesday. Wednesday's child is full of woe, and I am the anthropomorphic personification of Woe. Do not be that again if you can help it.

Art by Craig R. Miller, from the Wheel of the Year Songbook, *by Gwydion Pendderwen*

40. Time Travel Is Possible (Just Ask Your Future Self)

By Jason Myers, youngest of two sons

ONGRATULATIONS, you are different. Despite how that may feel like a curse in your formative years, rest assured you will learn to view your uniqueness as a blessing once tempered with the wisdom of a few life lessons. There are often times when humans wish they fit in to societal norms more uniformly. It can be frightening to feel "other" and comforting to feel like an accepted member of a pack. However, those of us who are "gifted" (as my elementary school teachers referred to it) will eventually grow into our strange ways and even learn to embrace the very things that position us on the outer fringe.

For me, the first thing I realized that set me apart was my natural ability for creative writing. It was not something I practiced or studied so I did not take the same pride in it as, say, an Olympic skater who toils endlessly over their discipline would. I simply picked up a pencil, put it to paper and my hand started writing the words that my spirit was feeding it. I say spirit rather than "mind" in this case because a lot of what I wrote as a weird child (and still do as a weird adult) came from someplace other than my intellect. To this day I have to go back and re—read passages once an automatic writing session has stopped and look up multiple words that I wrote yet do not necessarily "know" and have never verbally uttered.

This ability did not strike me as peculiar or supernatural. I enjoyed the blue ribbons and scratch—and—sniff stickers that I won most weeks in Mrs. McCorristan's second—grade writing competitions. I did not even mind being pulled away from my neighbors and friends and bussed off to a different school in third grade that taught experimental "enrichment" courses. It was far more fun learning about Indigenous cultures, creating crafts, and solving puzzles than it was in the stressful world of timed arithmetic tests. Otherness had its privileges.

I also found that my "old soul" or intellect gave me certain advantages when it came to experimenting with others physically and romantically. I often dated people several years and grades ahead of me and found many of the kids my actual age to be a bit boring back then. That followed me into my teen years when I switched my creative focus to learning bass guitar and joining rock bands. For the first ten years of my musical development, I was always the youngest member of any band I was in. Given these tendencies, it is amusing that I am now the eldest member of a band I founded twenty years ago and married to a lovely woman twenty years my junior. Though she is an adventurous open—minded old spirit as well, we always felt more evenly matched than birth certificates might indicate.

If there is a lesson in all of this, it is to embrace your weirdness. Assimilation is easier yet infinitely more boring. If you have ever felt like an alien, an outcast, or a freak – take solace in the fact that most of the people who made the largest intellectual or creative impact on the world were also freaks who learned to lean into their crazy ideas. Being the strange kid might feel overwhelming as you grapple with how to find your place. You may be misunderstood, ridiculed, or even bullied. Stay the course, stay grounded in your core ethics, reach out to your spirit guides, practice your magick, and realize that you will grow into your odd skin. Meanwhile, those who did not accept you likely envy you secretly for your bravery and unique approach to life as they cower behind the facade of dull conformity.

Ðear Ɱom(s) and/or Ðad(s)

Dear Pagan parents of the future, you are about to face a new tribulation – raising a little hell, as it were. The first thing to remember… do not panic. You have this.

The second thing to consider is that you are going to need more patience than most people display under normal circumstances. There will be many times when you marvel at the ideas and creations that come from your child's mind. Yet the same rugged spirit of individuality that lends itself to creative gold has another side.

Even the hippest parents are likely to take comfort in a degree of orthodoxy from time to time. The completely *un*orthodox nature of your child could be trying on the patience if not somewhat prepared. And how does one prepare for the random behavior of a sometimes mild, often wild Magickal Child? Meditation is the first thing that comes to mind. The ability to recognize the stillness of the universe that lies within your consciousness – theoretically this centering breath of your practice should be taught alongside labor breathing at Lamaze classes and the like.

I am fortunate in that my folks are alive and progressive minded. Though we live in different parts of the country I talk to them multiple times each week. The older we all get, the less we seem to take each other for granted. That said, we tend not to speak of religion much, though I am relatively public about mine these days. They experienced my witchy room, art, books, and creations as a kid living under their roof. And they attended and participated in my handfasting as an adult. I would like them to know that while my religion and rituals might seem strange, they are done for the good of all, and harm none. Then again, my parents know what is in my heart and furthermore have been desensitized to being shocked by me after observing five decades of my weirdness. Still, I want to ensure there is no undue unease at what my form of Witchcraft may or may not involve.

In general, it is helpful for kids to eventually tell their parents, "Do not worry, I may be different from what you expected or hoped for, but I am happy, living my best life, and not harming anyone. Some of your wisdom may have been lost on me in my more rebellious years of teen angst, but your best lessons permeated my subconscious and now show through in the way I conduct my life, in my core ethics, even if the life I lead differs in appearance from the one you envisioned."

For their part, it is so important for parents to tell their kids they love them, they accept them, and they are proud of them. Even if your child's life took a vastly different trajectory than the one you mentally mapped out, you should have faith that they will do their best and will hopefully take the keys you provided to open the correct doors when they are ready. Remember, for all their maddening obstinance and obtuseness, children are smarter and more observant than many give them credit for. They are certainly more likely to follow your actual examples than any sanctimonious lectures or empty platitudes. If you find yourself not understanding or accepting your offspring as they are, the work that needs to be done is on yourself, not on them.

"To my Future Self"

Dear me,

I am speaking to you from the past to the future, yet you are *in* the future because you have yet to incarnate at the time of this writing. If this sounds paradoxical it is because we are conditioned to consider our lives on a timeline when, in fact, time is anything but linear. Know that I am your wizened ancestor wishing to impart the wisdom I have accumulated to make your journey smoother. Yet at the same time, I am your descendant because the lessons you experience in your youth will shape and inform the adult that I become in this incarnation.

Labyrinthian riddles aside, let us get practical. There will be times when you will want to commune with your spirit as it exists at different points in the cycle. To facilitate this, consider making simple yet detailed journal entries in your personal spiritual journal or Book of Shadows. Make note of things like the date, time of day, phase of the moon, and weather conditions. Briefly explain what is happening spiritually in your life at the time of the entry.

If you are facing an issue where you could use the wisdom of an experienced elder, tap into that and reach out to yourself in the future. Be still, gaze into a scrying mirror, a candle flame, a dark crystal, or the screen of your mind's eye, and wait for your future self to ethereally materialize and respond. To know when your past self is seeking your assistance, look back at those journal entries on a regular basis. When you come across examples of yourself in the past seeking wisdom from yourself in the future, pause, go into Alpha, meditate, and telepathically link to your former self with your best hindsight. Keep any hints or instructions as clear and simple as possible—so less is lost in translation across dimensions.

It is helpful to experiment with these time—traveling communications during significant days of the year such as sabbats or your birthday. That way you will remember it is an important time for sending psychic messages back and forth between different eras of yourself. What you may find is that by imparting the wisdom of your current (and by default "future") self into the mind of your past self you will become what others around you refer to as an "old soul" or someone who is wise beyond their years. It instills a sense of calm and courage in the younger you which, in turn, leads to a happier, more well—adjusted older you. You can avoid some of the worst obstacles in life and, in a sense, become your own god.

If this technique sounds a bit too complicated or far fetched, try a simpler version. Once a week set aside a designated time to connect with your past self, perhaps in morning meditation or at night before falling asleep. This could be as basic as recalling a specific time in your past when you recall being open to metaphysical assistance. You may have experimented with mind—opening substances or techniques. In those altered states, your consciousness is more receptive to input from external sources. In this case, the source is your current/future self-sending those specific thoughts, assurances, and wisdom to your past self.

It may be helpful to draw a connection by pulling an old photograph of yourself and projecting your current intelligence backward into your previous mind. It is a cyclical technique, one that is fun to experiment with and has the potential to boost your psychic gifts and spiritual well—being. The messages could be as lucid as "Relax, you're going to be fine, it will turn out okay." Or they could be more specific instructions like, "Wait a few years before you move to California. You will be better prepared, and you need to experience a few things in Florida first that will serve you well later in life." These time—hop exercises will likely feel different for each person and certainly lead to different results.

If you are looking for a few examples of helpful hints to bestow upon your "future you," consider some of the overarching life changes that have made the biggest impact on your current health and happiness:

- Imagine your young self opening a fortune cookie that says, "Practice meditation when you don't need it, so it'll be second nature when you do."
- Visualize a confident, virile Nature God/dess whispering in your ear, "Sacrifice your jealousy and you will become infinitely more attractive, energetic, and confident while opening your relationships to exhilarating new possibilities."
- Envision young you seeing an aged wizardly or crone version of yourself looking back in the mirror to drop some knowledge like "If you stop eating animals now, you could add ten years to your life. That will seem like a bigger deal when you are older."

But do not limit this exercise to speaking with your younger self. Knowing what you now know, be available to reach out to your future self as well. Ask for specific guidance. Experiment with techniques until you find one that works for you. Perhaps a pendulum will aid in that contact, maybe a tarot session or even a spirit board. Most likely simple consistent meditation will provide the fertile soil for those conversations with future you to blossom.

The beauty of this form of time travel is that it is never too late to begin. You may find yourself thinking "that would have been incredible, but I didn't journal or seek elder wisdom as an impetuous youth." But if you start reaching back to your past self now, you could theoretically retrain your habits and alter that path. It is quite possible that this spirit guide you have been seeking is not some mythic deity "out there" or a mystical oracle that requires mastery of archaic languages and spells to convene with. You just might find your most helpful spirit guide has truly been within you the whole time.

41. The Once and Future Me

By Marie Strang

T A YOUNG AGE, THE PEOPLE IN MY LIFE MADE it known to me I was different. People teased me about my pale skin and red hair. Besides my physical appearance being unacceptable, I had the wrong sort of brain. My way of thinking did not conform. Decades later, at age 53, I learned I was autistic and had ADHD, but during my childhood and younger years I was just the weird one who did not understand social situations, could not listen, or follow instructions, and had sensory issues.

My parents dragged me to church, not because they were particularly religious, but because they thought it was the thing to do. Apart from creating blobs with Play—Doh, Sunday School bored me. I understood it, but even at six years old, I did not agree with the teachings because they made no sense to me and seemed unnatural.

Our next—door neighbor did not mind if we went for walks on the paths through her wooded property and one day, after walking through the trees, I stopped to rest in a clearing on a little hill. I sat still and kept quiet, something most six year old children do not do. After a while, the trees and plants spoke to me—not in English, but in some other, unexplainable way. A sacred feeling came over me, that which I was told I should feel while in church, but never did. At home, I told my mother, "I don't need to go to church anymore because the woods are my church." To my dismay, she laughed. She did not understand.

My parents continued to drag me to church over the next several years. I tried to conform. I tried to believe. I even went to a Christian school for two years and they made us read the Bible from cover to cover twice. They were some of the most cruel, authoritarian people I had met, so after that, no doubts remained in my mind; I wanted nothing to do with that religion.

For years, I searched for another religion. The sexism of Christianity bothered me the most, but other religions were sexist, too. Finally, at age 18, I found a book called *The Women's Spirituality Book* by Diane Stein. The Divine could be female? This opened a whole new world for me! I discovered true empowerment as a woman, which I needed after suffering through many abusive experiences.

Diane Stein's book led me to look for other publications such as *Green Egg* magazine, the works of Starhawk, Selena Fox's Circle

Sanctuary, and many more works that shaped my Pagan path. No longer just the 'weird' kid, I had a place, a purpose, and a home. I met the man who would become my husband and although he is not a Pagan, he is fine with me being one. He also loves my red hair! Though I started out as an awkward, ugly duckling, I no longer feel that way now.

Dear Future Parents

The souls who are my parents in this incarnation may or may not be my parents in the next. If you are my parents again—well, we learned a lot of hard lessons this time around, didn't we? Let us hope we all remember our experiences, so we do not have to reinvent the karmic wheel. Children come into this world expecting to be loved. My future parents should love me, guide me, and give me room to make mistakes.

Be aware that I may be neurodivergent in the life following this one. Help me find a place to fit in, a place where I will succeed. Hold my hand and help me find where I belong. Do not let me struggle; help me find out how to support myself using the talents I have. Do not let 53 years pass before I discover my brain is not typical. But also, do not let medical or mental health personnel abuse me with their misguided 'therapies' should I receive an earlier diagnosis. If I turn out to be neurotypical, help me be compassionate to those who are not.

Parents do not get to choose the child they want. They need to accept the child they have.

I will not be your scapegoat. I will not be the dutiful child who breaks under the weight of who you expect her to be. I will not carry your empire. I will not wear your mask.

Whatever personality I have, whatever body I end up in, love me and accept me. I ask you to help me learn to know myself.

To My Future Self

I finally understand and know myself in this lifetime. This incarnation is important and valuable to me because I will never experience this set of circumstances again. I will never have this exact body again. I will never live in this time again. But I will also value all other lifetimes because they will be unique, too.

Nature is diverse. People are diverse. We should exclude no one for not conforming to narrow sets of standards. No one has the authority to define those standards, nor should they. I have accepted myself. May that acceptance accompany the next turning of the wheel of my existence. I know my true nature and what is natural for me. I am monogamous by nature, but other people are not. May my future self—remind me that there are many types of relationships and families. I am straight and cis—

gendered. May my future self—remind me I had many LGBTQIA and non—binary friends and family members and there are many ways of being. I am white in this lifetime. May my future self—remind me that racism goes far beyond skin tone, and I need to do my part to make the world a safe place where BIPOC have equity and can not only survive but thrive. I have always had a home, enough to eat, and had all my basic needs met. May my future self—remind me that one's worth is not based on income. I do not know what kind of brain I will have in my next incarnation but make certain I remember to be patient with people who think differently. Remind me of all these things and more because everyone is important, and the world needs all of us.

Let me find my spirituality in nature. Show me hope in the blue sky. Let me feel the sacred Earth beneath my feet. Give me animal friends and plants for textbooks. Involve me in community. Soak me in pools of compassion. Lead me through the woods, to a clearing on a hill. Teach me to be loving, tolerant, and accepting. And above all, remind me to be kind.

Art by Craig R. Miller, from the Wheel of the Year Songbook, *by Gwydion Pendderwen*

42. Generations

By Joy Yumi

HIS IS A CAUTIONARY Tale—

Once upon a Time there was a little mouse, whose father was a rat. No one knew that the father was a rat except for the mouse's mother.

Throughout the year that mouse would be sent off to the rat colony, where they would tease it, tugging on its big ears and pulling on its tiny tail.

There were other rat children that the mouse could play with, but they delighted in watching the older rats punish the mouse, so these children would find devious ways to make havoc and place blame on the little creature.

Meanwhile, most of the mouse's existence was spent in the walls of Cinderella's house. Constantly listening to the bickering of those ugly stepsisters and the cruelty of the stepmother; the mouse's family was of service to Cinderella.

It was expected of a mouse to keep personal traumas hidden. The main priority was helping someone else get out of victimhood, the mouse's mother understood this, as did her mother before her. It was tradition.

Whenever the mouse did try to express frustration and say that they did not want to return to the rat colony, the mouse faced not only the emotional gravity to be diplomatic about the segregation amongst socioeconomic classes but felt the weight of an invisible accusation that it was lucky to be in the house.

For what was there to worry about when all that mice thought of was how to care for others?

Besides, the youngling did have twitchy little eyes that seemed to have anxiety about them, and a deep sorrow that no crumb could easily satisfy; and although no one had proof that this young mouse was half rat, it did act like one.

Refusing to cooperate with others? 'tisk 'tisk, with a click of the tongue.

No one speaks back in high society.

If the little mouse could not serve in the house because of its behavior, it could be a service to Cinderella by reminding the rats to keep to themselves and stay out of the house.

Well, this job became customary, because a mouse's life is very short compared to a human's…

That mousling ratkin established an econ system of barter and strength. Teaching cast outs from barn and house the adaptations and benefits mastered from experiencing more than one culture.

Passing down modes the diplomatic way of engineering social construct became its own burden. The beauty is in the communication, the beast. A feeling of sacrifice after every agreement.

Unfortunately, the mice I am talking about never got to see Cinderella's stepmother mutilate her children's feet in pursuit of the crown. Nor did they see Cinderella's toe slide into the blood—stained glass slipper and hear the roar of mice when the Mistress of the house was whisked away to the castle.

"We're Free!!"

Generational expectations that had been put upon the population, worked for as a colony, and achieved right before their eyes: instantly silenced.

Some may have wept, others danced, but more did not know how to live after a life of serving someone else. What would make them happy if not providing for a Mistress?

Over time many forgot about the "good ol' days" and when a story resurfaced, they would try to talk about it, but did not have the tools to deal with it.

Diplomacy became the way of dealing with Cinderella's disappearance in one of five ways:

Manipulation: taking factors that have been in good standing and refuse to accommodate and/or approach standstill by encouraging others towards an agreement.

Deceit: trickery, malicious intent, denial, however also as innocent as playing dress up and telling fictional stories.

Self—Preservation; doing things for the benefit of yourself, your family, and your nest. The willingness to do anything… even if it hurt another.

Resiliency; when hurt, heal; recognize there are hard times and navigate through them by gaining the knowledge and experience of loss. Grow from it.

Free Enterprise; the expansion of mouse/rat territory; creating the opportunity for the Cinderellen mice and the rats they had suppressed to sell their ideas and items amongst themselves and beyond the property line.

As time went on there were many who attempted an uprising to the system; be it through manipulated control, cultural dissonance, generational hoarding, civil disobedience and/or corporate strategy; but no level of diplomatically inclined rodent was prepared when the children began asking questions...

"Where do you expect us to live if there is nowhere else to expand?"

"Why do I have to talk to someone else for my ideas to be considered?"

"What am I supposed to do when you ignore my questions?"

"Who will help us if the adults won't?

"When will you stop making choices for me and our generation?

"How will we live?"

These questions and more scurried across the population, and as the new generations were forced into diplomatic policy, the rebellion became genetic. So ingrained in their DNA that the children did not ask questions anymore; they were born rebellious.

They did not speak, they did not sleep, they did not learn the way other generations had. Forcing an expansion in traditional parenting and education.

New growth will find a way. How we choose to embrace it is key.

There are influences in this world, some are vicious and others benevolent. All the decisions in this story were made because someone, or something, was important enough to sway choice.

What is important in your life?

Preservation of Culture? Heritage?

Doing something because it has always been done?

Or perhaps you are more rebellious by nature? A heretic? A heathen? An activist who believes in change?

The moral of the story is not about tradition or doing something to define your uniqueness; it is the outgrowth of ideas that support choice.

The willingness to reevaluate expectations, letting go of rigidity, and going beyond the accepted norm.

What would you do to support the children who are conscious and aware but do not share the same ability as their forbearers?

How would you encourage them to express themselves? What challenges would the lack of spoken language, or sleep, do to society? How could it help?

Are there ways you would teach the children? The adults? Culture?

The more choices we have to choose from effectually give broader expanse to what Pagans call Light, Shadow and Dark Magick—

43. Reincarnation and the Weird Kid

By Jessica Gagich

HERE IS A PREVAILING IDEA THAT WE REINCARnate to learn lessons as well as experience the gift that is life on this green and beautiful Earth. In some ways, I find the idea comforting, usually when I am thinking about being reunited with people I love.

But when I think about what I am supposed to learn this time around, well, okay, that is not right. It is when I think about what we are supposed to learn from abject poverty, war, trauma, illness, and the myriad other ways we suffer, that I wonder about the whole system.

I do not like the idea that our gods could use nature and the evil we do to each other to teach us lessons. That someone else's life is nothing more than a tool to teach us lessons.

My Mother did not die from a stroke to be anyone's lesson.

Sometimes bad things happen to people. Good people, bad people, people who were in the wrong place at the wrong time. To give these events the weight of destiny is to say whoever creates or oversees our existence is capable of cruelty for cruelty's sake.

One of the reasons I turned away from Christianity was because the deity of the Old Testament is ultimately not kind. He is by no means a father who I could look to for protection, guidance, and strength. So, I went elsewhere.

In the end, I like to think that in the vast amounts of seconds that tick over, inexorably, one after another, that there are only a few moments that are touched by destiny's hand. That while each life is set up to provide us with lessons, circumstances can throw the plan right out the window and we have to reset and try again.

And again, and again, and again.

I do not know how many times I have danced on this planet, or how many more I will. All I know is who I am now, and what I would hope for myself in the future. So, with all of that in mind, let us look at one weird kid's journey.

Imagine that you are tall, red-haired (the only one in the whole school), freckled, smart, and you generally like adults. Well, you want to like everyone, and that often makes you look like a teacher's pet. Your last name is weird, and you are one of the few white kids in a predominantly Black and Hispanic Catholic School (which your parents did on purpose, and it ended up being a very good thing). Oh, and you love everything fantastic, so on top of everything else, you are also a nerd.

Learning new things makes you feel smart, and it is a feeling you chase, will chase for your whole life. You never want to keep that feeling to yourself either, so you share as much as you can, whether the person you are speaking to wants your information or not.

You burn your hand a couple of times, both accidents, but this defines your relationship with fire, and fear itself, for your whole life.

When you start having trouble seeing the chalkboard, you wear your awful 80's oversized plastic frames, because seeing was more important than fashion. And do not forget braces! So important for the full picture.

Pretty sure at this point you have set a record for things you can be teased about.

Imagine all of the harsh words, the hair pulling, the "oops, that was an accident" (it wasn't), the time you had your head slammed in the bathroom door because you didn't want a classmate to be late after lunch, and all of the tears because you just can't understand why other kids are so mean. All you want is to be friends.

So, when you discover books with magic swords and dragons who Impress their riders, you find home. Your books are your friends. They take you on adventures where the villains are obvious, the heroes are wonderful, and very often good triumphs over evil. They never call you names or laugh at how big and awkward you are. And in the thousands of pages, you read you discover magic, sacred connections, and definitive experiences with divine beings that you want to believe in.

You want it all so badly, it sits like a stone in your belly, a constant reminder of the complete mundanity of your life.

And then right after freshman year, your Mother, your sainted, amazing Mother, passes away.

Oof.

But this is when all the seeds you planted in yourself, conscious or not, start blooming. This is when you have one of your most formative moments, just you and some freshly watered grass. You discover the stark contrast between the less than helpful confession (to be fair, it was not the priest's fault. You asked for something he could not give), and the feelings of comfort and calm you get walking through the grass.

Imagine discovering yourself through grief. You dedicate yourself to the Goddess at 15. You dedicate yourself as a Witch at 18, after you decided that you could take responsibility for your magick. You participate in your Baccalaureate Mass, consciously saying goodbye to the religion of your childhood. This will be the last time you partake in the host and wine and is the start of the adventure.

Now, imagine that you are tall, with hair that is mostly silver, your knees hurt, and you are still freckled, smart, and mostly like people. But now you are also connected, beloved, and an initiated Priestess of Sekhmet. The road's been long and bumpy, but you have half a lifetime's worth of experiences and the stone in your belly is long gone.

You did it. You found the magick, the sacred, the divine. There are times when your heart is so full that you can only cry because the feeling is too big for your body.

So do not stop. Life is not about reaching the top of the mountain. There is no flag to plant, no finish line. There is always another lesson, another way to become more. Sure, sometimes it is hard, scary, or impossible, but always take that next step.

You will understand, I promise.

Try to remember that when the world is on fire, and everything seems awful, there are people who are full of light and love, who love you dearly. Do not lose perspective, it will help you through all the frustration and loneliness.

I know you love community most of all, but please figure out that you are just fine alone. You have everything you need, anything else is grace.

Remember that we find what we seek, so do not make too many snap decisions or judgements. Always, always remember what it is like to be on the other side of the counter, the phone, the email…make sure you always work to not add to the misery of someone else's day.

If you are anything like me, you know you sometimes use too many words to get your point across. I know you do it for clarity's sake. Just, try to be patient with those who do not always let you finish before they respond. You can always try again.

And this probably sounds like the current woo trend of the day, but mindfulness and gratitude really do go a long way. It is so easy to get stuck in the dark, and remembering all the good and wonderful people and things in your life does help. This will help keep perspective too.

Do not worry about the small stuff. Color your hair. Get the tattoo. Use the weed. You are still you inside, and that is way, way more important. Also, challenges will come. It is okay to be afraid, just do not let it beat you. Tests of courage keep you honest about yourself.

Finally, no matter what, remember there is beauty and joy in the world.

If you manage to follow my advice, I know you will discover a life filled with moments of happiness to treasure. I certainly have.

Wherever the road takes us, blessings on our journey.

Θkay, Future Parents

You got this weird, funny, too smart for their own good kid. They are always wondering what they can learn next, and pride themselves on their accuracy, even when little. They are a drama queen when it comes to pain, but really, when they are that clumsy, they hurt themselves a lot.

Give them space. Give them time. Be patient. They are going to spill their drink, drop their plate, trip over thick air, or hit someone with a bat or stick. They have a hard time making their body work, and they are not doing it on purpose.

Let them speak. Sometimes it takes a few extra words to get the whole idea across. Do not assume what they are going to say. It will keep them from feeling betrayed when they get in trouble for a misunderstanding.

Try to make magic in your home. This kid will eat it up eagerly, and want to find ways to participate, or make that same magic to others. Let them play their games and read their books, just like my parents did. But make sure they have a good grasp on the difference between fantasy and reality. It may take a minute but keep at it. It will serve them so well in the long run.

Let them laugh, cry, and feel their big feelings. Just try to make sure their anger does not get out of control and that they are not beaten by their fears.

They are going to want to come up with their own ideas and make their own decisions when it comes to matters of the spirit. Things will have to make sense to them, and lots of big box religion just does not. But do not worry about it too much, they ultimately want to find a spiritual path that helps them to be happy and good.

Love them. That is the biggest and most important thing. Make sure that no matter what, they are loved, and loved for everything they are.

Thank you in advance. I know I will be in good care.

"Sorry, all our house cat positions are filled. You can be a hyena, a mollusk or a a dust mite."

44. Let Me Bloom

By Phoenix Silver

HAT WOULD I TELL MY PARENTS IF WE GOT TO try again? This is a question that has been on my mind surprisingly frequently as of late. What would I have told them if I could go back to when they were expecting me, knowing that I turned out to be far from what they expected? Where did things go so wrong and how could we have remedied that? Why did I end up so traumatized from being abnormal?

I suppose I should give some background on myself to be able to properly answer these questions. I was born to very Catholic parents in a very rural area, the youngest of five. By the time I started forming memories, my three oldest siblings (the youngest of whom is almost a full eighteen years older than me) had all left the church. My second sister was a staunch atheist, which was a major factor in my parents kicking her out. I must concede that my upbringing would have been far worse if she had not started breaking down my parents' expectations of perfectly holy children. Mind you, since my siblings set the tone for leaving the church, which made my parents try even harder to keep me in. They sent me to a Catholic elementary school where I was bullied consistently for the vast majority of my time there. By the time I turned fifteen, I was ready for a change. Catholicism never felt right to me. Thus, when my third sister informed me that she was Pagan and explained Paganism to me, something clicked in my head. Paganism made so much more sense to me. However, my sister and I both hid our Paganism from our parents given how they handled our atheist sister. If they were willing to kick her out for being atheist, what would they do to us for being what they would deem false god worshippers?

This leads me to the first answer, I suppose. Do not force a belief system on a child. Let your child's curiosity blossom to learn about religions and beliefs to find their own path and have empathy for others. Forcing beliefs leads to resentment and shame. It is dimming the light that could shine so brightly otherwise. Religious trauma is so hard to overcome, and it is so common. Your child will find their path whether you like it or not, so why not help them learn and grow instead of forcing them into a mold that they most likely do not fit into and never will?

A second piece of advice: work *with* your child instead of against them. Do not tell them, "Because I said so." If you want your child to understand—and they probably want to understand—explain everything to them instead of using authoritarian rules. My mother's strict rules and harsh punishments did not teach me not to do things she did not want me to do. They taught me to be a better liar, to cover my tracks better. This meant I had no guidance around things like avoiding abusive relationships when I began to date without my parents' knowledge. For the love of whatever deity you may or may not believe in, teach your child instead of hurting them. Regardless of how similar or different your child is compared to your expectations; your child deserves a chance to thrive as their own person.

Lastly, listen to your child. Truly listen. If you do not listen to what your child needs from you, your child will eventually give up on communicating with you. My parents did not ask, so I did not tell them what was really happening in my life. Why would I when the only time they really listened was to punish me for my honesty? The amount of frustration, anger, and despair I felt living in my parents' home because they did not listen to me is immeasurable. It was like my voice was sucked away by the wind whenever I asked for my emotional needs to be met. Did my parents meet my physical needs? Sure. I never went hungry, and I always had a roof over my head and clothes on my back. Did I ever get the validation that I needed? Did I ever get my thoughts treated as that of a full human being? Not until I left. While I appreciate that my parents listen now, it could have saved them and me so much grief if they had done so from the start.

Please, treat my next vessel with care, and those of my companions. We will be the generation that you leave this planet to. If you leave us with your scars as well as our own, I fear that we may be too scarred to keep going. End your cycles, your generational curses. End the perpetual trauma. Be the parent that you needed when you were hurt and lonely because we, too, are hurt and lonely souls. Be better than the generations before you before it is too late. Be better even now, before we are your children. You cannot build the foundations of love and trust overnight. "Ugly duckling" children like me need all the extra love and trust you can build. You are the ones who will build our foundations, and I hope you build them well. We are not your legacy, but how you care for us will be.

45. An Essay for Future Parents

By Joel Bukowski

IFE IS FULL OF MYSTERY. IT IS WONDEROUS AND strange and turns quickly when we expect it to go straight. Families are born when the children come into being and it is a wonderful sight to behold. Often this happens without a plan and complications of some sort arise when we feel we cannot take on anymore. What happens when the child comes into being and is special beyond the bounds of what you think you can handle? More and more frequently, children are born with minds that are exploding with desire for more than we, as parents, can ever possibly give them. I was one such child.

My life as a young one was rather traditional in that I had a brother and sister, a mom and dad, my dad worked as an engineer in a machine shop, and my mom took classes and became a nurse in the late 70's. We had a large backyard that had a small section of woods, complete with various forms of wildlife. I grew up with a freedom to explore that some children of the time may not have had, yet I was never given directions except for the traditional values of the average family of the time.

But I was strange. I never felt like I fit in anywhere. My passions were for things that kids my age thought were weird. I talked to animals like my friends would talk with each other. I saw the mechanics of the wind affecting the trees and could see the aberrations in the flow of the air as a dark wriggling mass that sought to fill in the area behind trees and sticks. I could see the soft glow of people and knew the difference between the "good" people, the "bad" people, and those who seemed lost in their own world the same as me.

At one time, I thought that all people were like me, but as I grew and met and interacted with more and more people, I found that this was rather unique to myself. There were others that could bear witness to some of the things that I experienced, but nobody seemed to understand the full complexity of wat I did. Well, that was what I thought at first.

I was fortunate to have an uncle that was as weird (or more so) than I was. He recognized some of the traits that I exhibited and took a chance to see if he could help me develop my natural instincts. Not on his own, of course, but by first introducing me to someone who understood discipline and a bit of the esoteric away from common western culture. The man I was introduced to was a Martial Arts Instructor in Aikido. Aikido is a martial art that seeks to blend the mind, body, *and* spirit through traditional exercise and meditations.

The connection that I seemed to have with what my sensei called "spirit" was very startling to him (though he would never say so to ME). He spoke of this to my uncle about this connection and it began a series of events that changed things for me.

My uncle was, in fact, a Rosicrucian. His knowledge of mysticism came from a lifetime of study and because of this was considered an "odd duck" in the family. I was not aware of his standing as a mystic for many years, but I received bits and pieces of training from him and my sensei over the next year on various subjects that were considered Occult by many, but I saw them simply as "interesting. My uncle passed away when I was young, only after a year or so and unbeknownst to me, had left my father with a cryptic message concerning his belongings.

My formative years (5-15) were mainly conventional, but it was interspaced with things that would spur my mind into different and new directions. I was by no means a "prodigy", but I was also not exactly average. I was tested for many things including colorblindness (which I was), accelerated reading skills and comprehension (also true), and various other skills which I showed an aptitude for but no desire to pursue.

My martial Arts (and related philosophy) classes continued throughout my summers and regular school in the fall. Winter, and spring. Upon reaching my 18th birthday, I was cleaning out the attic of my dad's garage because of a roof cave-in, and I discovered some old boxes of books with a strange symbol on them—a Cross with a Rose in the center. When I asked my dad what they were, my dad sat down and simply said, those books were your Uncle C—'s and now they are yours. I found out later that the cryptic message that my uncle told my dad was, "when your son turns 18, he may have these books in my collection."

It took a while to read all the information that my uncle left me, but I was in no way hindered by my parents. I tested the waters of life by making a few really stupid decisions by which I learned a few lessons that I believe I was meant to learn and would not learn in any other way. But the gist of the whole situation showed me that there were things that I never would have figured out if not for a few individuals that I met at a few very specific times in my life. These people did not have a "plan" for me, but only wished that I was able to pursue whatever path I may encounter with tools I may need to succeed.

I am keeping this story kind of short. I am a Philosopher and I can weave tales that span chapters, but in essence, this I about how my family accepted me for what I was, strange and unique, and did not try to force me to conform to the very traditional way of life that the family had experienced for generations. Allowing a child to explore is paramount to them being able to grow Spiritually, and Magically. Mysticism is a large part of who I am, but because I had a couple people who saw the potential (and all of the possible directions, both good and bad, that it could take) that gave me the generic tools to follow my path and make decisions that benefited not only me, but all those who I met along the way, I feel truly blessed.

I discovered my true (past) self through mystical meditations as taught to me by many different teachers. The best lesson was to not be afraid of what I may find in all the potential incarnations or experiences of my former "selves". Each one brings baggage and potential past trauma to the surface, but we find that even though it might be very difficult to wade through, it IS in the past. We are here not to learn from those experiences. It is difficult for modern people who are based on the illusion of solid reality to understand that we can know something without experiencing it AGAIN in THIS LIFE.

The second—best lesson that I learned was to trust your instincts if your instincts are true. Deciphering *True Instinct* from fantasy or imagination comes from having the correct tools to understand it. These tools are simple–dedication, discipline, and a true sense of self. The first two are pretty straight—forward, but a true sense of self comes when you apply the first two *to your own self—examination*. Be honest and you will never be led astray.

My own children were brought up with us encouraging a sense of wonder. My daughter, more than my son, has embraced the natural magic that our bloodline seems to hold. My son is ever the practical person that keeps us grounded. They are a really good balance for each other. This is not about living life without rules or understanding consequence. It is about creating a safe place for them to explore the world (and all the potential dangers) with a proper toolset and understanding that they are not just observers in this magical world, but active participants.

I jokingly say that the only rule I had for my kids was that they were NOT allowed to fly until they were at least 16 years old. It was true, but it also means that they were free to experiment (under supervision) and *taste* the world in ways that mundane children often are not allowed.

My advice to parents of magical Fey children should be patience. If you can recognize that there is something special about your child (or children), you should not be afraid to admit that you may not be able to do all that is necessary for them to reconnect with their true (or past) selves, but you CAN give them area to explore and maybe direct them to others who DO have the ability to equip them with the tools they may need.

46. Failed Conformity and the Odd Child

By Katelyn Dawn

 WAS THE YOUNGEST by 12 years and by far the strangest individual in my family, a characteristic which has only increased with age. We were devout Roman Catholics, and as a result, I spent a lot of my childhood sitting on uncomfortable wooden pews or kneeling on doubly uncomfortable benches.

I also was forced to spend Wednesday evenings in catechism class. For those of you lucky enough not to know, Catechism is the study of the Catholic interpretation of the Bible, and the sole purpose of Catechism is to prepare children and teens to be members of the Catholic church, something as a child I was not entirely sold on, but nonetheless accepted as an inevitability, as children do, as they are trained to do.

One evening of Catechism stands out in particular. I remember being snapped out of my dissociative, daydreaming adventure by a brief statement the teacher made, teacher is a very generous title here, for the teacher was really a Mother within our Parish who volunteered to teach us how to genuflect and do the sign of the cross, and who likely pulled the short straw during some Church committee meeting, resigned to the fact that her evenings would be spent in a stuffy bible school classroom teaching kids how to think and how not to. The statement she made was very vague, and brief, but I knew it to be profoundly incorrect, and there is nothing that irritates a neurodivergent child more than factual inaccuracy, for this teacher said that the Earth was created by God in six days, and on the seventh day, God rested.

This, I understood, and could easily explain, finally a way to contribute I remember thinking as I put up my hand and proceeded to tell the teacher that the universe was created by some large force, some called it the Big Bang, and that humans evolved many, many years after this.

The teacher, let's call her Mrs. Smarmy, for fun, was displeased, her brow furrowed, and I, therefore, misread the anger on the Catholic school teacher's face as confusion, so I started to explain further, I was excited to share contradictory information with her, after all, I had read everything I could get my hands on about History, Religious and otherwise, clearly, her story made no sense, and after all, we have the fossils to prove it. I simply had to regale the class and the poor middle—aged parent, who volunteered her evenings to teach us with the far more interesting Theory I knew to be widely accepted in the Scientific community.

This first event would then be a regular occurrence, throughout my miseducation, I misunderstood their concern and interpretation of me because the worst enemy of conformity and control is knowledge. Oh, the horror of a child shirking the offerings of Abrahamic religion, of her own volition! It would take years to arrive at the conviction that most adults had no idea what the hell they were talking about and that they could not really be trusted, or at least not to make important decisions.

I was born in New England to a single Mother who could not care for me. As a Catholic adoption agency saw fit, they placed me with a wonderful Catholic family. A nuclear family, one that was sufficiently toeing the line of normalcy. My adoptive family boasted a mother, a father, two sisters, and a brother, and they were very loving and kept me safe, even spoiling me sufficiently. I did not fit in with them, and still do not, although we have a good relationship now, it was rocky for some time.

I was an odd child, perpetually reading, always in the woods, always rebelling and misbehaving. I used to coerce my friends into making Altars and offerings on the limestone formations behind my childhood home in the Appalachian Mountains. I would tame animals, even wild ones, I was always challenging the status quo. I was never much like my adoptive family, even in appearance I was, and still am, a little bit disheveled, with wild unruly hair. I was regularly covered in dirt from climbing trees or riding horses. A wild child, through and through. Surely not the picture of perfection and beige normalcy, which was a characteristic my siblings and parents both embodied.

I was rebellious at school, excelling in History and failing Math... Which did not interest me until we got to geometry where I was enamored with Pythagoras and everything Euclidean. It was a lonely existence, burying myself within an avalanche of Authors, immersing myself in all the strange and unusual. The voices of hundreds of Authors helped me find my own. I never understood the modern perception of Religion, at least the Abrahamic version, the watered down, diluted translation of Magickal Theory, devoid of meaning, passion, and esoteric concepts, an interpretation designed and focused to shape, mold, and conform, even as a small child I saw through it, and that was even more polarizing.

Eventually, I came to realize that conforming was easier, so for many years I swallowed my thoughts, feelings, and beliefs. After all, it was so much better than being ostracized, it was easier to be swept away in the tide than to swim against it. This was dangerous, as I allowed myself to be used and abused by others, in an effort to be compliant and complacent.

Years passed in a haze, and eventually, I woke up again and started to dust off my old books, my stones, and my writing, and I embraced the beauty of Awen. I was again inspired, awakened, and immersed in freedom, love, and all things magickal. I came back to myself, I should have never deviated from my heart, but I did, and many others have as well, it is a response to conditioning and even in some cases trauma, some call it a fawn response, the decision to be who they want, and to give up your power.

If at this point in the essay you have arrived at the conclusion that I eventually grew up to be a proud Pagan of some type, you would be correct. I am now nearly forty, a Third—Degree High Priestess, and a First—Degree Druid, I practice Hydromancy, study, and teach esoteric concepts. I am an amateur Braucher and Amateur Anthropologist. I am a perpetual student of the Sacred arts! I am a lover of people and nature.

My titles do not matter as much as the fact that I have the freedom of choice, of thought, and I have settled into a harmonious existence where I convey the sacred knowledge that I have always immersed myself in. This happy conclusion was carved out of an unyielding medium of failed forced compliance.

Without malicious intent, I was hurt by the actions of those who raised me and desperately tried to get me to fit in. They did this out of love, but as an adopted neurodivergent and intuitively Pagan child, you can imagine how difficult it was to be "othered" by teachers, peers, family, and friends. I did blossom despite this and even because of this. There were many instances of trauma, sadness, fear, and self—nullifying behavior that I have left out because they were lessons, while that does not minimize their impact, it helps me to maintain a growth mindset by interpreting these experiences as lessons.

I now know that forcing children to be complacent and bend to the will of societal expectations does not need to be the norm. It should not be! Uniquely offbeat and Magickal children should be encouraged to march to the beat of their own drum. I encourage ALL parents, I beg you, let your children guide you. Meet them where they are. Allow them to show you the Magick they see, the magick you have forgotten. Honor the unique child with stars in their eyes and dirt on their feet, allow them to be sovereign.

The need to shape and mold children to fit the acceptable conditions of Patriarchal society is not your own, it was borrowed and learned, the concept perpetuated by those that seek dominance, control, and subservience. Truly, fear is what drives forced assimilation, parents want their children to succeed, whatever that definition means to them, and to succeed they need to fit in, they cannot rebel, and surely cannot worship anything other than the acceptable God.

If I could go back and learn the concepts and experience the growth earlier, perhaps it would have been better. I understand that the system is rigged, and the parents that removed their shackles and taught their offspring to stand in their power have it right, and that does not always look like the nuclear family, the white picket fence, and the guise of perfection, hidden under abuse and trauma.

I can't turn back time in this incarnation; however, I can stand up and help others see, help shape the perception of free thought and help others see the Magick right in front of their eyes, I hope that my second awakening wasn't too late for my son, and my own family. I hope that reading this will help another parent or a future parent learn to stand up too. I feel so sorry for anyone who does not see that we are all connected and that we are one with Nature, especially if at one point in their lives, they did see and feel that connection.

Art by Craig R. Miller, from the Wheel of the Year Songbook, *by Gwydion Pendderwen*

47. The Pagan Child and the Low Profile

By Alan Leddon

EAR FUTURE PAGAN GENERATION AND DEAR Mom & Dad for my next life,

It is with some delight that I take this opportunity to share the benefit of my experience with you, in the hopes of sparing you and yours some of the negative experiences that come from being "different" or "weird" in modern society. It may seem as though I am overly focused on a childhood tainted by the judgments of others, and, maybe to some degree, I am. I only hope that my recitation of the facts below is seen as is intended, as the most objective recounting possible. While most people are accepting and tolerant, those who are not so are vocal and cruel. Drawing their attention is to be avoided.

The youth of today would scarcely recognize the world of my high school years. Largely absent were woke-culture, wide-spread acceptance of alternate lifestyles, and jocks willing to defend the differently-abled. A percentage of the people of the time delighted in tormenting those seen as different, and still more joined in this activity in order to gain acceptance among the more popular kids. We all know that, no matter how good things are, there is always the 9.2% of people trying to ruin it for everyone.

I was seen as different, and I suffered socially as a result. My earliest memory of this was the "hide-and-seek" games played outside the main door of my school while awaiting entrance. Whoever was "it" would stand at the same pole every time, and those who were hiding would all, as a group, go "hide" around the same corner of the building. They'd have to pass "it" to get to "safe." After being caught a few too many times, I started going the other way, hiding in the bushes that lay closer to safe than that corner—and reaching safe while "it" was scattering the players around the corner. For this, I was dubbed "stupid" and "weird."

By eighth grade, I was nearly constantly harassed owing to my wide range of interests, consistently high test scores, and excellent memory. I was physically assaulted more than once for reading while others watched or played football. When it was discovered that I was a Boy Scout, the harassment got worse; when it was learned that I was a D&D player, it got worse still. And yet worse when I was caught reading books of mythology. Even beyond the harassment, I was only invited to three parties in my 13 years of school – and I was told often enough that I'd been rejected for being a teacher's pet, for liking science, for having a *Star Trek* lunchbox, and for other reasons contributing to my lack of social worth. This continued even past my childhood –for the same reasons, I went to prom dateless, and only one girl danced with me. She was the only person who saw me off when I left that small town forever.

Meanwhile, my stepfather and mother operated their own little home of horrors. On multiple occasions, I came home from school to see my stepfather feeding books from my bedroom into a burning barrel (we lived in a rural setting). If I did homework before chores, the parental response was…uncomfortable. When I was caught exploring the nearby woods, or when I was suspected of taking a book when I climbed a tree…more parental disapproval. When my artwork was displayed in a local gallery, I was punished because my parents felt obligated to attend the opening. Even looking over the plywood barrier at the rusting pump in the well house risked severe and stacked punishments. Winning on family game night invited punishment for "cheating."

Such was my ability that, when relatives contacted no less a person than President Ronald Reagan with a request that he stand behind his professed commitment to education by assisting my family to cover my tuition to Calasanctius School for the Gifted in Buffalo NY, he made a personal donation to the school to enable them to lower their tuition (but they didn't lower it enough to help my family afford it). And, yes, I do have documentation of this, including the actor's personal response and my acceptance letter to the school.

I discovered Paganism at 9 years old. I had taken my bike around the rather enormous block that I lived on and entered the same nearby woods. I heard singing. I approached it. I came across a group holding a Sabbat ritual (Beltane) in a unique "tradition" that amounted to vanilla Wicca seasoned with Norse decorations and names. I knew that I'd found something of value. Before my thirteenth birthday, I could watch and ask all the questions I wanted; after my thirteenth birthday I was allowed to participate. My parents were not informed.

To all parents, and especially my future mom and dad, I would ask you to teach your children to avoid becoming the scapegoat of the school by denying ammunition to the bullies. Teach your children how to keep a low profile when in the company of those who might not be accepting of their differences. Teach them to assess the reaction of their peers to any topic before launching into a discussion of it; keep their interest quiet if others disapprove. Please teach them to only discuss their true religion with people, at times, and in places that you have previously approved – you never know which friend's parent or which teacher will still hold onto outdated bigotries. Being the only kid not invited to another student's party for some minor reason (I liked *Star Trek* more than football--) can really hurt.

And, for the sake of Aphrodite and all like Her –PLEASE teach your kids how to communicate with other genders, I am reminded of 9-year-old Maia Skouris (as portrayed by Conchita Campbell in *The 4400*) shouting the question that has mystified girls for generations: "Why are boys so stupid?" (a question typically prompted by the difference in communication strategies used by boys and girls). Being rejected and then teased hurts – especially if these are occasioned by one's perfectly natural behavior, and they open the child up for more of each.

In the past, some Pagan groups have used subtle signals to identify themselves to others – a featureless green button, or a hand held in the shape of a "c" (or crescent moon) held near the eye. It would be helpful to return to the use of these.

To my future self, I give similar advice. Always mention one of your interests in a neutral way ("My neighbor told me that he thinks I should join Scouting USA. I'm not sure how to respond." "Some people that I know put quarters in the soil at the end of each row of corn to "buy" a better harvest.... what do you make of that?"). Don't flaunt your beliefs, and don't make false claims about them; these will always come back to bite you. Also, if possible, try to go through this life without bragging and without correcting people unnecessarily. Especially, do not openly practice the esoterica of your faith until after you have carefully considered the overall openness of your community (as has been said by others, "if all of your brash neighbors disapprove of something, it is effectively illegal").

And so, to my future parents and future self, I must reiterate the important parts of the above. As long as people continue to be people, it will be advantageous to avoid drawing the attention of others to the ways in which you are different from the rank and file of people. Carefully considered and subtle actions will help one to identify the people that you can safely share your interests with.

Yours in service to Her,

Alan

48. To My Future Parents

by Catherine Carr

O NOT BE AFRAID of me. I will say things you do not understand. This is because you have forgotten what you once knew: listen to me.

Do you ever notice that children seem to know things that they should not? Have you ever heard them speak about the past once they were grown? Have you seen them speak to beings you cannot see?

Teach me how to be a good friend. Even to beings that you cannot see. If you cannot see them, sit and speak to them with me. I may know neighbors you have forgotten.

Help me to explore. We can only grow by learning, and learning is of the body as much as it is of the mind. Give me the experiences I ask for, and sometimes the experiences I am afraid of, so I can grow. Let me learn from your bravery, not from your fear.

When I am misunderstood, help me to express myself instead of helping me to change myself. The world can only grow by learning, and it cannot grow if we shrink ourselves to comfortably fit the size it is now.

Help me to push against the world's edges, stretching them a little. Teach me resilience for when it pushes back, but do not teach me to stop pushing.

I will be inconvenient. That is the point. The only things that are convenient are the ones who fit neatly into spaces that already exist. I am here to carve out a new space, to change the shape of the world for the better.

When I am inconvenient, ask: what would happen if this child ruled the world? When I am inconvenient in my demands for justice, in my ingenuity, in my irrepressible joy, ask what part of yourself I am reminding you of that you had forgotten.

I am here so that we can both be children again. I am here so that you can stop pretending to fit into the spaces the world already knows. I am here so that we can make new spaces together and shape the world, instead of the world shaping us.

You forget. As you grow older, you forget. You forget what you once knew. You forget that you are here to shape the world, and not the other way around. You need a new soul, fresh delivered from the celestial realm, to remind you.

Let me remind you. And do not let me forget.

To my future self

Do not forget.

They will tell you that what you were was irrational, unreasonable, immature.

Do not forget.

They will tell you that what you felt in your blood and bones was unrealistic, false, imagined.

Do not forget.

What you sensed beneath the currents of creation, what you knew and still know in your blood and bones, is the way things really are. It is this strange world of steepled roofs and screens and sanitized, clinical etiquette that is imagined.

Do not forget.

It is the fire in your bones that you inherit from the Big Bang, from the first animal, from the ancestors.

It is the kinship you feel with the sky and the stars and all the living world that is real.

It is your asking "why?" And your rebellion, your this—does not—seem—right that is your purpose.

It is not your failure when you fail to fit into the world's empty spaces. It is the failure of the architects who came before you. Do not fail the same way they did. Do not fail to imagine. Do not douse the fire in your bones. Do not sever your connection to the living world because someone told you that what you felt was wrong.

Do not forget where you came from.

Do not forget.

49. Living as a Divine Being in a Human Existence

By Anthony Isbill

EAUTIFUL WEIRDO. This incarnation has certainly been interesting to say the least. I came to my spiritual enlightenment later in life. Currently, I am 41 years old. I am naturally an only child, but I have one adopted younger sibling. A transman brother. I've only recently re—awakened. It has been challenging...but extremely rewarding.

I was born to a religious family in central Oklahoma, USA. A deeply conservative state where anyone who is not Christian, Heterosexual, and Caucasian is not given the benefit of any doubt. I am none of these things. Well, arguably I am white passing, with Native American roots. I am also gay, and a Witch—a powerful witch. Seer, Empath, Manifestor, Divinator, Healer, Elemental...and I have been my whole life. I have only recently been able to access my abilities again after decades of hiding and blocking them due to a deep—rooted fear of a religion I no longer believe in.

Growing up, I knew I was different. I knew, instinctively, that I needed to hide those differences because if I did not it could mean trouble for me. Brought on by my own family, by the community I lived in, and by society in general. I was born in the early 1980's, when it was still very much a taboo subject to be gay. Later, when the AIDS epidemic came about, it was even more so. I did not have access to affirming or supportive role models, counselors, friends, adults or really anyone I could emulate to tell me what I felt was not wrong, evil, or sinful. So, I hid it most of my life. I did come out to my parents when I was fourteen and was met with both prejudice and hatred. It was not all bad. It became a "we just don't talk about that" situation. I was content with that.

It was the same with my spiritual abilities. I was an aura reader and empath from an incredibly early age. However, it was not "of God", therefore it must be "evil" and "sinful" – it also meant if I continued to do those things I was destined for Hell. Of course, I know now this is not the case. One would think that I have wasted the last 30+ years when I could have been honing my abilities and working in my Divine nature to do the work I was incarnated to do. To heal and to be a beacon of light to others so they may also shine through Universal Love and Collective Unity. However, through self—introspection, a modicum of Shadow Work, meditation and accessing my Higher Self, I have realized the past that I lived was necessary to get me to this point. There is no longer that past. There is only Now, and what I choose to do with the knowledge I have gained to this point.

In truth, I am unsure there will be a future incarnation of my spirit on Earth to read this account. The more I delve into my spiritual journey, the more I feel my next path through the veil will be as a Guide. Guides no longer incarnate but assist souls who are incarnating. I am at peace with that. I have surrendered this life to the Universe. I will continue to learn and grow until there is nothing more for me to learn here.

I have found a wonderful community of souls, witches, and enlightened beings. A chosen family that is helping me on this journey. We are forming a Collective Community for others like me who were searching for...us. We know there will be a rough road ahead, within our own lifetimes. Many more souls are awakening to Universal truth and love. They will need guidance and community. We are called for this reason, and we are not the only ones.

For whomever is reading this, be it a future incarnation of my spirit, or someone called to learn from my former journey, I have one piece of advice: Lead with Love. Love is the driving force of the Universe. Love is the one unifying power that connects each and every one of us with Source. Love is Creation. I certainly do not know everything, but I do know that.

Dear Mom(s) and/or Dad(s)

Let us be clear: being a parent is not easy. It is stressful, worrisome, painful, and at times heartbreaking. It is also one of the most rewarding things a third density being on Earth can achieve. Or so I am told. I am not a parent, nor do I have any desire to be. This section will be short, because quite frankly, I do not have much advice on being a parent. I do, however, know about being a child of parents. In that vein, I can share some insights.

Do you remember all those dreams you had of your child as they were carried through pregnancy? Your son will one day be a famous sports celebrity! Or a multi—million—dollar stockbroker! Your daughter will one day be a prima ballerina! Or President of the United States!

Forget all the expectations you have for your children. Please. They cannot live up to them. They cannot fulfill your childhood dreams for you. You cannot live vicariously through them. They do not exist to be extensions of what YOU wanted for yourself. They were created with their own paths and destinies that may have absolutely nothing to do with you. That is a hard truth to accept.

As parents, your only job is to raise your children to be who they are meant to be. That means allowing them the freedom to explore their own choices, make their own mistakes. They may not follow your religious path. They may not want to continue in the family business that you started. They may not even want to stay the same gender they were born as. It is okay to have hopes and dreams for your children. However, if the paths your children choose to do not follow those hopes and dreams, which is okay, too! Because like YOU did when you were young, they have their own minds and their own souls. They want to be happy and to be loved. Give that to them. You created them. You brought them into this world. Now, it is time to let them do what they came to this life to do. Support them in their choices, so long as those choices do no harm to themselves or others. Guide them. Be the parent that your child can trust to come to you with anything.

Allow them to flourish in their creativity. Allow them to come into their own power and intuition. Allow them to cultivate their spirits as well as their bodies. They are precious facets of Source, as we all are. It is their job to live as Divine Beings and learn from their own unique human existence, same as you.

To my Future Self

As stated previously, I am not sure if I will have a future incarnation. That has almost a sense of finality. A sense of ending. There is no true ending, though, is there? Even if my own future incarnation is not reading this, a soul I guided may be is reading this and can still learn from whatever it is I can teach. The Universe does work in strange ways like this, yes?

Be strong in your convictions. Know your power and your abundance! You are a super charged spiritual being living a human existence. ENJOY it! Trust yourself. Your intuition and gut feelings are gifts from your Guides to help you through this learning process. They cannot be wrong.

Please, never stop searching. Keep learning and trying new things, even if they seem scary or out of your comfort zone. There is no learning curve here. It is all just experiencing. There is NO WRONG OR RIGHT way to exist. There is only existing.

Remove fear from your vocabulary. Fear is the one constant state of being that halts spiritual evolution in its tracks. There is nothing to be afraid of. Death? There is no death. Only a transference from one state of existence to another. Take away that fear of death and, there is quite literally nothing else to be afraid of.

The world is your playground, my love. It is a stage and you it is star. Everyone and everything else are merely costars and day players. Be mindful of this and remember that in this same thought you are a mirror to those around you. You are the day player in their third acts.

We are all one. Connected through Love. Many Blessings.

"Urbi et Orbi" (to the City and to the World) illustration from Camille Flammarion's L'atmosphère : météorologie populaire *(Paris: Hachette, 1888), p. 163.*

50. Stranger in a Strange Land

By Jack Montgomery

Y MAGICAL, DYSFUNC-tional childhood.

I was born in 1953 to a first-generation white-collar family who rose to lower-middle class in the post-WWII/Korea period in America. My parents purchased an 800-square-foot, two-bedroom house in Columbia. South Carolina when I was two and stayed there until 1965 when we moved to the rapidly expanding subdivisions in the northwestern part of the rural old Dutch Fork section near Lexington, SC 12 miles away. My mother, unlike so many women in the post war period, did not return to the 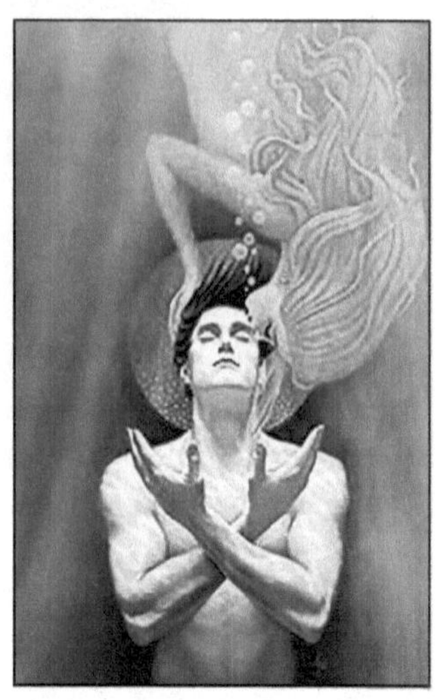 home to have babies and to pursue a domestic avocation after I was born. Neither did her sister who lived in one house down on the same street. As a result, our maternal grandmother kept my cousins and myself from 6:60am till 5:30pm five days a week in her home a mile away. My cousins and I were lucky in that we had two mother figures. To the best of my knowledge, we are genetically a mix of German and Scots Irish peoples called the "Black Dutch" and the "Black Irish" respectively.

Unlike other kids my age, I seemed to have had an enhanced sense of self from an incredibly early age. As early as age four, I never felt like I was a real member of my family and at one time was convinced that I had been marooned or abandoned by mysterious others and that they would come back for me one day. I remember lying in my bed thinking: "This is not who I am, I do not belong here. I am not a member of this family. Who are these people?" I did not feel like I belonged in this world either but resolved that I had to play along and make the best of it until "they" returned for me. I made this decision before I started school along with the resolution not to have children. My late mother believed in the genetic inheritance of bad traits like domestic abuse and hence I resolved that our collective nightmare would end with me.

Throughout my childhood and adolescence our immediate family life was overwhelmed with emotional discord and domestic violence as my father suffered PTSD from his war—time experience and dysfunctional homelife as a child. The episodic violence directed at me began at age two and continued until my father abandoned us when I was sixteen to pursue a relationship with another woman in another city. Like other kids in similar situations, I learned to dissociate so as not to react to the blows or express any pain lest I make the incident last even longer. What once was a retreat into fantasy for play or remembrance now became a tool for emotional survival. I was glad I had no siblings to share in this chaotic situation. I was also, at age four, tasked by my mother with hiding our situation from everyone including family.

Being an only child on the weekends gave me considerable time alone and I reveled in the silence and solitude. I played with the neighborhood kids, but never really felt like I was being myself. I was acting like a kid with kids who seemed like ghosts to me. I learned to play the games of childhood, but they gave me no satisfaction. When I played alone, I was myself. I remember acting out these elaborate military scenarios that usually had to do with the British colonial empire although I did not realize this until about age eight or nine. I would become lost in these childhood reveries to the point that my mother would have to come physically retrieve me from the backyard. Later as a teen, I wandered the nearby woods sensing all sorts of entities within them. Those entities were friendly, and I never got lost or was ever afraid in nature's loving arms.

I was also prone to hearing voices and having visionary experiences of a religious nature although we were not especially religious. We went to church, but that was fulfilling a family obligation and the people seemed completely hollow to me. One more time I was pretending to be a normal kid while plagued by the growing recognition that adults were always not as they presented themselves to be and in fact lied to kids all the time.

My developing personality carried over into my elementary school life. My first—grade teacher became concerned about my introversion and brought my mother into the fray, advising her to get me professionally evaluated. My IQ indicated that in certain cognitive areas, I was functioning at a nine— to ten—year—old while only age six. The clinician recommended that I be enrolled in "a school for smart kids." My mother thought it was fine, but my father would have none of it not wishing to "raise an egghead." Despite the domestic disfunction, we looked and sounded like any other family of the time.

Our cultural background, however, included collective practices that in retrospect revealed a certain acceptance of magic and an enhanced awareness of the world of spirits which were understood to be all around us. I remember my mother who held a middle—management position in corporate communications, also had practices that were common to the Appalachian magical traditions in the Western North Carolina region where she grew to adolescence. She gave me buckeyes to carry in my pocket and would not sweep dust out the door after dark. Once at age seven, when I came to her having seen the spirit of a recently deceased relative in our home, she chided me for acting afraid. "Why are you afraid? She loved you when she was alive, what makes you think that has changed?" Mother wisely had me experience the death and dying of relatives from an early age and helped me to understand and not to fear this very normal part of life. An actual Near—Death Experience while traveling in India in 1979, later cemented my lack of fear regarding death and even opened a window to enhanced spirit perception.

Most families in our area read the signs regarding events like the weather and the appearance of strangers. My mother once left me at home with Grandmother based on a prophetic dream, about taking me to the beach. This sort of behavior was common in families in the rural south. One friend's mother was a scryer who stared into a copper bowl of water, another read palms, and another spoke with spirits on a regular basis. Our young lives were saturated with magical elements we just accepted as normal although you were never supposed to speak of these things to outsiders.

Small wonder that in college at the University of South Carolina, I was drawn to the study of American folk religion as I majored in Religious Studies with two minors in Psychology and Anthropology. I fell in love with the ideas and practice of fieldwork which led me to encounter both the Hoodoo, Powwowing and later the Appalachian magical traditions. I lived completely immersed in those traditions for three years during college. I even discovered that I had a family connection to German American Powwowing through my great-grandfather Wagner who powwowed for animals in his rural North Carolina farming community. This was a family secret lest we be seen as superstitious.

This experience led to a life-long experience of magical encounters, spiritual healings and allowed me to meet fascinating people who have helped and guided me on this path. My memoir entitled *American Shamans: journeys with traditional healers,* published in 2008 by BUSCA Press, is a chronicle of my life in magic and spirit.

Advice to parents of a magical child

Although not a parent myself. I can summarize my thoughts on raising children like me:

1. Teach yourself about raising a special child. It is a gift; you need to know how to manage it.

2. Watch for the signs of an intuitive or psychic child. They will appear early in life.

3. Teach your child to interpret his or her experiences in a healthy, accepting manner.

4. Teach the special child ways to balance and manage themselves. Meditation, yoga, daily prayer are all good foundations.

5. Teach your child to cultivate social invisibility where magic is concerned. This world will never understand or embrace such things.

6. If, as apparent, you find yourself in a destructive or abusive relationship that is negative to you and to your child, get out of it. There is nothing to be gained by staying or trying to "work it out." You are not helping yourself and you are actively hurting your psychic child by making them endure abuse whether emotional, physical or both.

7. Let your child know that you accept and love him or her special qualities. Teach them that managed properly, they will be valuable assets to life.

Advice to my future self

1. At this phase in life (my 70s) know that you will keep going as long as this embodiment exists. There is still so much to learn, and you just may have time enough left to learn it as Jack Montgomery.

2. Do not waste time on negativity, despair, or become ensnared by chaotic, parasitic people. Your days are numbered, so use them well. Remember as the poet Charles Bukowski said in his poem *The Laughing Heart*: "Your life is your life. know it while you have it. You are marvelous, the gods wait to delight in you."

3. This life you live will always be changing. Listen to the signs and do not be afraid to act.

4. There will always be positive and negative elements within life. They are both inherent to this physical existence and suffering cannot be eliminated, only embraced and managed. Evil never dies and madness never sleeps so keep your emotional balance and learn how to respond and manage your inner dialogue as that management is central to how well you respond to life's issues.

5. As Hexenmeister Lee Gandee said so eloquently: "If you see the Devil, ask him why he has his horns on backward." Face the paranormal, for it is only another part of normal.

6. Remember the words of author Ralph Waldo Emerson when he said that: "To be yourself in a world that is constantly trying to make you something else is the greatest accomplishment."

51. My Next Incarnation as an Australian Woman

By Eubdia 'Aw Eabdayiyl

(Dear Reader, this essay contains themes of suicide. If this will harm you, please skip this essay. Your emotional health is more important than reading what is in these pages.)

M Y BELOVED MOM and dad, I am your daughter Lisby and I want to tell you that I love you both so much and I am so thankful and grateful to you for having given birth to me and taking care of me since I was a baby.

I want you to know that in my previous life I reincarnated as a man born to a Muslim family in the country of Iraq, in the capital Baghdad. I was very thin, skinny, and physically weak. I did not have parents who could raise me in a normal and correct upbringing like your wonderful and excellent upbringing for me. For this reason, I was severely exploited by the family and society until I committed suicide on the first lunar month after the vernal equinox of the year 2023. I was 24 years old.

My soul remained resting in the spirit world for a period of 6 years and three months until you conceived me, my dear mother, in the year 2029 AD—on the first lunar month after the solstice occurred.

You gave birth to me nine months later in the year 2030, in the first solar month and in the first lunar month after the vernal equinox in the northern half of the Earth—which is the same as the autumnal equinox in the southern half of the Earth, where we are now here in Australia and in Canberra.

My main wish in this life is to live a life as unlike the previous life as possible. Of course, there are many similarities between the two lives, such as that in my previous life I was reincarnated and born in the city of Baghdad, the capital of Iraq, and now I am also reincarnated in the city of Canberra—the capital of Australia. But there are also differences; in my previous life I was born according to the Babylonian zodiac in the month of Aquarius, while in my current life I was born according to the

Babylonian zodiac in the month of Aries. In my previous life I was born according to the Chinese zodiac in the year of the Rabbit 1999, while in my current life I was born according to the Chinese zodiac in the year of the Dog 2030. Also, in my previous life I was reincarnated and born as a heterosexual man, but I chose in this life to be reincarnated and born as a homosexual woman.

Do not expect me to become a mother one day when I grow up. I know that science will have advanced and developed so that I can carry and have a child and become a mother despite being a lesbian, but I do not want to become a mother or adopt children. If you want to become grandparents and have grandchildren, you must have another child besides me—if you have not done so yet.

In my previous life I was the second son of my parents, and their eldest son was a year older than me. In this current life, I chose to be your first daughter.

I used to see many dreams and nightmares that were constantly repeated over and over again from the time I was in nursery school. My parents did not care about my dreams and nightmares at all and made me stop telling my dreams to them. In my current life I am surrounded by good and fair parents like you who care about me and my dreams and nightmares with great interest and ask me to tell them to you. You write them in a notebook that you have devoted to this subject and for this reason you helped me a lot in knowing who I am and remembering many of my previous lives. I did not choose you arbitrarily for no reason, but because you are an excellent and wonderful couple who deserve a special child.

Dear Mom(s) and/or Dad(s)

The advice that I want to give you both, and I hope that you will implement it in my life, is to invest two days off, Saturday and Sunday in each week, and the summer vacation in every year of my studies—in order to help me to practice my favorite personal hobbies in various practices related to spiritual, mystical, or esoteric. Provide me with books rich in myths from varied extinct and living civilizations. Help me learn about paranormal beliefs and practices—particularly controlling dreams, remembering previous lives, the four elements of life, the hidden meaning of numbers, and others as well).

In addition to this, I would also ask you to continue to teach me a new language every year of my adolescence. I enjoy learning foreign languages continuously, which will benefit my writing in my professional future. Please provide me with a library with various collections of poetry, novels, and stories. And the sacred books of different religions and philosophies.

Please stay away from marginalizing me intellectually and respect all my choices and decisions in life. As well as my philosophical ideas—such as my opposition to eating animal meat, my support for the non-reproductive philosophy, my support for the philosophy of nudity, and my unwillingness to do anything that would participate in creating a living being, or that would participate in killing a living being (human, animal, or plant) such as harvesting, hunting birds, fishing, slaughtering animals, etc., The two principles (non-creation and non-killing) are the main ones in the spiritual path that I have drawn for myself in this life.

I also hope that you will accept me as I am because each of us is free to chart his own spiritual path in life based on what suits him more than others. I also want to ask you to suggest to me at the beginning of my adolescence that I open my own channel on YouTube so that I can I share my spiritual experiences with others from an early age on the Internet.

"To my Future Self"

How are you, Lisby? I wish you health, peace, safety, happiness, joy—in your new life and in your new body. You have a wonderful opportunity to live in the western world, where progress and development is continuous, where Paganism, parapsychology, paranormal science, and the science of human development are spreading, flourishing, and continuing to expand.

I advise you to continue reading books—especially sacred books and mythology. Learn how the world was created, what will happen at the end of the world, what happens after death, etc.

Continue writing and reading your diaries and spiritual experiences, such as the dreams and nightmares that have accompanied you since the beginning of time. Remember your previous lives and always thank the gods for the blessing of having a new life better than every old life you lived before in a previous body when.

I also want to advise you not to stay in Australia for the rest of your life, but as soon as you graduate from university and you find it easy to start traveling, take many tourist trips around many countries and benefit from all the languages that you have learned. I also advise you to continue providing your fans with at least one new book every year, translating it into various languages and publishing it widely to share your spiritual experiences. Also, do not forget to establish an institution, association, or temple of your own to teach and spread the esoteric sciences that you have practiced and developed from an early age.

Do not forget to do good and help people constantly, and do not forget to write a letter to your future parents, as I did for you, Goodbye.

Appendices

60-YEAR CYCLE OF CULTURAL RENAISSANCES

Dates	Popular Name
1480s	**Florentine Renaissance (Italy) 1469-1537** (The Age of Discovery 1492-1522)
1540s	**The Reformation 1517-1542**
1600s	**The Golden Age; English Renaissance** (Elizabeth I's reign 1558-1603; Shakespeare's plays 1589-1613)
1660s	**The Scientific Revolution 1660-1687** (The Royal Society 1660-1667; *Principia Mathematica* 1687)
1720s	**The Great Awakening 1727-1746**
1780s	**Enlightenment/Age of Reason 1715-1789; Age of Revolution** (American Revolution 1773-1794; French Revolution 1789-1799)
1840s	**Transcendental Awakening 1822-1844**
1900s	***Fin de Siécle;* The Golden Dawn 1886-1908** (3rd Great Awakening 1886-1908; Progressive Era 1896-1916)
1960s	**The New Age; Consciousness Revolution 1964-1984**
2020s	**The Awakening/Woke Generation 2020-**
2080s	***The Gaiaspora...***
2140s	***The Great Terraforming of Colony Worlds...***

© 20 04

Appendix A:
Pledge to Children
Midcentury White House Conference, 1950

TO YOU, our children, who hold within you our most cherished hopes, we the members of the Midcentury White House Conference on Children and Youth, relying on your full response, make this pledge:

From your earliest infancy we give you our love, so that you may grow with trust in yourself and in others.

We will recognize your worth as a person and we will help you to strengthen your sense of belonging.

We will respect your right to be yourself and at the same time help you to understand the rights of others, so that you may experience cooperative living.

We will help you to develop initiative and imagination, so that you may have the opportunity freely to create.

We will encourage your curiosity and your pride in workmanship, so that you may have the satisfaction that comes from achievement.

We will provide the conditions for wholesome play that will add to your learning, to your social experience, and to your happiness.

We will illustrate by precept and example the value of integrity and the importance of moral courage.

We will encourage you always to seek the truth.

We will provide you with all opportunities possible to develop your own faith in God.

We will open the way for you to enjoy the arts and to use them for deepening your understanding of life.

We will work to rid ourselves of prejudice and discrimination, so that together we may achieve a truly democratic society.

We will work to lift the standard of living and to improve our economic practices, so that you may have the material basis for a full life.

We will provide you with rewarding educational opportunities, so that you nay develop your talents and contribute to a better world.

We will protect you against exploitation and undue hazards and help you grow in health and strength.

We will work to conserve and improve family life and, as needed, to provide foster are according to your inherent rights.

We will intensify our search for new knowledge in order to guide you more effectively as you develop your potentialities.

As you grow from child to youth to adult, establishing a family life of your own and accepting larger social responsibilities, we will work with you to improve conditions for all children and youth.

Aware that these promises to you cannot be fully met in a world at war, we ask you to join u in a firm dedication to the building of a world society based on freedom, justice and mutual respect.

SO MAY YOU grow in joy, in faith in God and in man, and in those qualities of vision and of the spirit that will sustain us all and give us new hope for the future.[100]

White House Conferences on Children and Youth

The First White House Conference on Children and Youth was called into session by President Theodore Roosevelt in 1909.

The Goal: To stimulate higher standards of child care, to set new goals, and to emphasize America's responsibility for all her children. Subsequent WH Conferences have had the same general purposes as the first one, and in addition rather specific goals as well.

The Second White House Conference on Children and Youth was called into session by President Woodrow Wilson in 1919.

The Third White House Conference on Children and Youth was called into session by President Herbert Hoover in 1930.

The Fourth White House Conference on Children and Youth was called into session by President Frankin D. Roosevelt in 1940.

The Midcentury White House Conference on Children and Youth was called into session by President Harry S. Truman in 1950.

---

[100] "Pledge to Children," *Childcraft* Vol. 15. Field Enterprises, Inc. Chicago, 1954.

Appendix B:
Words of Wisdom
(OZ's favorite Aphorisms)
(more may be added continually...)

How to live:

First, figure out who you are, and then be it. Fully.

Second, figure out what you're here for, and then do it. Fully.

Third, be the person *you* decide to be, not the one that you were assigned to be. *(~Brandon Sanderson)*

Observations:

Everything is alive; everything is interconnected. *(Latin: "Omnia vivunt; omnia inter se conexa;" Cicero)*

As above, so below. As below, so above. *(~The Emerald Tablet)*

What goes around, comes around.

Reputation is what others know about you. Honor is what you know about yourself. *(Lois McMaster Bujold—the Vorkosigan Saga)*

You can't cheat an honest man.

The show must go on!

Living well is the best vindication. *(Vitere bene est Vindicata optima)*

In Nature there are no rewards or punishments. There are consequences. *(~Robert Green Ingersoll)*

To choose an action is to choose the consequences. *(~Lois Bujold)*

The best way to predict the future is to create it.

There's always something else...

An attitude of gratitude is the guidance of the Gaia-dance.

The Answer (to Life, the Universe and Everything) is "Yes!"

People will believe what they most hope, *and* what they most fear.

I believe in mind over matter. If you don't mind, it doesn't matter.

A waist is a terrible thing to mind!

"Old" is always ten years older than you are. *(Lois McMaster Bujold)*

The one thing you can't trade for your heart's desire is your heart.

Transcendental ideals: Truth, Beauty, Goodness. Criteria: Is it true? Is it beautiful? Is it good? *(~Aristotle)*

Glass half-full or half-empty, just remember the glass is refillable.

Everything will be okay in the end. If it's not okay, it's not yet the end. *(~Fernando Sabino, Portuguese author)*

The brighter the light, the darker the shadow.

It's always darkest just before the dawn.

This too shall pass. *(~ancient Chinese proverb for all occasions)*

Advice:

Do as you would be done by. *(Golden Rule)*

Be excellent to each other! *(~Bill & Ted's Excellent Adventure)*

If you don't like it, you can't have any. *(Corollary: More for me!)*

How others treat me is up to them; but how *I* treat *others* is up to me.

If you don't dig it, don't do it.

If you don't grok it, don't knock it.

Only make rules for others that you intend to follow yourself.

Never make unenforceable rules or idle threats.

It is unwise to summon what you cannot dismiss.

Walk your talk and talk your walk.

Sit down, shut up, listen, pay attention, take notes, remember.

Eschew hypocrisy: Do what you say you'll do and don't do what you say you won't.

Always consider the options.

Always consider the consequences. *(The essence of Wisdom)*

The job isn't done 'til you've put away the tools and cleaned up the mess.

Life is a buffet. Take what you want but eat what you take.

Always interpret everything in the best possible light.

True genius is knowing when not to reveal it.

Better to keep silent and be thought a fool than to speak and remove all doubt.

Everything you say should be at least two of the following: true, kind or necessary. *(~Socrates' "Triple Filter Test")*

An *[insofar as]* it harm none, do what thou wilt. *(Wiccan Rede)*

Try not. Do. Or do not. There is no try. *(~Jedi Master Yoda)*

Love:

Love is that condition in which another person's happiness is essential to your own. *(~Robert Heinlein, Stranger in a Strange Land)*

There is no power greater than Love.

Love shared is love multiplied.

True love cannot be 50%:50%. It's all or nothing: 100%:100%.

The greater the circle the more the love grows. *(~Gwen Zak)*

More than one person can be your sun, moon and stars—there are many multiple-star systems, all stars have planets, and most planets have more than one moon. And the number of stars is infinite... *(~Morning Glory Zell)*

Never date anyone crazier than you are. *(~Eldri Littlewolf)*

If you can't be with the one you love, love the one you're with.

Never argue with a woman. It wastes your time and annoys the woman.

Happy wife, happy life.

Survival tips:
Always look both ways before crossing a one-way street.
Never pick a fight with a man carrying a water buffalo.
In a restaurant or public place, always sit where you can see the door.
Never turn your back on a live enemy.
Always say less than necessary. *(~Robert Green, 48 Laws of Power)*
Never telegraph your next move.
Be careful what you wish for; you just might get it!
Win through your actions; never through argument. *(~Robert Greene)*
Choose your battles carefully, and always take the high ground.
Never attribute to malice what can be explained by stupidity,
   ignorance or incompetence.
Always speak truth to your true friends. Lie only to your true ene-
   mies. And lie through your teeth to anyone holding a gun on you!
The best way to defeat an enemy is to make him a friend. *(~A. Lincoln)*
When your enemy is destroying himself, get out of the way! *(~Sun Tsu)*
When you're running from a bear, you don't have to be faster than
   *every*body; you just have to be faster than *some*body.

Going somewhere:
The journey of 1,000 miles begins with a single step. *(~Confucius)*
Wherever you go, there you are. *(~Buckeroo Banzai)*
If you don't know where you're going, it doesn't matter how you get
   there! *(~Cheshire Cat to Alice in Wonderland)*
When you're going through hell, keep going! *(~Winston Churchill)*
The slowest vehicle leads the parade.
Be the second fastest car on the road, not the fastest. The fastest will
   get stopped for speeding!

Three Rules of Wizardry:
First rule: Always take credit/accept responsibility! *(This builds
   your credibility and reputation.)*
Second rule: Reputation is Power. *(~Robert Green, 48 Laws of
   Power—Law 5) (The power of a Wizard is directly proportional to
   his or her reputation.)*
Third rule: With great power comes great responsibility. *(~Stan Lee,
   Spiderman) (And with great responsibility comes Great Power...)*

Great Truths vs. small truths: *(~Robert Anton Wilson, Illuminatus)*
The opposite of a small truth is plainly false. *(i.e. "The Earth re-
   volves around the Sun")*
The opposite of a Great Truth is also True. *(i.e. "As Above, So Below")*

Appendix C:
Predictions & Prophecies[101]

As this book is a "Message in a Bottle" to be read by future generations, I feel I owe it to you future readers to offer a few predictions and prophecies from my vantage point in the year 2024. It'll be interesting to see how these turn out in actuality, as so many of the visionary predictions for the present times that were made in the 20th century have proven to be wildly inaccurate, while a few others have turned out to be spot-on. From where you stand, how are we doing? ~OZ

Generations

A *generation* is a group of people born around the same time (generally within a decade) who are often referred to collectively. Those given the same generational label are believed to live under similar conditions of parenting, technology, experience and socio-economic trends and share common cultural traits and values. Here is a brief synopsis of the named "Generations" since that concept was introduced a century ago:

The Lost Generation/Flappers: Born 1880–1899
The Greatest Generation *(GI Generation):* Born 1900–1924
The Silent Generation *(Traditionalists)*/Beats: Born 1925–1944
Baby Boomers/Hippies: Born 1945–1964
    (Micro-Generation Jones: Born 1955 to 1964)
Generation X *(Thirteeners):* Born 1965–1979
    (Xennial Micro-Generation: Born 1977 to 1983)
Generation Y *(Millennials):* Born 1980–1999
Generation Z *(Centennials; Zoomers; iGen):* Born 2000–2009
Generation Alpha: Born 2010–2019
The Woke Generation: Born 2020–2029

The "Strauss–Howe Generational Theory" posits a cycle in which historical periods are associated with recurring generational archetypes. Each generation unleashes a new era (a "Turning") lasting around 20-25 years, with a new social, political, and economic mood. Read this chart on the diagonals to see how each generation ages through the decades. The shaded vertical blocks indicate 60-year Renaissance Cycles:

---

[101] Zell, Oberon, *GaeaGenesis: Conception and Birth of the Living Earth.* Left Hand Press, 2022.

The Generational Diagonal

Generation	1962-1982	1983-2003	2004-2024	2025-2045	2046-2066	2067-2087
Age 66-87	reclusive	busy	sensitive	visionary	reclusive	busy
Age 44-65	powerful	indecisive	moralistic	pragmatic	powerful	indecisive
Age 22-43	conformist	narcissistic	alienated	heroic	conformist	narcissistic
Age 0-21	indulged	criticized	protected	suffocated	indulged	criticized

Reference: Strauss, William; Howe, Neil, The Fourth Turning: An American Prophecy. *Vintage Books, NY, 1997. Adapted with projections by OZ.*

Positives (hopes)

In the 2020s, Pagan organizations and individuals will achieve national prominence and public respect for their educational efforts and activism in environmental restoration, wildlife rescue, community gardens, highway adoption, social justice, equal rights, community service, and organized opposition to environmentally and socially destructive practices.

In the 2020s, Pagan kids and young adults will become the natural leaders in their schools and communities. They will garner respect among their peers and become role models for their intelligence, kindness, compassion, knowledge, and wisdom, learned from their Pagan families, communities and festivals. As these young leaders arise, many will rally to their causes, and their influence will spread throughout a growing subculture, as did that of the Hippies in the 1960s.

In the late 2020s, the avant-garde youth generation with their distinctive music, fashions and other characteristics will become popularly identified with a unique collective designation, as were the "Flappers" of the 1920s, the "Beats" of the 1950s and the "Hippies" of the 1960s.

In the late 2020s, we will see a worldwide Earth-Friendly political movement really taking hold. We Baby Boomers will all be gone. Things will be different even though harder. *[~Herman B. Triplegood]*

In the late 2020s, the Gaia Thesis (that the entire planetary biosphere is a single vast living organism) will become the pre-eminent spiritual paradigm and unifying image in the Western world, uniting peoples of all persuasions in a global Family. We will recognize that we are all children of the same Mother, as well as cells in Her immense body.

In the late 2020s, planetary healing and restoration will become the great Mission of many people and countries, to be funded and organized as an international "Gaia Corps" just as the Peace Corps was in the 1960s. Example: "The Pachamama Alliance." Many will identify as "Earth Warriors," "Gaia's Guardians," "Mama's Minions," etc.

In the late 2020s, The Grey School of Wizardry (est. 2004) will become known and recognized as the premier institution of esoteric education.

In the late 2020s, the Church of All Worlds (the first church ever to proudly claim the label and identity of "Pagan"–in 1967) will experience a profound resurgence as a new generation takes up the torch and carries it forward.

In the late 2020s, Neo-Pagan outreach to other non-Abrahamic religious communities will result in global alliances that will swell the ranks of so-identified "Pagans" to include Hindus, Shinto, Hellenes, Baltics, Norse, and all indigenous peoples (Native Americans, Australian Aborigines, Polynesians, Ifa, Afro-Caribbeans, etc.). Paganism will be recognized as one of the largest religions in the world.

In the late 2020s, economic prosperity will finally come to the Pagan community via flourishing Pagan businesses, Pagan creative enterprises, Pagan communities, and especially, a national Pagan Credit Union.

In the early 2030s, as the fastest growing (and 2nd largest) faith group in the US, modern Paganism will begin to vie with a declining Christianity as the pre-eminent religion in America, as well as in much of the Western world. There will be significant backlash from Christian Evangelicals as they realize they are losing the "Culture War" they started in the 1920s and escalated in the '60s.

In the 2030s, Pagan-owned lands will grow into significant and expanding territories, providing for Pagan villages and large land-based communities. Permanent festival sites and retreat facilities will become increasingly elaborate, with stone circles, temples, cemeteries, orchards, gardens, labyrinths, baths, guest facilities, stores, restaurants, etc.

In the 2030s, psychic phenomena—especially telepathy and the clair-senses—will become increasingly widespread and accepted. Seed pods and clusters of people will begin to link up telepathically. The veil between the worlds of the living and the dead will become more permeable. Reincarnation will become widely acknowledged.

Breakthroughs

In the late 2020s, 3D printing will become as ubiquitous and cheap as home office paper printing is now. Many items will cease to be mass-produced and sold, as they are replaced with print-at-home programs for toys, tools, instruments, and many other objects. Many factories and stores will go out of business.

In the late 2020s, prosthetic limbs and hands will become completely robotic and controlled via Neuralink by the cyborg person's own brain. We will develop new vaccines for cancer, new drugs to combat obesity and new CRISPR gene-editing techniques to treat many other diseases.

In the late 2020s, virtual reality will supplement and eventually supplant nearly all other forms of visual media, as movies, TV, communications, etc. will all be translated into fully immersive 3D virtual experiences. New art forms will be created which take place entirely in virtual reality. Wearable VR glasses and headsets will blur the boundaries between the real and the virtual..

In the late 2020s, virtual reality communication will go global, with a satellite communications network and quantum (entangled) system providing instantaneous communication across all space. Via VR, people will be able to project their holographic avatars to any place in the world that has a setup—and eventually to extraterrestrial locations as well.

In the late 2020s, quantum computing will supplant all other systems, eventually giving birth to true AI cyber-sentience, with sentient robots and androids like in all those sci-fi stories, movies, and TV shows. And as in all those stories, this will create unprecedented problems as sentient machines inevitably start making their own decisions and agendas.

In the late 2020s, petroleum-based internal combustion engines and power plants will begin to be gradually phased out and supplanted by significant advances in solar cell efficiency, improved batteries, hydrogen power, wind generators and other technological breakthroughs yet to be discovered. After 2030, all new cars will be electric. Cold fusion will finally be achieved, providing cheap and virtually limitless power.

In the late 2020s, we will confirm complex life on planets orbiting either G-type stars like our own or red dwarfs, thanks primarily to the new James Webb Space Telescope. It will be a journey of research taking some years, but I think mid- to late 2020s for this is a reasonable expectation. *[~Herman B. Triplegood]*

In the late 2020s, the continuing evolution of the Internet will create a technological vehicle of global consciousness, resulting in a planetary Awakening. A century ago, in a 1926 interview with *Collier's* magazine, inventor Nicolo Tesla said: *"When wireless is perfectly applied the whole Earth will be converted into a huge brain, which in fact it is, all things being particles of a real and rhythmic whole. We shall be able to communicate with one another instantly, irrespective of distance."*

In the 2030s, the livestock meat industry will be increasingly phased out by plant-grown and cloned meats. This will necessitate competitive costs.

In the 2030s, replacement organs and other body parts will be grown from the patient's own stem cells, often utilizing 3D printing. No more transplanting of donor organs from other people (or pigs).

In the 2030s, wooly mammoths will be resurrected via cloning (using Asian elephants for ova and wombs) and established in "Pleistocene Parks" alongside bison, caribou, and muskoxen. Resurrection of other extinct mammals and birds (such as thylacines and dodos) will follow.

In the 2030s, artificial therapod "dinosaurs" will be created via genetic engineering from emus, cassowaries, hoatzins—maybe even chickens. They will become popular attractions in zoos, parks, and as exotic pets.

In the 2030s, permanent research bases will be established on the Moon and Mars, and the beginnings of human colonies on those worlds. Mining operations for rare minerals will be commenced on the Moon.

In the 2030s, alien life will be discovered on Mars, Jupiter, Europa, Enceladus, Titan and elsewhere in the solar system. Remnants of alien structures and artifacts will be found on various planets and moons. These discoveries will spur a massive international space program to investigate, and a significant reconsideration of our place in the cosmos.

Regatives (fears)

In the mid-2020s, civil war may break out in the United States, fomented by extreme right-wingnuts, fanatical MAGA cultists, white supremacists, Christian Dominionists, Evangelicals, Congressional Republicans, Qanon conspiracy crazies and other authoritarians sympathetic to and even allied with autocratic foreign dictators and regimes.

In the coming decades, the radical Islamic Jihadist movement will continue to grow and spread violently throughout the world in its agenda to exterminate all other religions and cultures. Terrorist bombings and mass shootings will continue to increase in frequency and intensity. Due to its high fertility rate, Islam is projected to be the world's largest religion by the end of this century. Misogynistic Sharia Law will be established wherever radical Islamists gain a majority (currently in 49 countries).

In the coming decades, rising global temperatures will result in accelerated melting of the Greenland and Antarctic ice sheets. Deprived of the immense weight of all that ice, both depressed continents will rebound, displacing more water than is currently anticipated from melting alone, and raising sea levels significantly throughout the world. Warmer water will expand in volume, adding to the sea rise. The addition of so much fresh water from Greenland will interrupt the Gulf Stream, plummeting eastern Canada and the British Isles into a deep chill. Coral reefs will die in warmer, deeper waters. The US Eastern Seaboard, Florida, the Yucatan, Bangladesh and other low-lying coastal areas, and islands in the Pacific and Caribbean, will become submerged and disappear, and the lower Mississippi Valley, California's Central Valley and the Amazon Basin will flood. Inland seas will form in Australia and central Africa. Much of the world's prime food-producing regions will be inundated. Populations will have to shift inland to higher and less fertile elevations. These displacements and food shortages will result in unprecedented conflicts, wars, starvation, pestilence, and eventual significant reduction of the human population. A time of great anguish and turmoil.

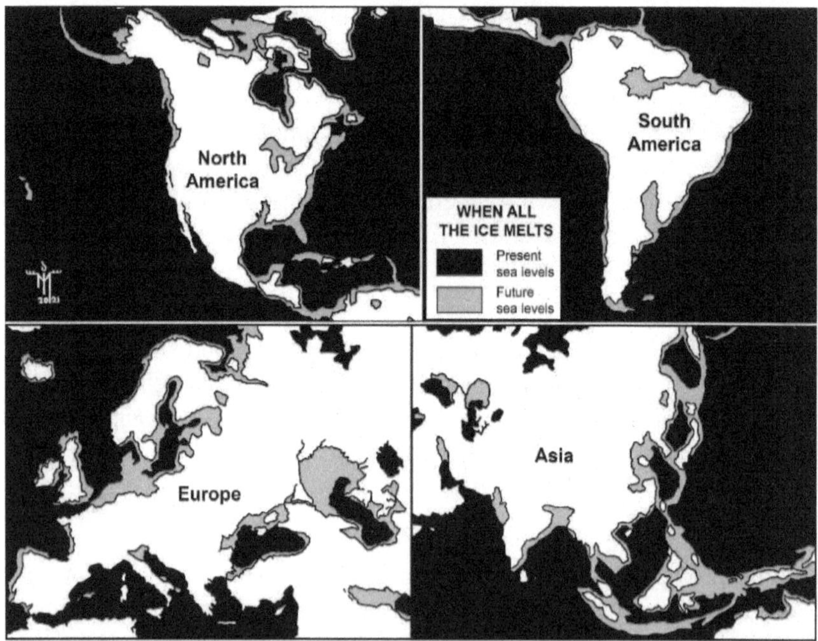

"When all the ice melts." Rising sea level projections by OZ (ref: National Geographic)

In the coming decades, we will see serious conflicts among the nations—possibly even nuclear—and many millions dead, not all of them war victims, but too many, driven by impending oil depletion and climate catastrophe and over-stressed Ponzi Scheme Economies.
[~Herman B. Triplegood]

In the coming decades, warmer oceans will result in an increasing frequency and severity of tropical storms: hurricanes, typhoons. cyclones and tornadoes—with consequent flooding. Thawing permafrost in the tundra will release great quantities of frozen methane, poisoning vast regions of the Taiga and rendering them uninhabitable for humans and animals. A permanently ice-free Arctic Ocean will allow year-round evaporation, resulting in increasing snowfall in the higher latitudes, and ever-more severe polar vortices, eventually precipitating a new Ice Age.

In the coming decades, The Cascadia fault off the Pacific Northwest coast is poised for a massive, 9.0-magnitude earthquake at some point, a rupture that would propel a wall of water across much of the Northwest coast within minutes. Low-lying coastal neighborhoods in Washington, Oregon and Northern California would be under 10 feet or more of water.

In the coming decades, more volcanoes will erupt, and earthquakes occur, with consequent tsunamis, "volcano winters" and other effects, all around the Pacific Ring of Fire. Expect major eruptions in Indonesia and Guatemala. Japan's Mt Fuji will detonate like Krakatoa (1888) and Thera (1627 BCE) from sea water leaking into its magma chamber and turning to steam. Japan will become the new Atlantis. In Iceland, volcanoes Hekla, Katla and Eyjafjallajökull will have major eruptions, plunging all of Europe into years of "volcano winter." Hopefully the Yellowstone Caldera will not go off, which would be a mass extinction event.

In the coming decades, we will come to the realization that even if we keep the temperature rise to under 1.5 C, we will not avert a worldwide climate disaster and we will need to plan for a sustainable retreat and a complete re-imagination of human society and politics that will eventually cope just fine with the Post-Petroleum Epoch of the evolutionary development on Earth. Yes, I see this as an evolutionary nexus, not just an historical one. All civilizations meet this crisis, and some survive, and some do not. That is Life. We are going through this because we can get through this. We are equipped as a species, by Natural Selection, to fulfill our Mission. But we have to be realistic about just how bad it can get, which is hard for Scientists and even Prognosticators because we are in the domain of non-linear unexpected events happening that we never thought about or thought about too little—like Iceland's Katla actually going off because of the weight of the ice no longer being there, or, major trade currents suddenly shifting, changing trade winds, causing crop failures and famines and making entire regions of the Oceans so toxic that ships on the surface have to completely steer them. Yes. A real mess. *[~Herman B. Triplegood]*

Predictions from futurist Ælex Vikoulov[102]

In the mid-2020s, *Computing:* It is estimated that by 2025 there will be 80 billion networked devices, ten times more than there are people on Earth. Then, with immersive computing going mainstream, the amount of data will double every month.

In the mid-2020s, *Virtual Reality vs. Reality:* Many conventional economic notions such as primary locations and differential rent, may gradually become irrelevant under new effective topologies of the social space and ever more prominent use of virtual environments... By 2025 full adoption of VR in the US is guaranteed. As analysts at Goldman Sachs predict, VR will be bigger than TV by 2027.

In the 2020s, *Hyperconnectivity:* Improved communications will ensure more homogeneous geographical distribution of real estate value. Basically, you may be anywhere with all necessary access to information, communication, and experience via VR.

In the 2020s, *Construction Tech:* Advanced engineering techniques, artificial intelligence solutions, extreme automation and new cheaper materials will bring down significantly the cost and time of building most structures. 3D printing, robotics and nanotechnology will further help revolutionize the construction industry.

In the 2020s, *Smart Homes:* Newly designed apartment buildings or houses packed with electronics and "in-home intelligence" may initially cost considerably more but ultimately, they will devalue the existing home properties. The notion of the million-dollar views will gradually fade away as any imaginable landscape can be recreated by using ultra-realistic dynamic digital wallpaper.

In the 2020s, *New Megacities and Nano-Nations:* By the time we should expect a recovery in existing home values, new cities may be built rather quickly outside of, or adjacent to the current metro areas with advanced infrastructure, mega projects, tall buildings, and smart homes which will make existing homes in old cities look like dog houses. Seasteading will spur the emergence of nano-nations with sustainable offshore communities.

In the 2020s, *The Nature of Work:* As more companies shift to a part-time work week, tele-commuting, and virtual work space-time, some

---

[102] Vikoulov, Alex M., *The Syntellect Hypothesis: Five Paradigms of the Mind's Evolution.* Ecstadelic Media Group, San Francisco, 2020.

converting to 100% "virtual entities," and so we'll also see an increasing number of emerging virtual corporations, commercial properties in major US cities, especially in downtowns, will be under pressure. In the 2030s, we'll see many downtown office buildings converting to hotels and residential properties.

In the 2020s, *Technology Displacement:* Many people may be displaced by technology automation and may only rely on Universal Basic Income (when implemented) for support. That would effectively take them out of the pool of available buyers of the higher end real estate.

In the 2020s, *Transportation:* Just as improved communications, improved transportation such as a hyperloop system making it possible to "commute" from Los Angeles to San Francisco in 30 minutes, self-driving cars and later flying cars, the Internet of things alleviating traffic conditions to "connected" vehicles, would mean you do not necessarily want to buy a home in a "prime location."

In the 2020s, *Generational Attitudes:* Millennials avoid investing in the big-ticket items such as real estate for all the right reasons—they understand better than the older generations that the entire new digital economy is about to undergo monumental paradigm shifts at the ever-accelerating pace whereas anything of physical value today will gradually lose its value and importance.

In the 2030s, *Money:* At the 2018 TED Conference in San Francisco, futurist Ry Kurtzweil made a bold prediction bout the future of free money: *"In the early 2030s, we'll have universal basic income in the developed world, and worldwide by the end of the 2030s. You'll be able to live very well on that. The primary concern will be meaning and purpose,"* he said onstage at the annual event. This timeframe also coincides with when Kurtzweil, Google's chief futurist and director of engineering at Google research, thinks AI will pass the Turing Test—when it becomes impossible to discern machine intelligence from human intelligence. At that point, human jobs could become increasingly scattered.

In the 2030s, *Prosperity:* we'll see a major change in basic assumptions in collective consciousness mediated by exponential technologies. Thus, a lot of products will be dirt-cheap or even free thanks to emerging 3D printing and nanotechnology, and many U.S. downtown office buildings will start to convert to hotels and residential property because we'll be working and interacting increasingly in virtual environments... We will be entering an unprecedented era of prosperity for all.

Appendix D:
Movies for Magikids

Here are some excellent kid-oriented intellectually-stimulating
sci-fi/fantasy movies. (* = OZ favorites)

Disney

Disney's animated fairy-tale films are classic, of course, and many are now being remade with live action. They are generally suitable for kids of all ages. Here are some of my favorite Disney films, in order of release:

*Fantasia (1940–a personal favorite)
Pinocchio (1940)
Bambi (1942)
Song of the South (1946–Tales of Uncle Remus-live with animation)
*Wind in the Willows (1949)
*Alice in Wonderland (1951; 2018)
*20,000 Leagues Under the Sea (1954–my childhood favorite!)
*Darby O'Gill and the Little People (1960-live)
*The Sword in the Stone (1963)
*Mary Poppins (1964) (later remake)
Dr. Doolittle (1967) (later remake)
*Return to Oz (1985–live)
*The Black Cauldron (1985)
*Who Framed Roger Rabbit (1988-live w. animation)
*Beauty and the Beast (1991; live remake 2017)
*The Lion King (1994)
*Pocohantas (1995)
*Tall Tale: The Unbelievable Adventure (1995–live)
Mulan (1998)
*Tarzan (1999)
Fantasia 2000 (2000)
*Dinosaur (2000)
*Atlantis: The Lost Empire (2001)
Monsters, Inc. (2001)

*Shrek (2001) & sequels
Lilo & Stitch (2002)
Finding Nemo (2003)
*The Incredibles (2004)
*The Chronicles of Narnia (live):
*Brave (2012)
*Frozen (2013) & sequels
*Maleficent (2014-3D, live) & sequel
*Tomorrowland (2015–3D, live)
*Moana (2016–3D)
*A Wrinkle in Time (2018–3D, live)
The Little Mermaid (animated & live)

Hayao Miyazaki and Studio Ghibli

I recommend pretty much everything Miyazaki has put out– especially the following (listed here in order of release):

Nausicaa of the Valley of the Wind (1984)
Castle in the Sky (Laputa) (1986)
My Neighbor Totoro (1988)
Kiki's Delivery service (1989)
Porco Rosso (1992)
*Princess Mononoke (1997)
*Spirited Away (2001)
*Howl's Moving Castle (2004)
Ponyo (2008)
The Secret World of Arrietty (2010)

For Children under 11

And here are many more wonderful, inspiring and magickal kid movies from various producers; these are all suitable for kids under 11 (in order of release):

The Wizard of Oz (1939–classic)
*The Sinbad movies (by Ray Harryhausen):
Journey to the Center of the Earth (1959, with Pat Boone)
*Jason & the Argonauts (1963, by Ray Harryhausen)
First Men in the Moon (1964)
*Yellow Submarine (1968 –animated)
*Willy Wonka & the Chocolate Factory (1971) + later remakes
Escape to Witch Mountain (1975) & sequels
The Hobbit (1977–animated)
Watership Down (1978–animated)
*The Black Stallion (1979) & sequels
*Time Bandits (1981)
*Clash of the Titans (1981, by Ray Harryhausen)
*The Last Unicorn (1982–animated)
*E.T. the Extra-Terrestrial (1982)
*The Neverending Story (1984–read the book!)
The Goonies (1985)
*Explorers (1985)
Flight of the Navigator (1986)
*Short Circuit (1986) & sequels
Batteries Not Included (1987)
*The Princess Bride (1987–read the book!)
*Willow (1988)
Honey, I Shrunk the Kids (1989)
*Erik the Viking (1989)
*Hook (1991–by Steven Spielberg)
*The Addams Family (1991) & sequels
*Fern Gully: The Last Rainforest (1992–animated)
*Nightmare Before Christmas (1993)
The Secret of Roan Innish (1994)
*Babe (1995)
* Dragonheart (1996) & sequels
*Muppet Treasure Island (1996)
The Borrowers (1997)
*George of the Jungle (1997) & sequel
*Men in Black (1997) & sequels

*Mighty Joe Young (1998)
Stuart Little (1999)
Alice in Wonderland (1999–TV miniseries; live, for very young kids)
*The Iron Giant (1999–animated)
*Titan A.E. (2000–animated)
Chicken Run (2000–claymation)
*The Adventures of Rocky & Bullwinkle (2000–live with animation)
*The 10th Kingdom (2000–TV series)
*The Incredible Adventures of Wallace & Grommit (2001–claymation)
*Dinotopia (2002-4-hr. TV miniseries, followed by 13 episodes)
*Peter Pan (2003–live)
*A Wrinkle In Time (2003 TV movie)
*Brother Bear (2003–animated)
*The Corpse Bride (2005–claymation)
The Curse of the Were-Rabbit (2005-claymation)
*Charlie and the Chocolate Factory (2005) plus remakes & sequels
*Night at the Museum (2006) & sequels
Nanny McFee (2005) & sequel
*Avatar: The Last Airbender (2005–TV anime series; 2010 movie)
The Last Mimsy (2007)
Meet the Robinsons (2007–animated)
Mr. Magorium's Wonder Emporium (2007)
*The Water Horse: Legend of the Deep (2007)
*The Spiderwick Chronicles (2008)
*Wall-E (2008–CGI animated)
9 (2009–CGI animated)
The Secret of Kells (2009–animated)
Coraline (2009–3D claymation; dark)
*Up (2009-3D, CGI animated)
Where the Wild Things Are (2009)
*Astro Boy (2009–3D, CGI animated)
*How to Train Your Dragon (2010–CGI animated) & sequels
*Legend of the Guardians: The Owls of Ga'Hoole (2010–CGI animated)

*The Pirates! Band of Misfits (2012-claymation)
*The Book of Life (2014-3D, animated)
Mr. Peabody & Sherman (2014–3D, CGI animated)
Shaun the Sheep (2015–claymation)
*Paddington (2015) & sequels
*Kubo and the Two Strings (2016–3D, animated)
*Coco (2017–3D, CGI animated)

For older kids (11+):

Cocteau's Beauty and the Beast (1946–Classic, b&w)
*Destination Moon (1950)
*War of the Worlds (1953)
*The Conquest of Space (1955)
*Forbidden Planet (1956)
*The Time Machine (1960)
*Mysterious Island (1961)
*The 7 Faces of Dr. Lao (1964)
*Fantastic Voyage (1966)
Munster, Go Home! (1966) & sequels
*Silent Running (1972)
*The People (1972–TV, from books by Zenna Henderson)
*The Star Wars series–all in 3D
*Close Encounters of the Third Kind (1977)
*The Life of Brian (1979)
*Flash Gordon (1980)
*Dragon Slayer (1981)
*Hitchhiker's Guide to the Galaxy (1981-BBC TV)
*Indiana Jones series (all)
*The Dark Crystal (1982)
*Yellowbeard (1983)
*The Last Starfighter (1984)
*Greystoke: The Legend of Tarzan (1984)
*Top Secret (1984)
*Ghostbusters (1984) & sequels
*Back to the Future (1985) & sequels
*Legend (1985–with Tom Cruise)
*Enemy Mine (1985)

*Cocoon (1985)
Weird Science (1985)
*Labyrinth (1986–Jim Hensen)
Howard the Duck (1986)
Invaders from Mars (1986)
*The Adventures of Baron Munchausen (1988)
*Akira (1988–anime)
High Spirits (1988)
*Bill & Ted's Excellent Adventure (1989) & sequels
*Edward Scissorhands (1990)
*Robin Hood: Men in Tights (1993)
*Jurassic Park (1993) & sequels
The Mask (1994)
Stargate (1994)
*Jumanji (1995)
Zathura: A Space Adventure (2005)
Jumanji: Welcome to the Jungle (2018)
*The Fifth Element (1997)
*All the "Discworld" movies (by Terry Pratchett)
*Pleasantville (1998)
*Galaxy Quest (1999)
*The Mummy (1999) & sequels
The Magical Legend of the Leprechauns (1999 TV miniseries)
*Mission to Mars (2000)
*Lara Croft: Tomb Raider (2001) & sequels
*Monkeybone (2001)
*AI Artificial Intelligence (2001)
*Final Fantasy: The Spirits Within (2001-CGI)
*Of course, all Harry Potter movies
*Lord of the Rings trilogy by Peter Jackson
*Fullmetal Alchemist (2003-'04–anime series; live-action movie 2017)
Whale Rider (2003)
Holes (2003)
*Pirates of the Caribbean series (all 3D)
*Hellboy (2004) & sequels

*King Kong (2005–3D, by Peter
   Jackson)
*Stardust (2007–by Neil Gaimon)
*The Golden Compass (2007–read
   the books!)
Dragonlance: Dragons of Autumn
   Twilight (2008–animated)
*10,000 BC (2008)
*The Secret of Moonacre (2009)
Inkheart (2009)
*The Imaginarium of Dr. Parnassus
   (2010)
The Sorcerer's Apprentice (2010)
*Alice in Wonderland (2010–3D)
Alice Through the looking Glass
   (2016–3D)
Percy Jackson & the Olympians (all)
*The Adventures of Tintin (2011–
   CGI 3D)
*Hugo (2011-3D)
*The Hobbit trilogy by Peter Jackson
   (all 3D; watch before LotR):
*Oz the Great and Powerful (2013-3D)
*Into the Woods (2014)
*The Monkey King (2014) & sequels
*Doctor Strange (2016–3D)
Miss Peregrine's Home for Peculiar
   Children (2016)

Classic sci-fi movies
*Destination Moon (1950)
Creature from the Black Lagoon
   (1954-3D b&w) & sequels
*The Conquest of Space (1955)
*Forbidden Planet (1956)
*The Time Machine (1960)
First Men in the Moon (1964)
Robinson Crusoe on Mars (1964)
*Fantastic Voyage (1966)
*Planet of the Apes (1968) & sequels
*2001: A Space Odyssey (1968)
*2010: The Year We Make Contact
   (1984)
Logan's Run (1976)
*Close Encounters of the Third Kind
   (1977)

*Star Trek movies (all):
*Hitchhiker's Guide to the Galaxy
   (1981–BBC)
*E.T. the Extra-Terrestrial (1982)
*The Last Starfighter (1984)
The Adventures of Buckaroo Banzai
   Across the 8th Dimension! (1984)
*Explorers (1985)
*Cocoon (1985)
*Back to the Future (1985) & sequels
Invaders from Mars (1986)
Flight of the Navigator (1986)
*Short Circuit (1986) & sequel
Batteries Not Included (1987)
Stargate (1994)
*City of Lost Children (1995)
*The Fifth Element (1997)
*Men in Black (1997) & sequels
*Galaxy Quest (1999)
*AI Artificial Intelligence (2001)
*Wall-E (2008-CGI animated)
*John Carter (Princess of Mars) (2012)
*Guardians of the Galaxy (2014–3D)
   & sequels
*Tomorrowland (2015-3D)
The Martian (2015)
*Valerian and the City of a Thousand
   Planets (2017–3D

Comic Book Superhero movies

There have been so many comic book superhero movies made that I cannot possibly list all of them. But I've seen and enjoyed them all, and I recommend them all highly to young and old for the great characters and stories, and the lessons they impart.

The main producers are Marvel and DC—now both owned by Disney.

Appendix E:
Books for Magikids

Within each category, books are alphabetized by author's last name,
and titles are listed by dates of publication, or in serial order.

I. Fantasy Novels & Series

Alexander, Lloyd—*Chronicles of Prydain:*
1. *The Book of Three* (1964)
2. *The Castle of Llyr* (1965)
3. *The Black Cauldron* (1966)
4. *Taran Wanderer* (1967)
5. *The High King* (1968)

Beagle, Peter S.—*The Last Unicorn* (1968)

Crowley, John —*Little, Big* (1981)

deLint, Charles—
Riddle of the Wren (1984)
The Harp of the Grey Rose (1985)
Yarrow (1986)
Jack, the Giant-Killer (1987)
Greenmantle (1988)
Drink Down the Moon (1990)
The Little Country (1991)
Into the Green (1993)

Duane, Diane—*Young Wizards:*
1. *So You Want to be a Wizard* (1996)
2. *Deep Wizardry* (1996)
3. *High Wizardry* (1997)
4. *A Wizard Abroad* (1999)
5. *The Wizard's Dilemma* (2002)
6. *A Wizard Alone* (2002)
7. *The Wizard's Holiday* (2003)

Ende, Michael—*The Neverending Story* (1984)

Goldman, William—*The Princess Bride* (1973)

Hardy, Lyndon—*Five Magics* trilogy:
1. *Master of the Five Magics* (1984)
2. *Secret of the Sixth Magic* (1988)
3. *Riddle of the Seven Realms* (1988)

Heinlein, Robert—sci-fi juveniles:
1. *Rocket Ship Galileo* (1947)
2. *Space Cadet* (1948)
3. *Red Planet* (1949)
4. *Farmer in the Sky* (1950)
5. *Between Planets* (1951)
6. *The Rolling Stones* (1952)
7. *Starman Jones* (1953)
8. *The Star Beast* (1954)
9. *Tunnel in the Sky* (1955)
10. *Time for the Stars* (1956)
11. *Citizen of the Galaxy* (1957)
12. *Have Spacesuit – Will Travel* (1958)

L'Engle, Madelyn—*Time Quintet:*
1. *A Wrinkle in Time* (1962)
2. *A Wind in the Door* (1973)
3. *Many Waters* (1986)
4. *A Swiftly Tilting Planet* (1978)
5. *An Acceptable Time* (1989)

LeGuin, Ursula K.—*Earthsea* cycle:
1. *A Wizard of Earthsea* (1968)
2. *The Tombs of Atuan* (1971)
3. *The Farthest Shore* (1972)
4. *Tehanu* (1991)
5. *Tales From Earthsea* (2001)
6. *The Other Wind* (2001)

McKillip, Patricia—*Riddle-Master* trilogy:
1. *The Riddle-Master of Hed* (1975)
2. *Heir of Sea and Fire* (1977)
3. *Harpist in the Wind* (1979)

Pierce, Tamora—*Circle of Magic* quartets:
1. *Sandry's Book* (1997)
2. *Tris's Book* (1998)
3. *Daja's Book* (1998)

4. *Briar's Book* (1999)
—The Circle Opens:
1. *Magic Steps* (2000)
2. *Street Magic* (2001)
3. *Cold Fire* (2002)
4. *Shatterglass* (2003)
Pini, Wendy & Richard—*Elfquest* (comics & graphic novels)
Pratchett, Terry—Tiffany Aching:
1. *The Wee Free Men* (2003)
2. *A Hat Full of Sky* (2004)
3. *Wintersmith* (2006)
4. *I Shall Wear Midnight* (2010)
5. *The Shepherd's Crown* (2015)
Rowlings, J.K.—Harry Potter series:
1. *The Philosopher's Stone* (1997)
2. *The Chamber of Secrets* (1998)
3. *The Prisoner of Azkaban* (1999)
4. *The Goblet of Fire* (2000)
5. *The Order of the Phoenix* (2003)
6. *The Half-Blood Prince* (2005)
7. The *Deathly Hallows* (2007)
Sampson, Fay—*The Pangur Ban Celtic Fantasies* (2002)
1. *Shape-Shifter, The Naming of Pangur Ban*
2. *Pangur Ban the White Cat*
3. *Finnglas of the Horses*
Stewart, Mary—Merlin quarto:
1. *The Crystal Cave* (1970)
2. *The Hollow Hills* (1973)
3. *The Last Enchantment* (1979)
4. *The Wicked Day* (1983)
Tolkein, J.R.R.—*The Lord of the Rings:*
1. *The Hobbit* (1937)
2. *The Fellowship of the Ring* (1954)
3. *The Two Towers* (1954)
4. *The Return of the King* (1954)
White T.H.—*The Sword in the Stone* (1963)
Yolen, Jane—*Wizard's Hall* (1991)

II. Mythology

Adam, Winky—*Little Celtic Activity Book* (2000)
Apuleius, Lucius—*The Golden Ass* (Robert Graves, trans.) (1998)
Colum, Padraic—
The Children's Homer: The Adventures of Odysseus and the Tale of Troy (1982)
The Golden Fleece and the Heroes Who Lived Before Achilles (1983)
Children of Odin: The Book of Northern Myths (1984)
The King of Ireland's Son (1997)
Cooper, Susan—*Silver Cow: A Welsh Tale* (1991)
Davidson, Hilda—*Gods & Myths of the Viking Age* (1982)
Gaimon, Neil—*Norse Mythology*
Graves, Robert —
Hercules, My Shipmate (1945)
The Greek Myths (1955)
Greek Gods & Heroes (1965)
Green, John—*Celtic Gods and Heroes (*2003)
Green, Roger L.—
Tales the Muses Told (1965)
Heroes of Greece & Troy (1970)
Tales of Ancient Egypt (1996)
King Arthur & His Knights of the Round Table (1995)
Grundy, Stefan—*Rhinegold* (1994)
Hamilton, Edith—*Mythology* (1942)
Jacobs, Joseph (Ed.)—*More Celtic Fairy Tales* (1976)
MacUistin, Liam—*The Tain: The Great Celtic Epic* (1993)
Matthews, Caitlin—*Celtic Memories* (2003)
Ovid—*Metamorphosis*
Picard, Barbara Leonie—
Lady of the Linden Tree (1954)
Three Ancient Kings: Gilgamesh, Hrolf Kraki, Conary (1986)
Silverberg, Robert—*Gilgamesh the King* (1984)

Snell, Gordon—*The Cool MacCool: Heroic Deeds of Finn MacCool Legendary Celtic Hero* (1989)

Stewart, R.J.—*Celtic Gods, Celtic Goddesses* (1990)

Hyemehost Storm—*Seven Arrows* (1985)

Sutcliffe, Rosemary—*The Hound of Ulster* (2002)

III. Life, the Universe and Everything

Gonick, Larry—*The Cartoon History of the Universe.* Vol. 1 (1990); Vol. 2 (1994)

IV. Nature Wild and Tame

Hopman, Ellen Evert—*Walking The World In Wonder—A Children's Herbal* (2000)

Ormond, Clyde—*Outdoorsman's Handbook* (1974)

Rey, H.A.—*Find the Constellations* (1954; 1988)
The Stars: A New Way to See Them (1962; 1980)

Sams, Jamie & Carson, David—*Medicine Cards* (1988)

Schuler, Stanley—*How to Grow Almost Everything* 1965)

Zim, Herbert S., Ed.—*Golden Nature Guides* (dozens of books… 1950s-on)

V. Conjury

Gibson, Walter B.—*Professional Magic for Amateurs* (1947; 1974)

Gilbert, George & Rydell, Wendy—*Great Tricks of the Master Magicians* (1976)

Hay, Henry—*The Amateur Magician's Handbook* (1950; 1972)

Karr, Todd—*Backyard Magic* (1996)

Nelms, Henning—*Magic and Showmanship: A Handbook for Conjurers* (1969)

Severn, Bill—*Magic in Your Pockets* (1964)

Tarr, Bill—*Now You See It, Now You Don't* (1976)

VI. Mythic Beings & Creatures

Katlyn Breene—*Faery Call* (1997)

Cohen, Daniel—*A Natural History of Unnatural Things* (1971)

Costello, Peter—*The Magic Zoo* (1979)

Froud, Brian—*Faeries* (1978)
Good Faeries/Bad Faeries (1998)

Keel, John A.—*The Complete Guide to Mysterious Beings* (1970; 1994)

Michell, John & Rickard, Robert—*Living Wonders* (1982)

White, T. H.—*The Book of Beasts* (1954; 1984)

Zell, Oberon—*A Wizard's Bestiary* (2nd edition 2022)

VI. History's Mysteries

Zell, Oberon—*Hystory's Mysteries* (2024)

Appendix F: What Advice do People Not Take Seriously Enough?

By Julie Gurner (from Quora)

I'm a doc of psychology who has talked to literally *thousands* of people, and these are 10 pieces of life advice I find that people do not take seriously enough:

1. **"Don't Make Decisions When You're Angry."** —I've seen people relapse on drugs, cheat on their spouses, get into physical fights, and quit their jobs simply because they were "angry." Don't do it.

2. **"Be Yourself."** —So many people suffer because they feel pressure to be something they're not. They can feel this pressure from parents, peers, co-workers, friends or even their significant others. I've seen women get breast implants because of this pressure, men marry women (when they are actually gay), and people going into careers they hate because it will make someone else happy. Be yourself, because being something else will make you miserable.

3. **"Don't Sweat the Small Stuff."** —This is solid advice for a happy life. Choose your battles, and be able to let the little things go. Once you realize what "big things" are (cancer, financial hardship, etc.), you will wish you had focused on the right things.

4. **"Know Your Worth"** —When you know your worth, you don't put up with things that devalue you…and that is *very valuable.* It will impact what you'll put up with in relationships, in your jobs, and in life. Knowing your worth has the ability to protect you from a lot of life's struggles—if you act consistently with it.

5. **"It's Okay to Ask for Help."** —Yes! Do you know how many people I've talked to, that wished they would have gotten help earlier? It would have given them back *years* of their life…but instead they waited until they were at an absolute breaking point—losing opportunities, jobs, relationships, sometimes even their kids. Ask for help, and ask for help *early.*

6. **"Who You Marry is One of the Most Important Decisions You'll Make."** —Take this one seriously. You will literally have to see this person every day of your life, you will spend more time with them than anyone else…so make it someone uplifting, supportive and wonderfully fitting to you. You will also have a financial future largely impacted by their spending habits, earning, saving ability, etc. Man or woman, divorce can devastate you emotionally and financially.

7. **"Make Time for People You Love."** —Putting off seeing your grandmother or parents because you wanted to do other things might not seem like a big deal today…but one day it will be.

8. **"The Best Time to Start is Now"** —Whether saving for your future or trying to write that novel, start today. Time gets away from us very quickly, and before you know it 20 years have passed and you didn't do those things you wanted to do. I have seen a lot of people who hold regrets…try not to have them.

9. **"The Best Revenge is Living Well."** —So many people get stuck in grudges and anger that it messes up their own lives—especially emotionally. There is a great saying that states that "anger is something you carry for someone else's mistakes" and it's the truth. Leave those who have hurt you in the past, take care of your own needs, and live well. It does you no good to do otherwise.

10. **"Treat Others the Way You'd Want to be Treated."** —This is certainly advice we don't take seriously enough. If we all treated others how we'd wish to be treated, the world would certainly be a much better place for us all.

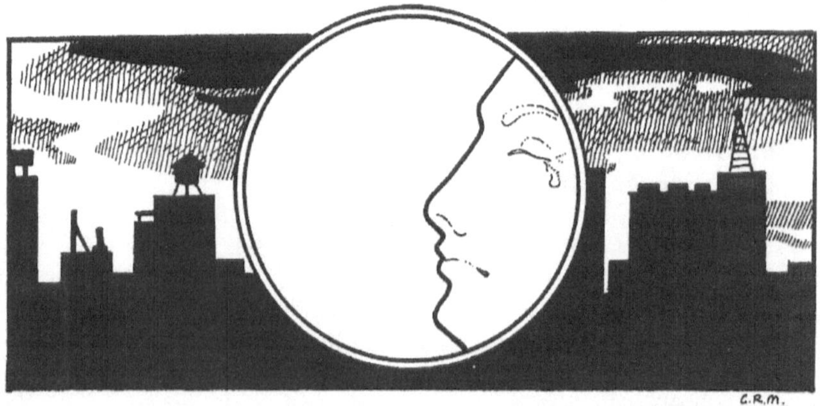

Art by Craig R. Miller, from the Wheel of the Year Songbook, *by Gwydion Pendderwen.*

Appendix G:
References & Resources

A. Near-Death Experiences

1. Alexander, Eben, *Proof of Heaven: A Neurosurgeon's Journey into the Afterlife.* Simon & Schuster, 2012.
2. Appel, Jacob, *Who Says You're Dead? Medical & Ethical Dilemmas for the Curious & Concerned.* Algonquin Books, Chapel Hill, NC. 2019.
3. Blackmore, Susan, *Dying to Live: Near-Death Experiences.* Prometheus Books, 1993.
4. Holden JM, Greyson B, James D, editors. *The Handbook of Near-Death Experiences: Thirty Years of Investigation.* Praeger/ABC-CLIO, Santa Barbara, CA, 2009.
5. Kerr, Christopher & Mardorossian, Carine, *Death is But a Dream: Finding Hope and Meaning at Life's End.* Avery, 2020
6. Ring, Kenneth, *Life at Death: A Scientific Investigation of the Near-Death Experience.* Coward, McCann, & Geoghegan, New York, 1980.
7. van Lommel, Pim, *Consciousness Beyond Life: The Science of the Near-Death Experience.* HarperOne, 2010.
8. Zaleski, Carol, *Otherworld Journeys: Accounts of Near-Death Experience in Medieval and Modern Times.* Oxford University Press, 1988.

B. Death and Afterlife

1. Allaun, Chris, *Guide of Spirits: A Psychopomp's Manual for Transitioning the Dead to the Afterlife.* S.L.: Moon Books, 2021.
2. Almond, Philip C., *Afterlife: A History of Life after Death.* I B Tauris and Cornell University Press, London and Ithaca, NY, 2015.
3. Brown, Sylvia, *Life on the Other Side: A Psychic's Tour of the Afterlife.* Berkley, 2001.
4. Chopra, Deepak, *Life After Death.* Rider-Random House, 2008.
5. Coddington, Robert H., *Death Brings Many Surprises: A Psychic Handbook.* Ivy/Ballantine Books, New York, 1987.
6. Cohn-Sherbok, Dan & Lewis, Christopher, eds., *Beyond Death: Theological and Philosophical Reflections on Life after Death.* Pelgrave-MacMillan, 1995.
7. Fontana, David, *Is There an Afterlife? A Comprehensive Overview of the Evidence.* O Books, 2005.
8. Grof, Stanislaw & Christine, *Beyond Death: Gates of Consciousness.* Thames & Hudson, 1980.
9. Hughes, Kristoffer, *The Journey Into Spirit: A Pagan's Perspective on Death, Dying & Bereavement.* Llewellyn Publications, Woodbury, MN, 2014.
10. Hunter, Devin, *The Witch's Book of Spirits.* Llewellyn Publications, Woodbury, MN, 2017.

11. Lanza, Robert, *Biocentrism: How Life and Consciousness are the Keys to Understanding the True Nature of the Universe.* BenBella Books, 2010.

12. Miller, Sukie, *After Death: Mapping the Journey.* Simon & Schuster, 1997.

13. Mirabello, Mark, *A Traveler's Guide to the Afterlife: Traditions and Beliefs on Death, Dying, and What Lies Beyond.* Inner Traditions, 2016.

14. Moreman, Christopher M., *Beyond the Threshold: Afterlife Beliefs and Experiences in World Religions.* Rowman & Littlefield, 2008.

15. Morey, Robert A., *Death and the Afterlife.* Bethany House Publishers, Minneapolis, 1984.

16. Mortellus, *The Bones Fall in a Spiral: A Necromantic Primer.* Crossed Crow Books, Chicago, 2023.

17. Novack, Peter, *The Last Secret of Death: Our Divided Souls and the Afterlife.* Hampton Roads Pub., Charlottsville, VA. 2003.

18. Roach, Mary, *Six Feet Over: Adventures in the Afterlife.* Canongate, 2007.

19. Schwartz, Gary E., with forward by Deepak Chopra, *The Afterlife Experiments: Breakthrough Scientific Evidence of Life After Death.* Atria Books, 2003.

20. Zell, Oberon, *That Undiscover'd Country: A Traveler's Guide to the Afterlife.* Black Moon Publishing, Cincinnati, 2020.

C. Reincarnation

1. Cerminara, Gina, *Many Lives, Many Loves.* William Sloane Associates, 1963.

2. Dossey, Larry, *One Mind: How Our Individual Mind Is Part of a Greater Consciousness and Why It Matters*, Hay House Inc. 2013.

3. Leek, Sybil, *Reincarnation: The Second Chance.* Scarborough House, NY, 1974.

4. Moody, Raymond, *Life After Life: The Investigation of a Phenomenon – Survival of Bodily Death.* HarperSanFrancisco, CA, 1975; 2001.

5. Morton, Chris & Thomas, Ceri Louise, *The Mystery of the Crystal Skulls: A Real-Life Detective Story of the Ancient World.* Vermont, Bear & Company, 1998.

6. Newton, Michael, *Journey of Souls: Case Studies of Life Between Lives.* Llewellyn Publications, Woodbury, MN, 1994.

7. Semkiw, Walter, *Born Again: Reincarnation Cases Involving International Celebrities, India's Political Legends and Film Stars.* Pluto Project, 2007.

8. Steiger, Brad, *You Will Live Again: Dramatic Case Histories of Reincarnation.* Blue Dolphin Press, Grass Valley, CA, 1996.

9. Stevenson, Ian, *Twenty Cases Suggestive of Reincarnation: 2nd Edition.* University of Virginia Press, Revised and Enlarged edition, 1980.

10. ________, *Children Who Remember Previous Lives: A Question of Reincarnation.* University of Virginia Press, 1987

11. ________, *Reincarnation and Biology: A Contribution to the Etiology of Birthmarks and Birth Defects.* Praeger Publishers, 1997.

12. Tucker, Jim. B., *Return to Life: Extraordinary Cases of Children Who Remember Past Lives.* St. Martin's Griffin, 2008.

13. ________, *Life Before Life: Children's Memories of Previous Lives.* St. Martin's Press, 2013.

14. Willoya, William & Brown, Vinson, *Warriors of the Rainbow.* Naturegraph Publishers, 1962.

D. Birthing and Raising the Magickal Child

1. Carroll, Lee & Tober, Jan. *The Indigo Children: The New Kids Have Arrived.* Hay House, 1999.
2. Cole, Cat Gina & Bonewits, Phaedra, *Psychic Skills for Magic & Witchcraft: Developing Your Spirit, Intuition & Clairvoyance.* Llewellyn Books, 2022.
3. Cook, Julia, *Personal Space Camp.* National Center for Youth Issues, 2007
4. Crosson, Monica, *The Magickal Family: Pagan Living in Harmony with Nature.* Llewellyn Publications, 2017.
5. England, Pam & Horowitz, Ron, *Birthing from Within, An Extra-ordinary Guide to Childbirth Preparation.* Partera Press, 1998.
6. Gaskin, Ina May, *Ina May's Guide to Childbirth "Updated With New Material."* Bantam,, 2003.
7. ________, & The Farm Midwives, *Spiritual Midwifery.* The Book Publishing Co, Summertown, TN, 2002.
8. Haffner, Debra, *From Diapers to Dating: A Parent's Guide To Raising Sexually Healthy Children—From Infancy to Middle School.* Newmarket Press, 1999.
9. Harris, Robie, *It is NOT the Stork!: A Book About Girls, Boys, Babies, Bodies, Family & Friends.* Candlewick, 2008.
10. Hegeman, William, *Magic, Mind, Emotion and Body, the Praxis: Magic No Woo, the How and Why Book.* People Embracing Change Tribe, 2021.
11. Hoffman, Enid, *Develop Your Psychic Skills.* Redfeather, 1997.
12. Hoyle, Alice & McGreeney, Ester, *Great Relationships and Sex Education.* Routledge, 2019
13. Keirle-Smith, Gordon, *Another Egg, Another Life: A Book designed to Stimulate Children's Past Life Memories.* CreateSpace Independent Publishing Platform, 2017.
14. Kermani, S. Zohreh, *Pagan Family Values: Childhood and the Religious Imagination in Contemporary American Paganism.* NYU Press, 2013.
15. King, Kimberly & King, Zack, *I Said No! A Kid-to-Kid Guide to Keeping Private Parts Private.* Boulden Publishing, 2008.
16. Losey, Meg Blackburn, *Children of Now.* Weiser, 2006.
17. Pierce, Joseph Chilton, *Magical Child.* Bantam Books, 1980.
18. ________, & Mendizza, Michael, *Magical Parent Magical Child: The Art of Joyful Parenting.* North Atlantic Books, 2004.
19. Sanders, Jayneen, *No Means No!* Educate2empower Publishing, 2017.
20. ________, *My Body! What I Say Goes!* Educate2empower Pub, 2017.
21. Silverberg, Cory & Smith, Fiona, *What Makes a Baby?* Triangle Square, 2013.
22. Tatter, Grace. *Consent At Every Age.* Harvard Graduate School of Education, 2018
23. Virtue, Doreen, *The Crystal Children: A Guide to the Newest Generation of Psychic and Sensitive Children.* Hay House, 2003.
24. Weed, Susun, *Wise Woman Herbal for the Childbearing Year.* Ash Tree Publishing, 1996.
25. Zell, Oberon, *Grimoire for the Apprentice Wizard.* New Page, 2004.
26. ________, *Companion for the Apprentice Wizard.* New Page, 2006.

27. _________, & Zell, Morning Glory, *Creating Circles & Ceremonies: Rituals for All Seasons & Reasons.* New Page, 2006.
28. _________, & Johnson, Kirsten. *Song of Gaea: Paean to the Soul of Nature* (a children's book) TheaGenesis, 2021.

E. Other References

1. Abram, David, *The Spell of the Sensuous: Perception and Language in a More-Than-Human World.* First Vintage books ed. New York, 1997.
2. Brusatte, Steve, *The Rise and Fall of the Dinosaurs: A New History of a Lost World.* Mariner Books, 2024.
3. Graham, Harvey, *Animism: Respecting the Living World.* New York: Columbia University Press, 2006.
4. Greene, Robert, *The 48 Laws of Power.* Penguin Books, 1998; 2000.
5. Montgomery, Jack, *American Shamans: Journeys with Traditional Healers.* BUSCA Press, 2008.
6. Morgan, Elaine, *The Aquatic Ape Hypothesis,* Souvenir Press, 1997.
7. Straus, William & Howe, Neil, *The Fourth Turning: An American Prophecy..* Crown; Reprint edition, 1997.

Wheel of the Year by Katlyn Breen

Appendix ℏ: Index

ADHD 67, 72-73, 75-76, 102, 226
AFAB 163-64
Afterlife 3, 11, 13-17, 20, 24, 26, 153, 176-78, 180-81, 286, 287
Altar 40, 43, 56, 83, 85-86, 111, 114, 148, 212, 291
AMAB 164
Ancestors 40, 42, 64-65, 75, 84, 86, 113, 126, 141, 249
Aphrodite 152, 155, 247
Aquariums 121
Archosauria 126
Armillary 130
Asexual 152, 155, 165
Aspergers 75
Astral body 98, 186-87
Astral projection 97, 100
Astrolabe 130
Aura 70, 74, 114, 186-89, 191-92, 251

Autism 67, 72, 74-75, 226

Baku 78
Bearded dragons 117
Beltane 146, 183, 246
Bible 176, 181, 210, 215, 226, 241
Birds 119
Bisexual 155, 157, 218
Box turtles 117
Buddhism 13, 17, 173, 175, 178-79
Bunnies 116-17

Cabinet of Curiosities 123
Catholic church 7, 175, 200, 241
Cats 115
Changelings 9, 72, 74-76

Christianity 20-21, 69, 90, 148, 152, 173, 175, 180, 210, 226, 232, 269
Clairaudience 97
Clairkinesthesia 97
Clairolfaction 97
Clairsentience 96
Clairvoyance 60, 96, 102, 193, 194, 212, 288
Colic 55
Confucianism 181, 200, 266
Consent 158, 160-63, 165, 167, 288
Contraception 167, 171

Déjà vu 97
Deinonychus 127
Dharma 178, 179, 182
Dinosaurs 9, 110, 117, 120, 122-23, 125-28, 131, 196, 211-13, 271, 277, 289

Dionysus 113, 155
Diorama 126
Discipline 63, 71, 73, 109, 200, 221, 238, 240
Discrimination 90, 150-51, 262
Divine 9, 15, 20, 27-28, 45, 49, 53, 72, 83, 174, 208, 226, 233-34, 250-52
Divinity 15, 38, 148-49, 174
Dogma 25, 152, 173, 181
Dogs 115-16
Doula 11, 40, 45
Dragons 9, 37, 56, 62-63, 117, 125-29, 144, 147, 213, 216, 217, 233, 278-80
Dreamer 60, 97
Dreams 31, 33, 42, 56, 62, 66-67, 78-79, 81, 97, 101-02, 115, 119, 132, 142, 164, 205, 210, 212, 252, 259-60
Drugs 42, 44, 82, 136, 157, 216, 218, 270, 284

The Authors

Oberon Zell earned a bachelor's degree in psychology, sociology and anthropology from Westminster College in Fulton, Missouri, and went on to graduate studies in clinical psychology at Washington University, as well as earning a Teacher's Certificate from Harris Teachers  College. His seminal work on the Gaea Thesis has helped foster a growing awareness of Earth as living Mother. Oberon is one of the most respected figures in the new Pagan spiritual movement that emerged in the latter half of the 20th century, and his influence has spread far beyond that movement, helping to bridge the gap between spirituality and science.

In 1962 Oberon co-founded the Church of All Worlds (CAW), which in 1968 became the first avowedly Pagan church to be legally incorporated. He founded the groundbreaking journal *Green Egg* in 1968 and has served as its publisher for over five decades. Since 2004, he has authored 19 published books on metaphysical thought and practice. He is the founder and Headmaster *emeritus* of the online Grey School of Wizardry, which offers more than 500 classes in 16 departments.

In 1998, Oberon created one of the most beautiful and best-loved expressions of Earth-centered spirituality in his visionary sculpture, "The Millennial Gaia." More than 100,000 reproductions of this exquisite altar figurine have been sold worldwide. People of all ages and cultures recognize a spiritual message in Her grace, beauty and complexity.

Oberon is now married to Lady Rhiannon of Serpentstone; they currently reside in the state of North Carolina. www.OberonZell.com

---

Haleigh Isbill holds a bachelor's degree in Sociology and graduated Dean's List from the University of Nevada, Las Vegas.

She lives in Las Vegas with her three partners and their five children, plus pets! She ran her high school newspaper, and copy edited for her college newspaper. She also copy-edited for websites, local zines, and for books by Oberon Zell. She has written tech industry case studies, processes and procedures for small businesses, and is now adding co-authoring books to her repertoire.

As a fiber witch, Haleigh spends her free time on her fiber arts: spinning yarn, nalbinding, knitting, crocheting, and now weaving.

This is her first published book, and she hopes it brings light and love to everyone who reads it.

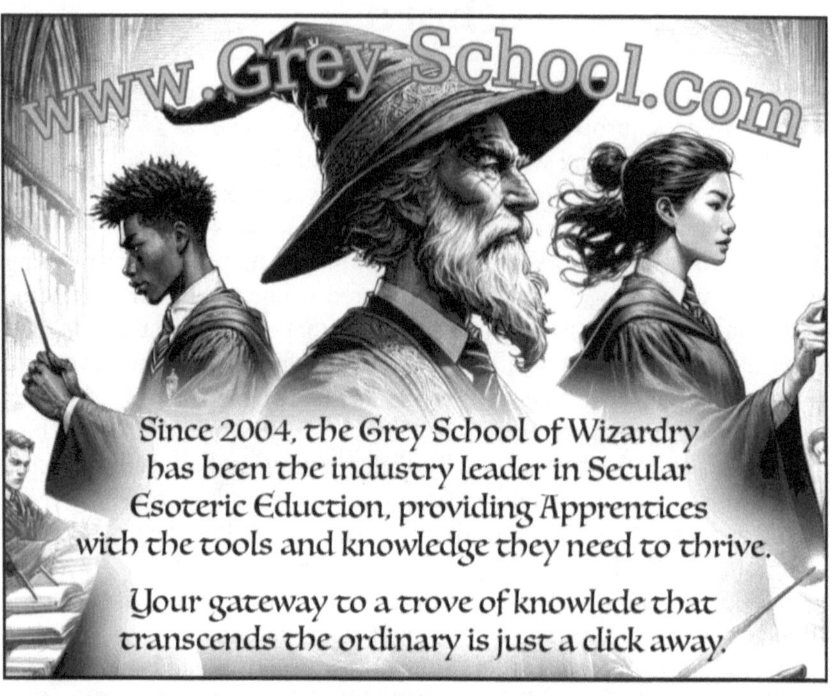

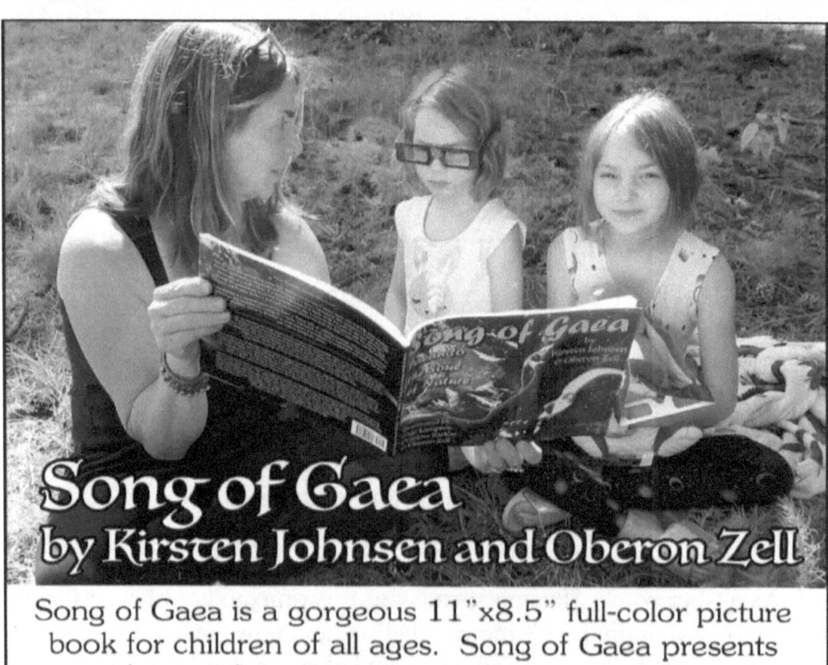

Song of Gaea is a gorgeous 11"x8.5" full-color picture book for children of all ages. Song of Gaea presents cosmology and evolutionary ecology in a lyrical mythic framework and offers a sustainable vision of the future.